Reading Salvation
Word, Worship, and the Mysteries

CONTRIBUTORS

Robert Louis Wilken is William R. Kenan, Jr., professor of the history of Christianity at the University of Virginia. He received his Ph.D. from the University of Chicago and has taught at Gregorian University, Institutum Patristicum Augustiniam, Hebrew University of Jerusalem, the University of Notre Dame, Fordham University, and Lutheran Theological Seminary. Wilken is the author of 10 books, including *The Spirit of Early Christian Thought: Seeking the Face of God* (Yale, 2003), *Remembering the Christian Past* (Eerdmans, 1995), and *The Christians as the Romans Saw Them* (Yale, 1984). He is also the translator, along with Paul Bowers, of *On the Cosmic Mystery of Jesus Christ: Selected Writings from St. Maximus the Confessor* (St. Vladimir's Seminary Press, 2003). His work is the subject of the festschrift, *In Dominico eloquio: Essays on Patristic Exegesis in Honor of Robert Louis Wilken*, edited by Paul M. Blowers (Eerdmans, 2002).

James Swetnam, S.J., entered the Missouri Province of the Society of Jesus in 1945 and was ordained a priest in 1958. He holds degrees in classical languages, philosophy, theology, and Scripture. His doctoral degree is from the University of Oxford. Since 1962 he has been a scholar of the Pontifical Biblical Institute in Rome, where he has held numerous posts, including vice-rector and dean of the biblical faculty. He has also served in an editorial capacity for several academic journals, including *Orientalia*, *Analecta Orientalia*, and *Biblica*. His area of specialization is the Epistle to the Hebrews. Swetnam is the author of *Jesus and Isaac: A Study of the Epistle to the Hebrews in the Light of the Aqedah* (Rome: Analecta Biblica, 1981) and *An Introduction to the Study of New Testament Greek* (Rome: Pontifical Biblical Institute, 1992)

Brant Pitre is assistant professor of pastoral theology at Loyola University in New Orleans. He received his Ph.D. in theology from the University of Notre Dame. He wrote his dissertation on "The Historical Jesus, the Great Tribulation, and the End of the Exile: Restoration Eschatology and the Origin of the Atonement." Pitre holds an M.T.S. degree in biblical studies and theology from Vanderbilt Divinity School and a B.A. in philosophy and English literature from Louisiana State University. His major areas of interest are biblical studies (both Old and New Testaments) and systematic theology (with an emphasis on Roman Catholic theology).

Sofia Cavalletti is a scholar of Hebrew and Semitic languages and biblical exegesis with a special interest in the religious development of children. In 1954 she co-founded the early childhood religious education program, the Catechesis of the Good Shepherd, which has since expanded to 23 countries in Europe, the Americas, Africa, and Asia. Cavalletti has collaborated on ecumenical editions of the Bible and has served on the ecumenical commissions of the Diocese of Rome, and the Italian Conference of Catholic Bishops. Her books include *The Religious Potential of the Child: Experiencing Scripture and Liturgy with Young Children* (1992); *Living Liturgy: Elementary Reflections* (1998); and *History's Golden Thread: The History of Salvation* (1999), all published by Liturgical Training Publications.

Jeremy Driscoll, O.S.B., has been a Benedictine monk since 1973. Ordained to the priesthood in 1981, he earned an S.T.L. degree in patristics from the Augustinianum Patristic Institute in Rome in 1983 and has taught theology at Mount Angel Seminary in Oregon since then. He was awarded an S.T.D. degree from the Pontifical Athenaeum of St. Anselm in Rome, writing his thesis on Evagrius Ponticus and ancient Egyptian monasticism. Since 1994 he has also taught one semester each year at the Athenaeum. In 2004, he was named a member of the Pontifical Academy of Theology and also a member of the Vox Clara Committee of the Vatican's Congregation for Divine Worship and the Discipline of the Sacraments. Father Driscoll translated and wrote the commentary for the volume *Evagrius Ponticus: Ad monachos* in the Ancient Christian Writers series (Newman Press, 2003). He is also the author of a collection of essays, *Theology at the Eucharistic Table: Master Themes in the Theological Tradition* (Gracewing, 2004), and a volume of poetry, *Some Other Morning* (Story Line Press, 1992).

Scott W. Hahn, founder of the St. Paul Center for Biblical Theology, holds the Chair of Biblical Theology and Liturgical Proclamation at Saint Vincent Seminary in Latrobe, Pennsylvania, and is professor of Scripture and theology at Franciscan University of Steubenville, Ohio. He has held the Pio Cardinal Laghi Chair for Visiting Professors in Scripture and Theology at the Pontifical College Josephinum in Columbus, Ohio, and has served as adjunct faculty at the Pontifical University of the Holy Cross and the Pontifical University, Regina Apostolorum, both in Rome. Hahn earned his Ph.D. in systematic theology from Marquette University, writing his dissertation on "Kinship by Covenant: A Biblical Theological Analysis of Covenant Types and Texts in the Old and New Testaments." Hahn is the general editor of the *Ignatius Study Bible* and is author or editor of more than 20 books, including *Letter and Spirit: From Written Text to Living Word in the Liturgy* (Doubleday, 2005); *Understanding the Scriptures* (Midwest Theological Forum, 2005), and *The Lamb's Supper: The Mass as Heaven on Earth* (Doubleday, 1999).

Christopher T. Baglow holds the Sue Ellen M. Canizaro Chair in Catholic Theology at Our Lady of Holy Cross College in New Orleans. He earned his Ph.D. at Duquesne University and his dissertation was published as *'Modus et Forma': A New Approach to the Exegesis of St. Thomas Aquinas with an Application to the Lectura super Epistolam ad Ephesios* (Analecta Biblica 149, Rome: Biblical Institute Press, 2002).

Marcellino D'Ambrosio is the founder of www.crossroadsinitiative.com, an apostolate of Catholic renewal and evangelization. He earned his doctoral degree in historical theology from the Catholic University of America, writing his dissertation on Cardinal Henri de Lubac, S.J., and his recovery of the biblical interpretation of the early Church fathers. He is the author of numerous books and video and audio courses, including *Exploring the Catholic Church* (Charis, 2001) and *The Guide to the Passion: 100 Questions about 'The Passion of the Christ'* (Ascension, 2004). He also contributed to Abingdon's *Dictionary of Biblical Interpretation*.

Hugh of St. Victor (d. 1141) was philosopher, theologian, and mystical writer. A monk and abbot, he wrote on topics ranging from grammar and geometry to history and mystical philosophy. An influential biblical exegete, he wrote numerous commentaries characterized by a concern to draw spiritual and theological meanings from the foundation of a literal and historical meaning of the texts. His works include *De sacramentis christianae fidei* (On the Sacraments of the Christian Faith) and *Didascalicon*, from which the excerpt in this issue is drawn. Used by permission of Columbia University Press.

F. X. Durrwell, C.Ss.R. (b. 1912) is a French Redemptorist priest who took his degree at the Pontifical Biblical Institute in Rome and is the author of several groundbreaking books of biblical theology, including *The Resurrection: A Biblical Study* (1960), *Holy Spirit of God: An Essay in Biblical Theology* (1986); and *In the Redeeming Christ* (1963), from which the excerpt in this issue is drawn. Used by permission of Rowman & Littlefield Publishers.

Augustin Cardinal Bea, S.J. (1881-1968) was a Jesuit priest with a long distinguished career as a biblical scholar, serving at the Pontifical Biblical Institute and the Gregorian University among other places. Cardinal Bea served on the Pontifical Biblical Commission under Pius XII and influenced the formulation of the pope's encyclical *Divino afflante Spiritu* (1943). He also collaborated from 1941-48 in the project to prepare a new Latin translation of the Psalms. A close adviser to Pope John XXIII, he had a shaping influence on the Second Vatican Council's documents on non-Christian religions, religious freedom, and divine revelation. His books include: *The Unity of Christians* (1963) and *The Word of God and Mankind* (1962), from which the selection in this issue is drawn. Used by permission of the Continuum International Publishing Group.

Introducing

Letter & Spirit

Welcome to *Letter & Spirit*. With this new journal we hope to foster a deeper conversation about the Bible—what it is and where it comes from; how we should read it; and what claim it should make on our lives, on the teaching and practice of the Church, on the world we live in.

We realize that wildly divergent answers to these questions have long been afoot in our churches, seminaries, and academies. Some have gone so far as to describe a "crisis" in contemporary understanding of the Bible. Indeed, we would suggest that a failure to think straight about the Bible risks confounding our worship, confusing our doctrine and morals, and rendering uncertain the Church's witness to the culture and to other believers.

That said, the readers of this journal deserve to know where we are coming from—our starting points, the prior judgments and assumptions we bring to this conversation. Without trying to put too fine a point on it, we read the Bible from the heart of the Church. That means we read the Bible as the Church hands it on—as *Scripture*, as a divine Word spoken by God to a faith community that acknowledges this Word as authoritative and normative for its life and worship. We read, then, from within a tradition that for more than two millennia has listened to and contemplated God's Word—preaching, praying, and interpreting that Word in liturgy, doctrines, and devotions, and applying its wisdom in countless pastoral settings.

The Bible is an ecclesial and liturgical document. As we see it, this is a statement of historical fact, not an article of faith. The Bible exists because the apostolic Church composed, collected, and preserved this Word, even to the shedding of blood by its martyrs. The Church continues to proffer this Word as essential for making disciples of the God revealed in its pages and for worshipping that God, revealed finally and fully by Jesus Christ (John 20:31; 1 Thess. 2:13).

The Word of God was proclaimed before it was written, heard before it was read. The site of this proclamation and hearing, since the first Easter night, has been the divine liturgy of the Church (Luke 24:13-49). The earliest Scriptures were composed to be read and interpreted in the Eucharistic assembly. And Scripture from the start has always been proclaimed and interpreted in order to anticipate a liturgical act—baptism or the Eucharist, for instance—by which the hearer of the Word is granted entry into the salvation promised in the Scripture. There would be no Bible without the liturgy and there could be no liturgy without the Bible.

The culture of the Church that gives us the Bible is a biblical culture. The words of Scripture quite literally form the basis for the Church's confessions of faith. Its art, music, and architecture are expressed in words and images drawn from the sacred pages. The Church's dogmas and doctrines are expressed in scriptural language and are themselves authoritative interpretations of the Scriptures. The "mysteries" of the faith, the Church's sacraments, are celebrated through biblical signs of water, oil, bread, and wine. As God addresses the Church in the human language of Scripture, in its liturgy the Church responds to his Word in prayers, songs, and vows drawn from those same Scriptures.

Again, these are statements of historical fact, not articles of faith. Much of what has led to the crisis in contemporary biblical scholarship could be overcome by acknowledging these historical realities. One certainly does not have to confess what the Church confesses, nor does one have to believe what the Church claims about the Bible, in order to read, study, or interpret it. But if we are seeking the true meaning of Scripture as it is written, and not merely to advance fanciful or private judgments, we cannot divorce Scripture from the ecclesial and liturgical culture in which it comes to us.

Reading Salvation—Word, Worship, and Mystery

What we are about and what we are up to in *Letter & Spirit* is perhaps best explained by the selections we present in our inaugural issue. Our theme for this issue tries to capture something of the enormity of what the Church claims for Scripture. In the Scriptures, according to ancient understanding, is narrated the history of the world's salvation—a history that each believer enters into through the sacraments, also known as the "mysteries." In this sense, to read Scripture is to be "reading salvation." In this reading we encounter the living Word of God who desires to lead all humankind to worship and communion in the mystery of his own divine life.

Our issue examines the many facets of this reading of salvation. In "Allegory and the Interpretation of the Old Testament in the 21st Century," **Robert Louis Wilken** looks at the Church's oldest and most enduring approach to biblical interpretation and shows the necessity of allegory for reading the Bible—not as an ancient document, but as the living voice of the living God. In a unique treatment of how certain psalms are interpreted in the Church's daily liturgy, Wilken illustrates how allegory helps the Church read the Hebrew Scriptures in light of the "prodigious newness" of the incarnation, of the Word of God becoming flesh. Wilken notes that this traditional Christian way of reading Scripture requires "more than what is considered interpretation today." Indeed, in the academy and in many parts of the Church, allegory has been rejected in favor of strictly historical and literary approaches to the text.

As does Wilken, our second contributor, **James Swetnam, S.J.**, questions whether it is possible to understand the historical and literary meaning of the biblical text without what he calls a "hermeneutic of faith." Swetnam's "The Sacrifice of Isaac in Genesis and Hebrews" is a penetrating study of a key and controversial biblical text—God's demand that Abraham offer his beloved son as a sacrifice (Gen. 22). Swetnam observes how both the original account and the interpretation of that account in the New Testament presume that readers share a certain faith perspective. He argues that in order to interpret these Scriptures as they were written—as historical and literary texts—one must acknowledge that their literal and historical meaning is intended to convey a religious truth. The interpreter must then, he says, take seriously the faith presumptions of the biblical authors. In this case, that means exploring not only the notions of covenant and sacrifice that underlie the Genesis text, but also giving due consideration to both authors' underlying core belief in the trustworthiness of God's promises and his power to raise the dead.

Brant Pitre also explores the interpretation of the Old Testament in the New in his contribution, "The 'Ransom for Many,' the New Exodus, and the End of the Exile." His paper exemplifies *Letter & Spirit*'s commitment to using the tools of historical and literary criticism to explicate the essentially religious meaning of the biblical text. Through careful consideration of the Old Testament background, Pitre demonstrates convincingly that Christ's "ransom" is presented in Mark's Gospel as more than the deliverance of individuals from bondage to sin. The "ransom" also evokes Israel's expectation for a new exodus that, like the first exodus, would atone for the people's sins, restore the people from exile, and establish a kingdom in the promised land. Pitre breaks new exegetical ground in this piece and sheds new light on the ecclesial and corporate dimensions of the paschal mystery.

Christian liturgy, born in the Last Supper, from the start was viewed by the Church in terms of the exodus and the celebration of a new "Passover" (1 Cor. 5:7; 10:1-4). In her contribution, "Memorial and Typology in Jewish and Christian Liturgy," **Sofia Cavalletti** explores the influence of the synagogue on the early Church. She shows how the portrait of Jesus in the gospels—particularly in the Gospel of John—is shaped by a kind of "literary dialogue" with the scriptural texts read in the great Jewish feasts. She argues that from the synagogue the Church also inherited its understanding of how God's saving words and deeds are to be grasped typologically in the reading of Scripture, and how the promises of salvation are experienced and realized in the liturgy.

These themes are further developed in "The Word of God in the Liturgy of the New Covenant," the contribution of **Jeremy Driscoll, O.S.B.** Proclaimed in the Church's liturgy, Scripture is far more than a written account of remarkable deeds done long ago. He notes how even the order of readings in the Eucharistic celebration charts the history of salvation—from the revelation of the old covenant to the revelation of the new. At the center of this history is the "event" of Christ, the entrance of the living God into human history. In the liturgy, the promise of that event is delivered anew to every believer. In Driscoll's words: "We see in the liturgy, the final accomplishment and actualization of God's will for the world, the meaning of salvation history—that we have access to the Father through the Son in the Holy Spirit."

The final article in this inaugural issue, "Worship in the Word" by **Scott W. Hahn**, takes a panoramic look at the story of salvation that unfolds in the pages of Scripture. Hahn sees what he describes as a *liturgical trajectory* and *liturgical teleology* in this history. By that he means that Scripture, read canonically from start to finish, presents a liturgical reason and purpose and "destiny" for the world and the human person. This scriptural vision, he contends, continues in the Church's liturgy, where each believer is made a part of biblical salvation history. As Driscoll does, Hahn reminds us that Scripture is written with the liturgy in view, that in the liturgy the purpose of Scripture is fulfilled—men and women enter into communion with God through worship expressed as a sacrifice of praise.

We also include in this issue two important shorter pieces highlighting the enduring legacy of two intellectual pioneers in biblical theology—St. Thomas Aquinas and Henri de Lubac, S.J. Arguing that Thomas should be a model for exegetes and theologians today, **Christopher T. Baglow** offers a line-by-line study of Thomas's method in reading the literal sense of the crucial "bread of life" discourse in John's Gospel. **Marcellino D'Ambrosio** reminds us of de Lubac's recovery from the ancient Church—that the spiritual interpretation of Scripture is not only essential to any authentic Christian exegesis, but is also "at the heart of Christian faith itself."

We round out our issue by sounding the voices of the Church's living tradition. In excerpts specially selected and edited for *Letter & Spirit*, we hear from **Hugh of St. Victor** (d. 1141), who outlines the classical Christian approach to the Bible, teaching that all interpretation is founded on the literal, historical meaning of the text. **F. X. Durrwell, C.Ss.R**, in a text written in the 1960s, considers the ancient teaching that Scripture, like the sacraments, brings us into contact with the "Word of salvation in the redeeming Christ." Finally, **Augustin Cardinal Bea, S.J.,** (1881-1968) provides a careful and authoritative reading of Catholic teaching on the nature and truth of sacred Scripture.

The Letter & Spirit Project

In the century just ended, enormous strides were made in studying the historical and literary contexts of the scriptural texts. This has greatly enhanced our understanding of Scripture. We believe the task for the century ahead is to join the scientific study of Scripture's literary and historical meaning to an equally vital recovery of Scripture's ecclesial and liturgical sense—that is, how these texts are used and interpreted in the "today" of the Church's living tradition.

Such a task is an adventure of the highest intellectual and spiritual order. That is what makes biblical scholarship so exciting, something worth devoting all our hearts, minds, and strength to. That is the sense of excitement that animates *Letter & Spirit* and the St. Paul Center for Biblical Theology which publishes it. The Center is a nonprofit research and educational institute that aims to advance the study of the sacred page at every level, from beginning students of Scripture, to seminarians, pastors, and priests. This journal appears as part of the Center's Letter & Spirit Project, which publishes dissertations and other scholarly studies of important themes in Scripture from literary, historical, and theological perspectives.

The St. Paul Center is guided by the belief that a renewal of biblical studies is an enterprise of urgent practical necessity. A primary symptom of the current "crisis" is that biblical scholarship has become a specialized discipline within the academy—far removed from and little concerned with the needs of pastors, seminarians, and ordinary believers. The result has not been a happy one, for either biblical scholarship or the Church.

Reading the Bible from the heart of the Church means, finally, bringing the interpretation and study of Scripture back home. We take heart that the very word for the Bible's original and rightful home—*liturgy* (from the Greek *leitourgia*)—means "public work." Classical authors used this word to categorize the labor of street sweepers and bureaucrats. The Church uses *liturgy* to describe the service by which the saving truths and great works of God recorded in Scripture are carried out in the here and now, making believers a part of the salvation history told in its pages.

There can be, then, nothing elitist or obscurantist about our study of Scripture. Biblical scholarship must serve Scripture's proclamation and its faithful reception. It must be in service to the ministry of the new covenant, whereby the written text becomes living Word, whereby the letter on the page becomes life-giving Spirit.

Such are our starting points and presumptions. And these are some of the things we hope to talk about in the pages of *Letter & Spirit*. We welcome you to join us in the conversation.

Letter & Spirit 1 (2005): 11-21

ALLEGORY AND THE INTERPRETATION OF THE OLD TESTAMENT IN THE 21ST CENTURY

• Robert Louis Wilken •

University of Virginia

Allegory is the Church's love affair with the Bible. It is the oldest and most enduring way of interpreting the Bible and is very much alive today in the selection of scriptural readings in the liturgy, in the Church's daily praying of the psalms, and in classic works of devotion, such as St. Gregory of Nyssa's *Life of Moses* or St. Bernard's *Homilies on the Song of Songs*. Each Lent in connection with my morning prayers I read from John of the Cross's writings and last year I was particularly impressed by his inventive interpretation of unexpected and often obscure passages from the Old Testament. Without allegory his spiritual writings would be much less penetrating and biblical. Though he lived in the 16th century he moved in a world that was formed by the biblical commentaries, homilies and sermons of the Church fathers.

Yet for generations, indeed centuries, biblical scholars have scorned allegory. With the triumph of the historical approach to the Bible in the universities and colleges and seminaries many took it as self-evident that only the original meaning of the text, presented to us with the tools of historical criticism, can claim the allegiance of modern readers of the Bible. Yet literary critics have always realized that the notion of a single sense does not carry us very far in the interpretation of great works of literature. One reason that the "classics" of our civilization endure is because each generation is able to discover in the texts depths of meaning that were not discerned by earlier readers.

This is even more true with the Scriptures, as the distinguished literary critic Frank Kermode wrote: "For the last century or so there has been something of a consensus among experts that parables of the kind found in the New Testament were always essentially simple, and always had the same kind of point, which would have been instantly taken by all listeners, outsiders included. Appearances to the contrary are explained as consequences of a process of meddling with the originals that began at the earliest possible moment. The opinion that the parable must originally have been thus, and only thus, is maintained with an expense of learning I can't begin to emulate, against what seems obvious, that 'parable' does and did mean much more than that."[1]

---

[1] Frank Kermode, *The Genesis of Secrecy: On the Interpretation of Narrative* (Cambridge: Harvard University, 1979), 25.

Allegory has to do with words and things and events meaning "much more than that." The term itself means "another meaning" in addition to the original sense and, significantly, it is used at a key place within the New Testament. In the famous passage in Galatians 4, St. Paul gives an allegorical interpretation of Abraham's two wives, Hagar and Sarah. "For it is written that Abraham had two sons, one by a slave and one by a free woman. But the son of the slave was born according to the flesh, the son of the free woman through promise. Now this is an *allegory*: these two women are two covenants. One is from Mount Sinai, bearing children for slavery; she is Hagar . . . she corresponds to the present Jerusalem, for she is in slavery with her children. But the Jerusalem above is free, and she is our mother" (Gal. 4:22-26).

In the early Church Galatians 4 is one of three texts that is cited consistently in support of the use of allegory. The others are 1 Corinthians 10 that speaks of the Israelites who were baptized in the cloud and in the sea, and drank from the supernatural rock that was Christ and Ephesians 5 where Paul quotes the words of Genesis, "For this reason a man shall leave his father and mother and be joined to his wife, and the two shall become one flesh." To which he comments: "This mystery is a profound one and I am saying that it refers to Christ and the Church." In the introduction to his *Literal Commentary on Genesis,* Augustine cites 1 Corinthians 10 and Ephesians 5 to observe: "No Christian will dare say that the [biblical] narrative must not be taken in a figurative sense."[2]

All of these examples, Galatians 4, 1 Corinthians 10, and Ephesians 5 have to do with the interpretation of the Old Testament. The term allegory is used so loosely today that it is sometimes forgotten that it is primarily a technique for interpreting the Old Testament, the Jewish Scriptures that the early Christian community made its own. In the words of a medieval Spanish exegete: The New Testament "*pro se stat sicut auditur; non est allegoria,*" the New Testament stands on its own, it does not need allegory.[3] The epistles of St. Paul do not call for allegory, and only occasionally is it appropriate for passages in the gospels, for example, in dealing with certain parables.

As the passages cited above indicate it was St. Paul who taught the Church how to use allegory for the interpretation of the Old Testament. By giving us "some examples of interpretation," writes Origen, the first great Christian exegete, Paul also pointed the way toward a rationale for the use of allegory by later interpreters. In 1 Corinthians 10, Origen observes, Paul says that the things that took place in ancient times and recorded in the

---

[2] *De Genesi ad litteram,* 1.1.1.

[3] PL 96: 958d. See Henri de Lubac, *Exégèse Médiévale,* 4 vols. (Paris: Aubier, 1962), 4:110.

Old Testament were "written for our instruction." What a text says about past events and persons is an integral part of what they mean, but the interpretation is never exhausted by the original meaning. These things happened "for us." The text belongs to a world that is not defined solely by its historical referent. For St. Paul this is not an enterprise in literary artifice, but a matter of divine revelation. For the same Christ "through whom are all things and through whom we exist" (1 Cor. 8:4), who was at work among the Israelites in the wilderness in ancient times, is alive and present in the Church today. This profound truth is disclosed in the words, "and all ate the same spiritual food and all drank the same spiritual drink. For they drank from the supernatural rock which followed them, and the rock was Christ" (1 Cor. 10:4).

Another example of how St. Paul became the Church's teacher and model in matters exegetical is his interpretation of Psalm 19 in Romans 10. There Paul writes: "How are they to believe in him of whom they have never heard?" and "how can men preach unless they are sent?" Then he says, citing the prophet Isaiah: "How beautiful are those who preach good news?" Faith comes by hearing and hearing by the preaching of Christ. Indeed, he adds that they have heard, citing Psalm 19: "Their voice has gone out to all the earth, and their words to the ends of the world."

In its original setting the first part of Psalm 19 (Psalm 18 in the Vulgate) celebrates the silent witness of the heavens to the majesty of God. "The heavens are telling the glory of God; and the firmament proclaims his handiwork. . . . There is no speech, nor are there words; their voice is not heard." Paul, however, interprets the text not in relation to the knowledge of God displayed in creation but as a psalm about the mission of the apostles. He gives the passage another sense than its obvious or plain meaning, that is, he allegorizes the psalm.

Even the biblical scholar Joseph Fitzmeyer, no apologist for allegory, recognized that St. Paul had done something significant when he interpreted Psalm 19 in relation to the apostles. In his magisterial commentary on Romans, Fitzmeyer says this of Paul's use of the psalm: "The psalmist sings of the works of nature proclaiming the glory of God everywhere; Paul accommodates the psalmist's words to the preaching of the gospel."[4] Fitzmeyer makes no mention or allegory or spiritual interpretation, but his word "accommodate" says all that is needful. Once a text from the ancient Jewish scriptures is brought before the eyes of a Christian reader it can no longer mean simply what it once meant, or what it means for Jews. Paul "accommodates" the words of the psalm to the new thing that has happened, the coming of Christ and the preaching of the gospel.

---

[4]   Joseph A. Fitzmyer, S.J., *Romans: A New Translation with Introduction and Commentary* (New York: Doubleday, 1993), 599.

In the words of Henri De Lubac, the French theologian who more than any other modern thinker has helped the Church rediscover the enduring worth of allegory: "With its varied panoply of nuances" ancient Christians exegesis "throws into relief 'the prodigious newness of the Christian fact'. It sets in motion a subtle dialectic . . . it defines the relations between historical reality and spiritual reality, of society and the individual, of time and eternity . . . . It organizes all revelation around a concrete center, marked in space and time by the cross of Jesus Christ. It is itself a complete and completely unified dogmatic and spiritual theology."[5]

Paul's accommodation of Psalm 19, to the apostolic mission was an interpretation with consequences. For his exegesis of the psalm passed over into the Church's worship, most notably in daily prayer. Whenever we celebrate the feast of an apostle, one of the psalms appointed to be read in the office of readings is Psalm 19, whose words "their voice has gone out to the limits of the earth, their words to the end of the world" are used as the antiphon. For those who pray with the Church the apostolic interpretation of Psalm 19 is as familiar and natural as the original or plain sense of the psalm.

This does not mean that the original meaning of the psalm is abandoned. It stands confidently as a testimony to the witness of creation to the mystery and majesty of God. At the same time the allegorical or spiritual interpretation became a precious and fixed part of the Church's life and worship. The two interpretations live comfortably side by side.

Of course it is significant that the interpretation of Psalm 19 as referring to the apostles has a foothold in the New Testament. Yet, if one looks at another psalm used in the daily office for the "common of apostles," Psalm 64, the New Testament offers no support. In its original setting Psalm 64 was a prayer for deliverance from personal enemies—"hide me from the secret plots of the wicked, from the scheming of evil doers who whet their tongues like swords, who aim bitter words like arrows. . . ." Confident of God's deliverance the psalmist wrote: "They will tell what God has done, they grasped the meaning of his deeds."

In the Liturgy of the Hours, the verse "they will tell what God has done" is used as the antiphon for Psalm 64. The English translator botched the matter by translating the verse differently in the antiphon from the verse in the psalm itself, but in the Latin breviary the antiphon and verse 9 are the same: *Et annuntiabunt opera Dei, et facta eius intelligent* (translated as "They will tell what God has done. They will understand God's deeds"). There is, however, one small but revealing change. In the antiphon the future tenses of the psalm, *annuntiabunt* and *intelligent* ("they will tell" and "they will understand") are changed into perfects, *annuntiaverunt*

---

[5]   De Lubac, *Exégèse Médiévale*, 1:16.

and *intellexerunt* ("they proclaimed" and "they grasped the meaning"). As with Psalm 19, here too there is an "accommodation" to the new setting in which the psalm is recited, the coming of Christ and the preaching of the apostles. In the Church's worship the psalm came to be interpreted not only in reference to the time in which it was written, but also as a celebration of what has come about since it was written. In other words, Christian interpreters followed the example of St. Paul when they interpreted the Psalm, even though there is no specific warrant within the New Testament.

The distinction (urged by a few writers in antiquity) between Old Testament texts whose meaning is given by the New Testament (for example. the serpent on the pole in John 3:14, or the rock in the desert in 1 Corinthians 10:4) and those whose spiritual sense arises later within the Church's worship or catechesis, collapses in actual practice. In Christian tradition, most notably in the writings of the first readers of the Bible, the New Testament was not viewed as a comprehensive commentary on the Old Testament. By its very nature it only provided a few examples, but those passages served as a guide for interpreters. In the words of St. Augustine: "By explaining one passage (1 Cor. 10), [Paul] shows us how to understand others."[6]

I have chosen interpretations of Old Testament texts from daily prayer because the most inviting portal to enter classical Christian exegesis is how it is used—the setting in which a passage from the Scriptures is read, recited, or sung within Christian worship. Take, for example, Psalm 42, "As the deer yearns for streams of living water, so longs my soul for you O LORD." This psalm was sung as the newly baptized were about to receive communion at the great Vigil of Easter.[7] So accustomed are we to think of the locus of interpretation as the scholar's study that we forget that liturgy is the most pervasive and enduring setting for interpretation. Even in the solitude of study early Christian interpreters were never far removed from the Church's worship.

Another text whose classical interpretation has no obvious support within the New Testament is the opening verses of Chapter 63 of Isaiah. Isaiah writes: "Who is this that comes from Edom in crimsoned garments from Bozrah, he that is glorious in his apparel, marching in the greatness of his strength?" According to scholarly opinion these are words of a watchman of the city demanding to know who the solitary terrifying figure with blood red vesture approaching from Edom could be. Astonished, the watchman challenges him, "Who is this?" In the next verses he receives an

---

[6] *Contra Faustum Manichaeum*, 12.29; for the same point see also Origen, *Homily on Exodus*, 5.1.

[7] Augustine, *Enarrationes in Psalmos*, 41.1.

answer: "It is I, announcing vindication, mighty to save." The one who approaches is the living God, the God of Israel, victorious over Israel's foes. What follows is a hymn of triumph celebrating the triumph of the divine warrior, the God of Israel.

Origen, however, took Isaiah 63 to be a depiction of Christ's passion and ascension. After his death, writes Origen, Christ returned to the Father "victorious and bearing trophies with the body that had been raised from the dead." When he is greeted by the heavenly host they ask him: "'Why is your apparel red and your garments as if fresh from a full wine press that has been trampled down (Isa. 63:2).' To which Christ answers: 'I trampled them' (Isa. 63:2). And his escorts say to those stationed at the gates of heaven: Lift up your gates and the king of glory will come in (Ps. 24:7)."[8]

This is an imaginative, even breathtaking exegesis characteristic of Origen. Yet his interpretation of Isaiah 63 was not idiosyncratic—it can be found in many early Christian commentators, even among those whose approach to the Old Testament differed from his. Cyril of Alexandria [who was not an Origenist] is a good example: "This prophetic oracle," he writes, "wisely and artfully gives a true to life portrayal of Christ, the Savior of all, as he makes his return to heaven. . . . He was seen by the powers above in the form which he had among us, that is, as a man [Cyril is thinking of 1 Tim. 3:16, "manifested in the flesh . . . seen by angels"], and displayed to them the signs of his passion. This passage teaches not only that the perforations from the nails and the others marks remained in his holy flesh after he rose from the dead, it also gives us to understand that as he showed the nail wounds and his side to Thomas . . . by ascending into heaven with the signs of his passion so Christ also showed to the heavenly powers what he had accomplished 'that through the Church the manifold wisdom of God might now be made known to the principalities and powers in the heavenly places' (Eph. 3:10)."[9]

Though on first reading this interpretation of Isaiah 63 may seem contrived, "a serious misapprehension of the spirit of the prophecy" as one modern commentator put it, it fills a space left vacant by the two verses from the New Testament: 1 Timothy 3:16, with the phrase "seen by angels," and Ephesian 3:10, where it is said that the manifold wisdom of God made known in Christ "might now be made known to the principalities and powers in the heavenly places." According to the Church fathers, at his ascension Christ's work on earth was announced to the heavenly host upon arriving, clothes stained with blood. On seeing him they called out, "Why is your apparel red?" to which Christ replied, "I trampled them." Just as the New Testament's interpretation of Isaiah 53 had led interpreters to other texts not cited in the New Testament—such as, "I gave my back to the

---

[8] Origen, *Commentary on John*, 6.287-292.

[9] Cyril of Alexandria, *Commentary on Isaiah 63:1-7* (P.G. 70: 1381b-1384b).

smiters. . . . I hid not my face from shame and spitting" (Isa. 50:6)—by the same reasoning it allowed them to give concreteness to the depiction of Christ's passion with phrases from Isaiah 63: for example, "I have trodden the wine press alone," and "I looked but there was no one to help. . . ." This reading of Isaiah 63 became something of an *opinio communis* in Christian tradition and passed over into the Eucharistic liturgy. Isaiah 63 was read on Wednesday of Holy Week in conjunction with Isaiah 53 until the reforms of the Second Vatican Council.

Now all would agree that context forms meaning. The few lines from Chapter 63 cannot stand alone, they need to be related to something other than themselves, be that the section of the book in which the passage falls, the historical setting in which the prophet lived, the meaning of the words established by usage in 6th century Hebrew, among other things. The most obvious context of this passage then is the book of Isaiah, or Second Isaiah, which portrays, after the lament in Chapter 62, God's vengeance on the nations for their abuse of Israel during the time of exile, and the vindication of Zion and the glorification of the city of Jerusalem. In this view the key persons in the text are Israel, the nations that surround Israel, such as Assyria and Babylonia, and the God of Israel. Context is defined historically and literarily. Without context as a guide interpretation, it is argued, will be arbitrary and captive to the caprice of the interpreter—as Northrop Frye, the literary critic, once quipped: like going to a hermeneutical picnic in which one person brings the text another the interpretation.

Context is, however, an elusive category. In dealing with ancient texts it is often assumed that what went before or what is contemporaneous with the text set the terms of interpretation. Yet one might ask why context should be restricted to what happened earlier. Is what went before more significant than what occurred afterward or what came about because of what happened, was said or was written down? With great political ideas, for example, it is only as they are played out in history that we know what they mean. In the telling of American history, President John Kennedy's achievements during his presidency would be remembered much differently had he not been assassinated in his first term.

Even in our personal lives and in relations with others we are constantly adjusting our view of the past and of the lives of others as new experiences unfold. We view a close friend who has patiently and heroically endured a grave illness differently than we did before his illness. Even the things done or said earlier appear different.

Fyodor Dostoevsky thought that any understanding of the past that did not see things in light of what came later produced the "worst kind of untruth." As an example he referred to a painting by the Russian artist, Nikolai Ge, in which Christ and his disciples were portrayed as average Russian men and women of the 1860s. Dostoevsky writes: "There sits Christ, but is that Christ? It may be a very good young man, deeply hurt by his quarrel with Judas, the latter standing there getting dressed to go off and denounce him, but this is not the Christ we know . . . [and] we must ask the question: where are the eighteen centuries of Christianity that followed? . . . How is it possible that from such an ordinary quarrel of such ordinary people gathered to have supper . . . there could arise something so colossal?" If we are to be true to what happened, a person or event from the past must be seen in light of subsequent developments "which had not yet occurred at the historical moment" which the artist was depicting.[10]

Dostoevsky's question is our question. Where are the 19 centuries of Christian life and history in our interpretation of the Bible? Echoing Dostoevsky we might say, "there stand the psalms as ancient Hebrew poems, but are they the psalms we know?" When I read this passage from Dostoevsky in the final volume of the magnificent biography by Joseph Frank, I was reminded of the words of another 19th century figure, Adolf von Harnack, whose ideas have dominated the interpretation of the history of theology in the 20th century (and, one might add, prejudiced generations of scholars against patristic exegesis).

Many years ago I wrote down this passage from his *Lehrbuch der Dogmengeschichte*: "No religion gains anything through time, it only loses." For Harnack, the Church's history had to be scoured by the acid of critical historical reason to uncover an earlier allegedly more pristine form of the gospel. Yet what is most characteristic of the Christian (and one might add the Jewish) interpretation of the Scriptures is that the words of the Bible do not arrive smooth and clean, scrubbed free of the experiences of centuries. Much of what we hold most dear in the Scriptures was discerned only over time.

Time has endowed the words and images of the Bible with a fulness that can be known only by reading the text forward, not backward. A particularly egregious example of the unanticipated and unhappy consequences of self-imposed amnesia is the New Revised Standard Version translation of *Beatus vir*, "Blessed is the man," in Psalm 1. By translating the verse according to the perverse and ephemeral logic of the moment, "Happy are *those* who . . .," the Christological interpretation of the psalm is swept away to become a forgotten chapter in the arcane specialty of the history of exegesis.

Allegory resists the tyranny of historicism and invites us to see things as they are, not as we imagine them to have been centuries ago. This is one reason for the formative power of the liturgy on interpretation. The Church at prayer spans the great divide separating what the text *meant* from what it *means*. Allegory is about what has come to be, the accommodation that is inevitable because of what happened in Christ, in the Church, and what continues to unfold.

---

[10] Cited in Joseph Frank, *Dostoevsky: The Mantle of the Prophet 1871-1881* (Princeton: Princeton University, 2002), 111-112.

There is then a realism in allegory as well as spiritual depth. The mystery of which the Bible speaks is realized historically and socially. St. Paul was not interested in ephemeral "meanings" that could be attached *ad libitum* to the ancient texts. He sought to discover what the authoritative documents of his religious tradition (and ours) meant in light of "the things that have been accomplished among us," to invoke Luke's memorable words.

Any discussion of allegory turns, in the end, on the Jewishness of Jesus and of his first followers. Because the things proclaimed by the prophets had taken place in their time and of which they were witnesses (something the readings from Acts during the Easter season remind us of again and again), the disciples believed that the end of the ages, the last days of Isaiah 2, had dawned. When they opened their sacred books anew, the ancient oracles could no longer be read as earlier generations of Jews had read them. Christian interpreters did not impose an evanescent superstructure on the text without root in history or experience. They shunned a strictly literal or historical reading of the law and the prophets, not because they preferred spirit to history, but because they were members of a community that had been transformed by a new series of events. Paradoxically, the spiritual sense was the historical sense.

Allegory is a form of translation. The most familiar is translation from one language into another. As any skilled translator knows, even in this type of translation the words and ideas of the Bible take on new coloring as they are expressed in the idiom of another language. The term translation is also appropriate when speaking about presenting and explaining the truths of the Scripture in the language of a new and alien culture. But there is also a translation that takes place within the idiom of the Bible itself, a rendering of what is found in one part of the Bible into the language of another part of the Scriptures. So in the example cited above, Cyril of Alexandria uses the words and the imagery of Isaiah 63 to express what is stated more straightforwardly in the gospels about the passion and ascension of Christ.

In practice, allegory is a way of thinking about what is given in the Bible using the words and images of the Bible. An impressive instance of this kind of translation is the use of the erotic imagery of the Song of Songs to interpret the words of Jesus, "You shall love the LORD your God with all your heart and with all your mind and with all your strength." It is a truth that Augustine recognized in *De Doctrina Christiana* when he said that it was more delightful to contemplate the Church as a beautiful row of teeth, using the image from the Song of Songs, "Your teeth are like a flock of shorn ewes . . ." than simply as Church.[11] It is something that Gregory the Great grasped in his *Moralia*, when he took a metaphor

---

[11] *De Doctrina Christiana*, 2.10-12.

from the book of Job such as "the waters wear away the stones" and applied it to temptations that come on gradually, "penetrating unobtrusively into the heart of man," like rocks worn down slowly.[12]

Allegory's playfulness and inventiveness grows out of the certainty of faith formed by a community of shared beliefs and practices. It keeps words from evaporating into nothing, from becoming simply things, not signs. It also introduces a welcome and necessary obliqueness into our reading of the Scriptures. Remember that according to Exodus, God showed only his back to Moses. Metaphor, symbol, image are the natural clothing of religious thought. "Tell all the truth but tell it slant," wrote Emily Dickinson, the American poet. By likening what is known to unexpected words or images within the Bible, allegory gave Christian thinkers a more subtle and versatile vocabulary to speak of the things of God. The language of the Bible became a vehicle of discovery.

Allegory is about privileging the language of the Bible. It assumes that it is better to express things in the language of the Scriptures than in another idiom. As the Church's great preachers have always known metaphors drawn from elsewhere, no matter how apt, lack the power of the biblical language to enlighten the mind and enflame the heart. Like rhetorical ornaments that momentarily delight the hearer, they are ephemeral and soon forgotten. The words of the Bible, however, are emblematic and weighted with experience. Unlike words taken from elsewhere, their meanings cannot be disengaged from the biblical narrative, from God's revelation in Israel, the sending of Christ and the pouring out of the Spirit on the Church. The range of possible meanings is never exhausted.

In spite of its many accomplishments, a strictly historical approach to the Bible is incapable of receiving the Bible as Bible. It can offer various kinds of syntheses, such as a cultural history of the ancient Near East, a chapter in the religious history of the Greco-Roman world, to mention the most obvious, but it cannot give us the book of the Church, the Scriptures that have been read, the psalms that have been prayed, the holy men and women whose lives have been imitated, the teachings that have been expounded. To be sure, the Old Testament is a book that has its origin in the ancient Near East, but the book the Church reads also belongs to another time and to other places.

It is of inestimable significance that Christians did not rewrite the Old Testament to suit Christian taste (or dispense with it). As Rémi Brague the French philosopher has reminded us, one of the marks of Christian civilization is "secondarity"—receiving what was earlier, reinterpreting, build-

---

[12] *Moralia on Job*, 12.18.22.

ing on it, not constructing new foundations.[13] There remains the book written in Hebrew and Aramaic, but the earliest Christians read it in Greek and in translations from the Greek. When read in conjunction with the apostolic writings, its words resounded with meanings they did not have before Christ. Words were singled out that had seemed commonplace, images that had lain dormant sprouted anew, persons and events once thought secondary became paradigmatic. It was this book that formed the Christian imagination. To understand the Christian Old Testament, the ancient Near East is the place to begin but hardly the goal toward which interpretation moves.

The unique vocation of the Christian exegetical tradition was to offer a comprehensive understanding of the Bible as the book of the Church centered on the Triune God. This required more than what is considered interpretation today. For the Bible of the early Church was a living voice, not only a document from ancient history. In its pages the fullness of Christian faith and life could be found in bewildering detail and infinite variety—all organized around the center which was Christ. Early Christian exegesis was not simply exegesis, but a distinctively Christian way of thinking. That we should find ourselves drawn to this synthesis does not mean that the exegesis of the early Church or the middle ages can be appropriated without being filtered through our experience and thinking, including our historical consciousness. But it does mean that at the beginning of the 21st century the time has come to take out of the closet and polish a very old word from the Christian lexicon, "allegory," and to discover anew why it is indispensable for a genuinely Christian interpretation of the Old Testament.

---

[13]   Rémi Brague, *Eccentric Culture* (Notre Dame, Ind.: University of Notre Dame, 2002).

Letter & Spirit 1 (2005): 23–40

The Sacrifice of Isaac in Genesis and Hebrews
A Study in the Hermeneutic of Faith

• James Swetnam, S.J. •

Pontifical Biblical Institute, Rome

One of the key texts in the Old Testament, both in its own right and as viewed by Christian authors, is the account of Abraham's sacrifice of Isaac in Genesis 22:1-18.[1] The present essay will attempt to understand the meaning of the account; to study how it is interpreted in the Epistle to the Hebrews; and to outline how Cardinal John Henry Newman's book, *A Grammar of Assent*, may offer grounds for a faith-centered hermeneutic that aids in the exegesis of both the Genesis and the Hebrews texts.

In the later history of biblical criticism, the sacrifice of Isaac by Abraham has proved a veritable storm center.[2] With the coming of the Enlightenment the sacrifice has often been viewed as an immoral action.[3] But such condemnations are normally based on a view of Abraham's decision to sacrifice Isaac which is divorced from its context. In the way in which Genesis 22:1-18 is customarily interpreted as part of the canonical

---

This article is an adaptation in English of a conference originally given in Italian on November 5, 2003, at the Pontifical Biblical Institute in Rome. It marks the conclusion of the author's thirty-six years of teaching at the Institute. The Italian and original English versions are available on the Institute's website, www.biblico.it.

[1] For a brief summary of the importance of Genesis 22 in scholarly biblical research and in the light of varying religious traditions, see R. W. L. Moberly, *The Bible, Theology, and Faith: A Study of Abraham and Jesus* (Cambridge: Cambridge University Press, 2000), 71-72. The expression "sacrifice of Isaac" does not mean to imply, of course, that in Genesis 22 Abraham was allowed to carry through God's command to offer Isaac in sacrifice. The traditional Hebrew expression, the "Binding [*Akedah*] of Isaac," is used to show how far the intention of Abraham to sacrifice his son was allowed by God to proceed. But there is no question that *as regards intention* Genesis 22 depicts Abraham as sacrificing his son. The Epistle to the Hebrews uses the perfect tense of the Greek verb προσενήνοχεν ("offer in sacrifice") in 11:17 to show how the author viewed Abraham's sacrificial stance towards his son as having a permanent witness in Scripture. In this sense, Genesis 22 is about the "sacrifice of Isaac."

[2] See Moberly, *The Bible, Theology, and Faith*, 132-161, for a brief presentation. A more detailed discussion can be found in David Lerch, *Isaaks Opferung christlich gedeutet: Eine auslegungsgeschichtliche Untersuchung* (Tübingen: J. C. B. Mohr, 1950); Shalom Spiegel, *The Last Trial* (New York: Behrman, 1979 [translation from the Hebrew edition of 1950]).

[3] See the forceful condemnation of Abraham's action in agreeing to slay his son by the influential philosopher Immanuel Kant as presented in Moberly, *The Bible, Theology, and Faith*, 128-129. See also some remarks of contemporary scholars, 162.

text of the Old Testament alone or of the Old Testament and the New Testament together in various religious traditions, the verses present no insuperable difficulty in this regard.[4]

There are three broad headings which seem to commend themselves in a brief discussion of the implications of Genesis 22:1-18 within the canonical text of the Old Testament: *covenant, sacrifice,* and *faith.* Taken together, these three headings provide a convenient way of entering into the text.

The Covenant Setting

For a proper understanding of Abraham's sacrifice of Isaac it is crucial to keep in mind the covenant setting of the canonical text. Verse 1 states that God is "testing" (Hebrew: נסה; Greek: πειράζειν) Abraham. That is to say, God is arranging a test to discover if his son is "faithful" (אמן; πιστός).[5] The text of Genesis 22 is the climax of a progression involving call, promise, covenant, and oath.[6] The call is found in Genesis 12:1-3, and consists of three blessings: a blessing which involves a land and nation (vv. 1-2a); a blessing which involves a dynasty (v. 2b); and a blessing which involves the entire world (v. 3 with v. 2).[7]

These three elements seem to correspond to the three covenant episodes presented in Genesis 15, 17, and 22.[8] In Genesis 15, the episode with the divided animals represents the making of a covenant by which

---

[4] This point is well made by Moberly, *The Bible, Theology, and Faith,* 129-130. On evidence from within the text that it was part of a canonical tradition (Moberly, 114).

[5] See Birger Gerhardsson, *The Testing of God's Son* (Lund: C.W.K. Gleerup, 1966): "'Faith' is a vital element here; faith meaning to 'treat YHWH as reliable' (אמן; πιστεύειν), to trust him, to believe that he will faithfully and lovingly keep his promises and honor his 'obligation.' What is required of the people in general is also required of each member individually" (26-27); "When the Old Testament speaks of YHWH testing his covenant son, 'tempting' him (נסה; πειράζειν), it means that God arranges a test to find out if his son is true to the covenant, is אמן, πιστόν. It is almost a formula that God tests 'that he might know' whether his chosen one is true or not" (27).

[6] See the discussion by Scott W. Hahn, "Kinship by Covenant: A Biblical Theological Study of Covenant Types and Texts in the Old and New Testaments" (Ph.D. diss., Marquette University, 1995), 181-211.

[7] See Hahn, "Kinship by Covenant," 183-184.

[8] Most commentators agree that the covenant between God and Abraham is a "grant-type," i.e., it comprises six basic elements: (1) oath of suzerain (i.e., God); (2) blessing by suzerain of vassal and curse of enemies; (3) unconditional obligation on part of suzerain; (4) naming of progeny of vassal as beneficiaries by suzerain; (5) suzerain's praise of "name" of vassal; (6) frequent reference by suzerain to virtue of vassal. See Hahn, "Kinship by Covenant," 168-171.

Abraham's descendants will live as a nation in a particular land. In Genesis 17, the emphasis is on Abraham's great "name," that is, there is question of a dynasty. And in Genesis 22:16-18, the climax, there is question of a blessing to all nations.[9]

Thus Genesis 22:1-18 can be viewed as the culmination of Abraham's life as it is portrayed in the canonical text of Scripture. Afterwards he enters into the story only in relation to the death of Sarah (Gen. 23) and the marriage of Isaac (Gen. 24). His definitive life and destiny in terms of his relation with God are outlined in Genesis 22.[10]

The oath sworn by God to Abraham can be considered the concluding high point in the series of covenant episodes.[11] It incorporates, so to speak, the successful outcome of Abraham's test into the blessing given to all nations, so that Abraham's faith is now a part of the destiny of his offspring.[12]

The context of the covenant in Genesis 22 is fundamental for ascertaining the precise point of the passage. For Abraham is being tested with regard to his faith in God and his faith in God's pledge to give him the blessings of the covenant despite the apparent contradiction of God's command to offer his only beloved son. Further, Abraham must have been aware that this was a test, that he was being faced with a cruel dilemma in which his filial affection must be secondary.

---

[9] See Hahn, "Kinship by Covenant," 185-186.

[10] "Within the Genesis portrayal of Abraham's life and his relationship with God, Genesis 22 is the climactic moment. It is not the final story of Abraham, for there are still two more stories in which he features. Since, however, his purchase of a burial place for Sarah anticipates his own dying and burial (Gen. 23), and in the lengthy story of the acquisition of a wife for Isaac the focus shifts away from Abraham himself to Abraham's faithful servant (Gen. 24), these stories provide a kind of diminuendo and prepare for the story line to move on from Abraham. Genesis 22 is the last dialogue between Abraham and God, and its content focuses on the nature of the relationship between Abraham and God" (Moberly, *The Bible, Theology, and Faith,* 72-73).

[11] See the discussion in Hahn, "Kinship by Covenant," 198-202.

[12] See R. W. L. Moberly, "The Earliest Commentary on the Akedah," *Vetus Testamentum* 38 (1988): 320-321.

At stake was not only the meaning of his God-centered existence but the meaning of the God-centered existence of Isaac and of all who were to be descended from him.[13] The command from God to Abraham to sacrifice Isaac, in other words, was a deadly serious affair for Abraham and for God.[14]

That the command of God to Abraham was a serious affair for God, as well as for Abraham, has perhaps not been sufficiently noted. For in ordering the test, God is implicitly endangering the whole enterprise of his covenant with Abraham. In terms of the story, God is waiting to see the result of Abraham's free reaction to the test: a refusal by Abraham to sacrifice Isaac would show that Abraham had not passed the test of his faith.[15] Hence the covenant enterprise and everything associated with it would presumably collapse and salvation history would have to take a radically new turn.

The Meaning of Sacrifice

A second major perspective according to which Genesis 22 should be interpreted is that of sacrifice. Sacrifice here is associated with the location in which the action of Genesis 22 occurs. There is ample reason to take that

---

[13] Moberly, after a discerning discussion (*The Bible, Theology, and Faith*, 102-106) of how God's omniscience can permit of the statement that "now I know" (cf. Gen. 22:12), has these summary remarks: "Issues about God with the Old Testament are never posed in separation from the relational dynamic through which Israel knows God. The most explicit raising of the issue of divine omniscience, Psalm 139, raises the issue entirely with the context of the psalmist's relationship with God. It would be a mistake to construe God's 'knowing' in relation to his 'testing' any differently. The concern of the texts is for a deepening of the encounter between God and people. Although the primary emphasis falls upon the appropriate human response, this response is relational at the same time as being moral, and this relationship is not conceived as one-sided but rather God is engaged within the encounter in such a way that the outcome is a genuine divine concern. When Abraham is depicted as 'one who fears God,' the divine pronouncement 'now I know,' rather than 'now people will know,' indicates that the deepened relationship is in some way an intrinsic concern of God even as it also constitutes the nature of mature humanity" (106-107). Moberly takes the "fear of God," which is the object of God's knowledge as a result of the test, as equivalent in Christian parlance to the "faith" of Abraham which is being tested (79). But this equivalence seems a bit too facile, and betrays a lack of recognition of the covenant dimension of faith. "Fear of God" in Genesis 22 seems to be the virtue of Abraham which is based on his faith and is evidenced by his obedience.

[14] See the discussion in Moberly, *The Bible, Theology, and Faith*, 97-98.

[15] "It is [the] dimension of human choice that is primarily signified by *nissah*, which characteristically, as in Deut. 8:2, poses Israel's response in terms of a fundamental choice—'testing you to know what was in your heart, whether you would keep his commandment[s], or not.' What marks out Abraham as 'one who fears God' is that he *chose* to obey God. What Deuteronomy holds out as a human possibility, all too often unrealized, is realized in Abraham. Human growth through choosing to obey God is the issue" (Moberly, *The Bible, Theology, and Faith*, 105).

location ("Moriah" מריה in v. 2) as Jerusalem.[16] If this is so, then Genesis 22 becomes the basic Old Testament text for understanding animal sacrifice as practiced in the Temple of Jerusalem. This, in turn, would solve the puzzle as to why so little is said in the Pentateuch about the meaning of such sacrifices.[17]

The principal type of sacrifice indicated in Leviticus and Deuteronomy is the whole burnt offering (עלה; ὁλοκαύτωμα).[18] This is precisely the type of sacrifice which Abraham is called on to make of Isaac and actually does make of the ram.[19]

The relevance of sacrifice in the interpretation of Genesis 22 has not always been given the importance it should. This lack of attention not only distorts understanding of the interpretation of Genesis 22 which must have guided generations of faithful readers in Israel. It further distorts the possible relevance which Genesis 22 should have for the modern reader of the canonical text. By showing exactly how sacrifice can have a purchase on human existence as personified in Abraham, Genesis 22 is of crucial importance in the understanding of God's revelation as contained in the Bible.

The Centrality of Faith

The perspectives involving covenant and sacrifice indicate the centrality of faith in Abraham's response to God. Covenant and sacrifice are focused on

---

[16] See Moberly, *The Bible, Theology, and Faith*, 108-116. Moberly notes that the emphasis given in v. 14 to the place of the testing as "YHWH sees" indicates that "the general truth about God is tied to a particular place where that truth is realized" (p. 109).

[17] See Moberly, *The Bible, Theology, and Faith*, 117-118: "Genesis 22 becomes the primary account within the Old Testament of the meaning of animal sacrifice (as practiced in the Jerusalem Temple). It has long been a puzzle that the extensive Pentateuchal prescriptions for sacrificial worship say so little about the meaning of what is prescribed. One explanation, at least in terms of the Pentateuch as a canonical collection, is that the meaning of sacrifice has been so clearly depicted in Genesis 22 that further explanation becomes superfluous."

[18] Lev. 1; Deut. 12:6,11,13,14,27. See also, Moberly, *The Bible, Theology, and Faith*, 118.

[19] Gen. 22:2,13. "Within Genesis 22 Abraham's sacrifice of the ram stands in place of his sacrifice of Isaac. Once Abraham sees the ram, he does not need to be told what to do, but directly grasps its significance and so he sacrifices the ram instead of Isaac. The meaning of this substitution of animal for child is provided by the preceding narrative of God's testing, Abraham's fearing, and God's providing. That is, the whole burnt offering is symbolic of Abraham's self-sacrifice as a person who unreservedly fears God. Sacrifice could, and no doubt did, mean other things within Israelite history (not to mention other contexts). But the canonical and received meaning is that of Genesis 22, where visible religious action and inward spiritual significance are knit together as one" (Moberly, *The Bible, Theology, and Faith*, 118).

God as he manifested himself to Abraham (covenant) and as Abraham replies to God's command (sacrifice). It is faith that motivates Abraham.[20] To have faith is to treat God as reliable (אמן; πιστεύειν), to trust him, to believe that he will faithfully and lovingly keep his promises and honor his obligations.[21]

Because Abraham's faith was based on his covenant with God, he was aware of what was at stake, and was cognizant not only of what was expected of him (obedience) but what God expected of himself (fulfillment of the promises)—Abraham's faith was a type of knowledge. And it was this knowledge which enabled Abraham to withstand the test God had prepared for him: Abraham *knew* that God would somehow provide a solution to what, outside the realm of faith, was an insoluble problem. In other words, Genesis 22:8 ("God will Himself provide a lamb for a burnt offering") is to be taken not simply as the anxious words of a distraught father to a questioning son, but as an expression of certainty based on faith.

In seeking the relevance of Genesis 22 for the reader of today, faith is thus the crucial element. It is this element which provides the basis for the religious significance of the original text for any application of that significance to a world contemporary with a reader of any time.[22] Hence any attempt to read Genesis 22, if it is to come to grips with the core relevance of the text for the contemporary world, has to be based on Abraham's faith.

But there are two basic ways in which Abraham's faith can be approached by the contemporary reader. The reader may choose to stand "inside the loop" of Abraham's faith, or outside of it. That is to say, the reader may share in the faith of Abraham as he undergoes the events of Genesis 22, or the reader may simply consider himself to be an onlooker of the events portrayed. Herein lies the crucial hermeneutical challenge of Genesis 22.

Nothing within the text will force the reader to opt for a reading in which he incorporates Abraham's faith into his own life. The stance here

---

[20] The result of Abraham's faith as seen in Genesis 22 is that he is shown to "fear God" (ירא אלהים). This phrase seems to situate Abraham in a broader context than the covenant, making his conduct a model for all those who react in obedience to God. See Moberly, *The Bible, Theology, and Faith*, 94-97.

[21] See above, n. 5.

[22] On the question of the religious meaning of a biblical text as a key element for the application of that text to the situation of a later age, see the remarks of Albert Vanhoye, former secretary of the Pontifical Biblical Commission, in Peter Williamson, "Catholicism and the Bible," *First Things* 74 (June-July, 1997): 36: "The Bible is a collection of religious writings. If one does not explain the religious meaning of a biblical writing, one has not explained the text adequately."

has to be dictated by the reader's own free choice. God's freedom in calling Abraham and in putting him to the test and Abraham's freedom in responding to this call and test are mirrored in the freedom which every reader enjoys before the text as it stands. This is not something peculiar to Genesis 22—it is a choice which faces every reader of the Bible. It is the peculiar merit of Genesis 22, however, that it sets forth this choice in all its starkness.[23]

Abraham in Hebrews

The Epistle to the Hebrews pays particular attention to Genesis 22. This attention can serve as a guide in understanding how the early Christians interpreted this key text in their search for understanding the reality of Jesus Christ.

Hebrews (11:17-19) singles out Abraham's faith in its understanding of the Genesis text:

> [17] By faith Abraham, in the act of being tested, stands as offering Isaac, that is, he attempted to offer up his only son in sacrifice, he who had received the promises, [18] he to whom it had been said that *In Isaac will your seed be named,* [19] having concluded that God was able to raise from the dead, and as a result he received Isaac back as a symbol.[24]

The text is theologically rich. "Faith" (πίστις) is highlighted. In Hebrews 11, faith is attributed to a variety of Old Testament heroes, and is described in 11:2-3, 6.[25] The word "offer [in sacrifice]" is used twice in v. 17. The first use is in the perfect tense (προσενήνοχεν, "stands as offering")— Abraham's sacrificial stance is the chief point of Genesis 22 upon which the author of Hebrews wishes to base his understanding of the whole text. The

---

[23] See the remarks of E. D. Hirsch, Jr., *Validity in Interpretation* (New Haven: Yale University Press, 1967), 24: "Since it is very easy for a reader of any text to construe meanings that are different from the author's, there is nothing in the nature of the text itself which requires the reader to set up the author's meaning as his normative ideal. Any normative concept in interpretation implies a choice that is required not by the nature of written texts but rather by the goal that the interpreter sets himself."

[24] My translation from the Greek. The text used is that of Nestle–Aland, *Novum Testamentum Graece* (Stuttgart: Deutsche Bibelgesellschaft, 1994[27]), 581. There are no significant textual variants.

[25] Any detailed study of the use of Genesis 22 in Hebrews would have to take into account these descriptions. But such a study is beyond the possibility of the present paper.

second verb is in the imperfect tense (προσέφερεν, "attempted to offer"). This conative imperfect describes how Abraham was "in the act of being tested" (πειραζόμενος).

The terms of the testing are made clear: he was offering up his "only son" (μονογενῆ) as "one who had received the promises" (ὁ τὰς ἐπαγγελίας ἀναδεξάμενος). The promise in question is specified: "He to whom it had been said, 'In Isaac will your seed be named'" (πρὸς ὃν ἐλαλήθη ὅτι ἐν Ἰσαὰκ κληθήσεταί σοι σπέρμα). These remarks indicate that the author of Hebrews has read the text of Genesis 22 with care, and has set out the parameters of the test with precision. What follows is a remarkable interpretation of the reasoning behind Abraham's faith in God: "having concluded that God was able to raise from the dead" (λογισάμενος ὅτι καὶ ἐκ νεκρῶν ἐγείρειν δυνατὸς ὁ θεός).

The apparently matter-of-fact way in which the author of Hebrews attributes belief in the resurrection from the dead to Abraham should not distract one from realizing the implications of what is being affirmed. Abraham's faithful inference would seem to be plausible, given his previous belief in the birth of Isaac from his own "dead" body and Sarah's "dead" womb.[26] In view of Abraham's heroic faith, there is nothing forced or artificial about the exegesis. If God's promise of offspring through Isaac (v. 18) had to be believed without qualification, and the command to sacrifice Isaac was for Abraham required by God, then his belief in the resurrection would seem to a possible—indeed, perhaps even the only possible inference.

What is remarkable is the attribution of belief in resurrection from the dead to Abraham. He stands at the very fountainhead of Old Testament belief and practice, and this belief and practice is traditionally understood as being agnostic with regard to resurrection from the dead.[27] Here, a Christian writer who had clearly reflected long and deeply on the Old Testament antecedents to his Christian faith, states decisively that Abraham believed in resurrection from the dead.[28]

---

[26] See Heb. 11:10-11; Rom. 4:19.

[27] The following texts are sometimes cited in support of belief in resurrection from the dead in the Old Testament: Isa. 26:19; Ezek. 37:4-14; Dan. 12:2. The first two texts are not conclusive. The third is much more probable as an indication of belief in individual resurrection from the dead, but it is quite late.

[28] One modern commentator on Hebrews remarks dryly: "This phrase and the belief thus attributed to Abraham go well beyond the scriptural data." See Harold W. Attridge, *The Epistle to the Hebrews* (Philadelphia: Fortress, 1989), 335. The explicit scriptural data, certainly. But what is implicit in the scriptural data, perhaps not. Another modern commentator on Hebrews notes: "What the present verse says about resurrection is clearly derived not from Old Testament or other pre-Christian sources, but from primitive Christian tradition." See Paul Ellingworth, *The Epistle to the Hebrews*, New International Greek Testament Commentary (Grand Rapids, Mich.: W.B. Eerdmans, 1993), 602. Agreed. But again the inference attributed to Abraham seems legitimate given the circumstances and given Abraham's faith.

If Abraham's interior attitude in sacrificing Isaac is to be understood as paradigmatic for the interior attitude of all subsequent Old Testament worshippers, this is a startling statement about what Hebrews' author regards as implicitly standing behind all Old Testament sacrifice. The author seems to be attributing this attitude, at least implicitly, to all those offering sacrifices in the Old Testament.

What seems to be happening in Hebrews 11:19 is that the author, guided by his faith in the resurrection of Christ (Heb. 13:20), is extrapolating this belief into the world of Abraham. But the extrapolation is perfectly in keeping with the words of the Old Testament text—that is, the interpretation does no violence to the parameters of the Genesis account as it stands. As we have noted, in the context of Abraham's presumed heroic faith in God, there is nothing out of character for such a belief on Abraham's part. The second part of Hebrews 11:19 confirms the view that the author of Hebrews was thinking of the restoration of Isaac with relation to the resurrection of Jesus, for he states that the restoration is a "symbol" of the resurrection of Jesus.[29]

The Oath Sworn to Abraham

Hebrews (6:13-18) alludes to the sacrifice of Isaac at 6:14 with a citation from the text of Genesis 22:17. The context of Hebrews is revealing:

> [13] For God, having made a promise to Abraham, since he had no one greater to swear by, swore by himself, [14]*with the words: With blessing shall I bless you, and with increase shall I increase you.* [15]And thus, having endured, did Abraham receive the promise. [16]For men swear by that which is greater; and at the end of every controversy among them comes the oath as a confirmation. [17]Thus God, wishing to show more clearly to the heirs of the promise the unchangeable nature of his design, intervened with an oath. [18]The purpose of the oath was that, through two

[29] Ellingworth (*Hebrews*, 604) suggests that the reference is more to the resurrection of believers than to the resurrection of Jesus, since the author of Hebrews is more interested in the former than in the latter. I wish to contest this view—the resurrection of Jesus is, for the author of Hebrews, that which brings to "perfection" the priesthood of Jesus. See James Swetnam, "The Structure of Hebrews 1:1–3:6," *Melita Theologica* 43 (1992): 58-62; in particular, n. 28. Also, see James Swetnam, "Christology and the Eucharist in the Epistle to the Hebrews," *Biblica* 70 (1989): 78-79 and n. 17.

unchangeable things in which it is impossible that God lie,
we have a strong source of comfort, we who have fled, so
as to lay hold of the hope before us.[30]

The author of Hebrews is here exhorting his addressees to show the necessary diligence and concern to imitate the heirs of the promises and receive
themselves what has been promised through faith and endurance (see Heb.
6:9-12, especially v. 12). Hence the presence of the introductory "for" in v.
16. That Genesis 22 is in the mind of the author of Hebrews is seen, not
only from the citation of v. 17 of that chapter at Hebrews 6:14, but also from
the allusion to the oath of Genesis 22:16 in Hebrews 6:13. This suggests
that for the author of Hebrews the oath has a close relation to the blessing
and multiplication of Abraham's offspring.

The precise content of the "two unchangeable things" mentioned in
Hebrews 6:18 is much canvassed.[31] The text at Hebrews 6:13-14 would
seem to furnish the first step towards an answer. The "two unchangeable
things" are the oath of Genesis 22:16 and the promise of Genesis 22:17.
They are juxtaposed in Hebrews just as they are juxtaposed in Genesis.
The words of the promise speak for themselves with regard to the content:
they have to do with the multiplication of Abraham's progeny.[32] The oath
serves to reinforce this promise, so that when Abraham receives the promise at the conclusion of his heroic show of patience at the call to sacrifice
Isaac (Heb 6:15), the promise has been reinforced by an oath. Abraham is
thus portrayed as having received the promise.

But it is clear from the way the author of Hebrews uses the verbs
ἐπιτυγχάνω (6:15; see 11:33) and κομίζω that even if Abraham had received
(ἐπιτυγχάνω) the promise reinforced by an oath, he had not received
(κομίζω) the thing promised—progeny (cf. 10:36 and 11:39).[33]

The mind of the Hebrews' author is revealed by the third use
of κομίζω—at 11:19, where he says that Abraham received (κομίζω) Isaac
after the attempted sacrifice "as a symbol" (ἐν παραβολῇ). In other words,

---

[30] My translation from N-A[27]; see n. 24, above.

[31] See the discussion of opinions in William L. Lane, *Hebrews 1–8*, Word Biblical Commentary, 47a
(Dallas: Word, 1991), 152.

[32] It is this promise which is referred to in the singular at Hebrews 6:17, "to the heirs of the promise"
(τοῖς κληρονόμοις τῆς ἐπαγγελίας).

[33] See also Heb. 11:13 where the verb κομίζω is a variant reading for the better attested λαμβάνω. The
use of the latter verb emphasizes the reality of the obtaining or not obtaining of the promises, while the
use of κομίζω takes in the emphasis on the reality of obtaining or not obtaining while adding an
eschatological nuance.

the thing promised to Abraham at the sacrifice of Isaac—progeny—is received only with the coming of Christ. Christ himself is that promised progeny.

If the content of the promise to Abraham is Christ, then the oath that God swore to Abraham is, at the most profound level, a symbolic action foreshadowing the definitive granting of the thing promised, which is Christ. That is why the author of Hebrews emphasizes the oath sworn by God to Jesus at the moment of his resurrection (Heb. 7:20-21). This is the oath which was foreshadowed by the oath of God at the sacrifice of Isaac. This latter oath results in the actual granting of that which was promised in the oath sworn to Abraham: definitive progeny. As Christ is the definitive progeny promised by God's oath to Abraham, that oath was a symbolic foreshadowing of the oath that God swears at the resurrection—that Jesus will be a priest forever.[34]

By identifying the oath of Psalm 110:4 with the fulfillment of the oath of Genesis 22:16, and by placing the oath in the explicit context of the multiplication of Abraham's seed, the author of Hebrews has brought about a profound transformation in the nature of this seed. For the Hebrews author, the true and definitive offspring of Abraham is effected not through his physical child Isaac, but through his spiritual offspring, Jesus Christ, of whom Isaac was a "symbol" with regard to Jesus' resurrection, as well as with regard to the accompanying oath of Psalm 110:4.

The author of Hebrews thinks that this offspring can be best described by evoking the Old Testament figure of Melchizedek, in the context of whom Jesus Christ emerges as the definitive High Priest. As the High Priest according to the order of Melchizedek, Jesus Christ replaces the Levitical high priesthood which had heretofore given identity to Abraham's descendants (Heb. 7:11). This new high priest is the Son of God himself (Heb. 7:3).[35]

He is the source of the definitively better hope which is the cause of the addressees' encouragement. The one through whom God made the ages (Heb. 1:2) is the one through whom God definitively blesses and multiplies Abraham's offspring. Through Christ's risen priesthood a new people has come into being (Heb. 7:12), one coextensive with the entire human race. Through a son who transcends time, Abraham's offspring is extended

---

[34] For the classic presentation of this interpretation of the role of Ps. 110:4 (though without some of the nuances given here) See Helmut Köster, "Die Auslegung der Abraham-Verheissung in Hebräer 6", in *Studien zur Theologie der alttestamentlichen Überlieferungen*, ed. Rolf Rendtorff and Klaus Koch (Neukirchen: Neukirchener Verlag, 1961), 95-109.

[35] See James Swetnam, "Hebrews 1:4-14," *Melita Theologica* 51 (2000): 51-68.

to all men who have ever lived and who will ever live—to those who existed before Abraham as well as those who will exist after him. This is the way
the author of Hebrews understands the meaning of Genesis 22:17, with its
promise that God will bless and multiply Abraham's offspring.

The Relevance of Faith

Just as the reader is faced with the choice of a hermeneutic when confronted with Genesis 22, so the reader is faced with the choice of a
hermeneutic when confronted with the interpretation of that text in the
Epistle to the Hebrews. The reader may opt to share in the obvious faith
the Hebrews' author had in the Christian relevance of the Genesis account,
or he may not. That is to say, the reader may opt to be a participant in
Christ's role and in Abraham's role in Genesis 22 as seen by the author of
Hebrews, or he may opt to be a spectator. Right here is the crucial
hermeneutical challenge of Genesis 22 as presented in Hebrews.

Every reader of Hebrews comes to the text with a certain set of presuppositions, just as every reader comes to Genesis with a certain set of
presuppositions. Such presuppositions determine in large measure the
reader's choice of a hermeneutic. A Christian who lets his Christian faith
enter into every facet of his life will identify automatically with the
Christian author of Hebrews. For such a believer, identification with the
faith of Abraham as presented in Genesis 22 will be subsumed into the
faith of the Hebrews' author in the Christ who gives to the Abraham-Isaac
story a new dimension.

According to the interpretation of the author of Hebrews, with
the coming of Christ the account in Genesis 22 assumes a more profound
meaning: the faith of Abraham becomes a faith in the power of God to
raise from the dead. Further, the oath made to Abraham finds its fulfillment in the oath made by God to Jesus at the moment of his resurrection
so that his earthly priesthood can become a heavenly priesthood according to the order of Melchizedek—that is, a priesthood which transcends
all human limitations.

One final, crucial truth about the faith of Abraham as seen by the
author of Hebrews should be noted: Abraham's obedience is rewarded by
God with the gift of Isaac as symbol of the resurrection of Jesus. Thus the
faith-trust of Abraham enters into the providence of God in achieving the
role of Christ as High Priest for all of humanity.

According to Hebrews 11:17-19, Abraham received Isaac back "as a
symbol" (ἐν παραβολῇ), that is, he received Isaac as a symbol of the escha-

tological reality which is the risen Christ.[36] Abraham's reasoning is expressed in Hebrews 11:19a: ". . . having believed that God was able to raise from the dead." The text goes on to say, "whence (ὅθεν) he received him back as a symbol" (Heb. 11:19b).[37] Abraham's trust (Heb. 11:17) leads him to believe in God's ability to raise from the dead (Heb. 11:19a) and this faith earns him a divine reward—not only the gift of Isaac, but the gift of Jesus, who is prefigured by Isaac.

Hebrews 11:17-19 is found in a section of the letter in which God is presented as a "rewarder" (μισθαποδότης; see Heb. 11:6) of those who seek him in faith. The inference to be made, then, is that the supreme gift of the resurrection of Jesus, and all that follows from it, is in a sense a "reward" for the faithfulness of Abraham, who has passed the test imposed by God.[38]

Thus, the final act of Genesis 22—God's oath to Abraham—contains something new for the author of Hebrews: the role of Abraham's faith enters into the gift of the risen Jesus and hence into all that the risen Jesus implies for humanity, as outlined above.[39] God has taken cognizance of Abraham's covenant faith and has responded in the language of his own covenant loyalty. And he has done so in a completely unexpected way.

The Preconceptions of Christian Belief

There is one final step needed to sketch a satisfying hermeneutic of Genesis 22 and Hebrews: the preconceptions which prompt the Christian believer to believe in a Christian interpretation of Abraham's faith

---

[36] Some authors maintain that the resurrection of Jesus is not as important for the author of the epistle as the resurrection of Christians (for example, Attridge, *Hebrews*, 335, n. 34). But this is to ignore much patristic evidence to the contrary on the relation between Isaac and Jesus, as Attridge himself admits. The view represented by Attridge also depends very much on his interpretation of Hebrews 2 with regard to the expression "Son of Man," in which Attridge follows common views for the most part. For a different view, see Swetnam, "The Structure of Hebrews 1:13–3:6," 58-62, in particular, 64, n. 28.

[37] See the discussion of ὅθεν in Ellingworth, *Hebrews*, 603.

[38] See the discussion of Hebrews 11:6 in Attridge, *Hebrews*, 318-319.

[39] This inference of the author of Hebrews follows the sense of the Old Testament of Genesis 22, where the oath following on Abraham's successful completion of the test contains something new with respect to the original promise of descendants made by God to Abraham: the plans of God for Abraham's descendants are henceforth based on the will of God and the obedience of Abraham (which two elements, obviously, do not enjoy equal billing). See above, n. 12.

must be explored. No one approaches any written text without precon-
ceived ideas. If this is true of any written text in general, all the more so
is it true of a religious text such as the Bible. In particular it is true of
Genesis 22 and the Christian interpretation of Genesis 22 in the Epistle
to the Hebrews.

It was argued above that the only proper way to approach the
interpretation of Genesis 22 is on the basis of its place in the larger context of Scripture. For the sacrifice of Isaac by Abraham was intended by
the author of Genesis 22 to be understood in a much broader context than
the text itself.[40] This broader context takes in such fundamental questions of religious cult and morality that Genesis 22 frequently serves as a
focus of discussion on man's relations with God.[41]

Given the fundamental nature of the questions involved, then, it
is impossible that the reader not approach Genesis 22 with certain preconceptions. These preconceptions may be of a believer or of a nonbeliev-
er. Whatever their nature they are present, and their presence, since it
inevitably involves subsequent interpretation of the biblical text, should
be taken explicitly into account. As was argued above, hermeneutical
stance is a matter of choice: one chooses one's approach to a text.[42] But
this choice is not made in a vacuum of values. One's preconceptions are
inevitably the basis for one's choice of hermeneutical stance. Hence the
choice of one's hermeneutical stance must be investigated in the light of
one's preconceptions.

It is in this context that it seems appropriate to introduce John
Henry Newman's *An Essay in Aid of a Grammar of Assent* (1870).[43] The
core insight of the book is that the act of assent of the human person is
not the result of a reflex act which is called certitude; rather the act of
assent is the result of a variety of contributing causes working together

---

[40] For example, the use of the word "test" implies the context of covenant, as was mentioned above
(cf. n. 5); the mention of "Moriah" suggests the context of Jerusalem, as was mentioned above (cf. above,
n. 16); the mention of "holocaust" suggests the context of sacrifice, as was mentioned above (cf. n. 19).

[41] See Moberly, *The Bible, Theology, and Faith*, 71-72.

[42] See above, n. 23.

[43] The edition used in this article is John Henry Cardinal Newman, *An Essay in Aid of a Grammar of
Assent*, with introduction by Nicholas Lash (Notre Dame: University of Notre Dame Press, 1979).

in what he calls the "illative sense."[44] The illative sense, for Newman, is the personal use of reason about some concrete matter.[45] He insists on the personal nature of any such use of reason.[46] As authorities for this view he cites Aristotle and Scripture.[47]

Given the personal nature of any such use of reason with regard to some concrete reality, the role of conscience in religion is for Newman unavoidable:

> Our great internal teacher of religion is . . . our conscience. Conscience is a personal guide, and I use it because I must use myself; I am as little able to think by any mind but

---

[44] Newman, *Grammar of Assent*, 271: "I have already said that the sole and final judgment on the validity of an inference in concrete matter is committed to the personal action of the ratiocinative faculty, the perfection or virtue of which I have called the Illative Sense, a use of the word 'sense' parallel to our use of it in 'good sense,' 'common sense,' a 'sense of beauty,' &c.; –and I own I do not see any way to go farther than this in answer to the question." In his discussion of faith Newman tends to think in terms of what is believed as a result of the use of the illative sense ("*fides quae*"). But this conception of faith as being that which is believed logically presupposes a prior faith in the biblical sense ("*fides qua*"), i.e., the trust in God which is the basis for what is believed.

[45] Newman draws a contrast between a judgment about something "scientific" and a judgment about something "practical." It is necessary to study the chapter, "The Illative Sense," (Grammar, 270-299) to understand his approach. A detailed discussion is impossible here. As with any other imaginative suggestion, this suggestion of Newman's must be corrected, refined, and deepened.

[46] Newman, *Grammar of Assent*, 321: ". . . in any inquiry about things in the concrete, men differ from each other, not so much in the soundness of their reasoning as in the principles which govern its exercise, that those principles are of a personal character, that where there is no common measure of minds, there is no common measure of arguments, and that the validity of proof is determined, not by any scientific test, but by the illative sense."

[47] Newman, *Grammar of Assent*, 321-322. He gives no explicit references, but does give citations. For example, "Young men come to be mathematicians and the like, but they cannot possess practical judgment, for the talent is employed upon individual facts, and these are learned only by experience; and a youth has not experience, for experience is only gained by a course of years. And so, again, it would appear that a boy may be a mathematician, but not a philosopher, or learned in physics, and for this reason—because the one study deals with abstractions, while the other studies gain their principles from experience, and in the latter subjects youths do not give assent, but make assertions, but in the former they know what it is they are handling" (322). Newman is referring to a passage in Aristotle's *The Nicomachean Ethics*, bk. 6, chap. 8 (cf. J. A. K. Thomson, *The Ethics of Aristotle: The Nicomachean Ethics Translated* [Harmondsworth: Penguin Books, 1971], 182). Among the Scripture texts alluded to by Newman is John 7:17: "If anyone wishes to do his will, he will know whether the teaching is from God or whether I speak on my own" (my translation). Cf. also Epistle VII of Plato [#344A-D] (Plato, with an English Translation: *Timaeus, Critias, Cleitophon, Menexenus, Epistles*, by R. G. Bury [Loeb IX; London: William Heinemann / New York: G. P. Putnam's Sons, 1929], p. 538]).

> my own as to breathe with another's lungs. Conscience is
> nearer to me than any other means of knowledge.[48]

The use of the word "knowledge" in the last sentence should be noted:
Conscience, in matters of religion, is a means of knowledge. From this it follows that Scripture is not merely a collection of abstract truths, but an
authoritative teaching.

> And the whole tenor of Scripture from beginning to end is
> to this effect: the matter of Revelation is not a mere col-
> lection of truths, not a philosophical view, not a religious
> sentiment or spirit, not a special morality . . . but an
> authoritative teaching, which bears witness to itself and
> keeps itself together as one, in contrast to the assemblage
> of opinions on all sides of it, and speaks to all men, as
> being ever and everywhere one and the same, and claim-
> ing to be received intelligently, by all whom it addresses,
> as one doctrine, discipline, and devotion directly given
> from above.[49]

This view, of course, is the result of Newman's own exercise of
conscience as a means of knowledge. He reached his judgment about "the
whole tenor of Scripture" as a result, in part, of the personal guidance of his
conscience, and to this judgment he gives real assent.[50] He concludes his

---

[48] Newman, *Grammar of Assent*, 304. See further the remarks of one recent commentator: "His
[Newman's] concern is not with finding *more* knowledge of the divine, but rather with showing that
religious experience can help us *realize* the more abstract knowledge of God we already have. The
question he poses to himself in the Grammar is this: 'Can I attain to any more vivid assent to the Being
of a God, than that which is given merely to notions of the intellect? Can I enter with a personal
knowledge into the circle of truths which make up that great thought? Can I rise to what I have called
an imaginative apprehension of it? Can I believe as if I saw?' The religious experience in conscience
enables him to answer these questions in the affirmative, because God is there perceived and
encountered, not as an abstract essence, but as a concrete reality. The difference that such an
experience makes in our conception of God, and in our relation with him, is analogous to the difference
between actually meeting a person and just hearing about him." J. van Schaljik, "Newman and Otto on
Religious Experience," *Communio: International Catholic Review* 28 (2001): 734.

[49] Newman, *Grammar of Assent*, 302.

[50] Newman, *Grammar of Assent*, 82-83: "Real assent . . . calls as the experience which it presupposes,
is proper to the individual, and, as such, thwarts rather than promotes the intercourse of man with
man. . . . I call the characteristics of an individual accidents, in spite of the universal reign of law,
because they are severally the co-incidents of many laws, and there are no laws as yet discovered of
such coincidence."

book by showing his own reasons for believing in the Catholic Church as God's providential gift to be accepted by faith,[51] a faith, however, which is associated with an accumulation of probabilities yielding the certitude which results from the legitimate use of the illative sense.[52]

Newman offers a hermeneutics of exegetical preconceptions that gives grounding to the hermeneutics of exegetical choice advanced above in regards to Genesis 22 and its interpretation in Hebrews.

Conclusion

The present study began with a presentation of Genesis 22, with all its attendant challenges to interpretation. Because of its explicit connections to covenant and cult, an exegesis was advanced based on the acceptance of that covenant and cult as part of the religious dispensation whose written record is the Old Testament. The proper response to Genesis 22, it was argued, is one of faith mirroring the faith of Abraham. This interpretation of the propriety of faith was occasioned by the content of Genesis 22, not mandated. It was argued that the acceptance of Genesis 22 in a spirit of faith was the result of a hermeneutics of free choice.

An interpretation given to Genesis 22 by the Epistle to the Hebrews was next suggested. This interpretation revolved around the faith of Abraham and the oath of God sworn to Abraham following the successful outcome of his test. The faith-inspired interpretation given by the author of Hebrews was seen as a function of faith in Jesus Christ. The propriety of a reading of the text accompanied by faith was again proposed. And once again, this faith was seen as the result of a hermeneutics of free choice. The Old Testament faith of the believing Jew was subsumed into the New Testament faith of the Christian.

Finally, an attempt was made in this paper to ground this hermeneutics of exegetical choice on a hermeneutics of exegetical preconceptions. Newman's "illative sense" was proposed as a key factor in understanding the exegetical preconceptions that the Christian believer (in Newman's case, of the Catholic believer), brings to the biblical text. Because of the importance of conscience in the formation of the preconceptions which

---

[51] Newman, *Grammar of Assent*, 321: ". . . instead of saying that the truths of Revelation depend on those of Natural Religion, it is more pertinent to say that belief in revealed truths depends on belief in natural."

[52] Newman, *Grammar of Assent*, 319-320; see also, 299.

underlie the Christian's act of faith, the role of moral choice is evident here as well.

Following Newman, it can be argued that, when all is said and done, it is the individual exegete who is responsible for the exegetical stance adopted for interpreting a given text of Scripture—first with regard to the preconceptions which govern his choice of an exegetical approach, and then with regard to the choice itself.

It is clear that Genesis 22 portrays Abraham as a man of faith; it is clear that the Epistle to the Hebrews portrays Abraham in Genesis 22 as a man of faith and presents Jesus Christ as the fulfillment of that faith. Whether the exegete will put himself in tune with this faith is a matter of his own choosing, a choosing both remote and proximate.

In attributing hermeneutical stance to personal choice one should not neglect the bias built into the biblical text itself: the text itself is an invitation to believe as its authors believe. It is clear from the way Genesis 22 is framed, and from the way that the Epistle to the Hebrews enters into a development of Genesis 22 in terms of Jesus Christ, that the authors of these texts are believers who have written these texts for other believers, actual or potential.

The Hebrews' author speaks frequently of "we"—"we believers" (cf. 1:2; 2:3; 3:6; etc.). He believes, and writes to others who believe. At the most profound level, these texts call for participation in the faith of those portrayed, not simply a contemplation of that faith. As Kierkegaard remarks about the biblical passage involving the widow's mite (Mark 12:41-44), acceptance of the story on its own terms, that is, presupposing the faith of the widow, transforms the gift "into much." This faith-challenge is the challenge of Genesis 22 in its Old and New Testament guises as well.

> . . .that sympathetic person who accepts the book and gives to it a good place, that sympathetic person who, by accepting it, does for it through himself and through his acceptance, what the treasury did for the widow's mites: hallows the gift, gives it significance, and transforms it into much.[53]

---

[53]   Translated by T. Jacobsen from the preface to *Fire opbyggelig Taler*, Søren Kierkegaards samlede Verker udgivne of A. B. Drachmann, J. L. Heiberg, og H. O. Lange, 2nd ed. IV (Copenhagen, 1923), 7. Used by Jacobsen in his article "The Myth of Inanna and Bilulu," *Journal of Near Eastern Studies* 12 (1953): 160-187, and reprinted in Thorkild Jacobsen, *Toward the Image of Tammuz and Other Essays on Mesopotamian History and Culture*, ed. William L. Moran (Cambridge, Mass.: Harvard University Press, 1970), 61. Jacobsen uses the quotation to invite the reader to invest credibility in an ancient Sumerian myth written in an "old book of clay." As it is used in the conference above, it invites faith in the Bible. A "literary faith" of the type advocated by Jacobsen has, of course, its own value, but a "religious faith" that saves presents a dimension that is completely different. A faith that saves, obviously, is dependent ultimately on a gift of God.

Letter & Spirit 1 (2005): 41-68

THE "RANSOM FOR MANY," THE NEW EXODUS, AND THE END OF THE EXILE
Redemption as the Restoration of All Israel (Mark 10:35-45)

• Brant Pitre •

Loyola University, New Orleans

Of the many difficult sayings of Jesus in the Gospels, the famous statement about the Son of Man having come to give his life as "a ransom for many" (Mark 10:45) is arguably one of the most enigmatic. While exegetes continue to offer various competing interpretations of the statement, and while it has been traditionally interpreted as somehow referring to an atonement for the sins of humanity, the precise meaning of Jesus' words continue to remain veiled in obscurity.[1] Moreover, the passage has been the subject of a long-standing scholarly debate about whether or not the "Servant Songs" of Isaiah, in particular Isaiah 52-53, are being alluded to in Jesus' references to the Son of Man "serving" and "giving his life" for "many."[2]

---

[1] See discussion below for examples of scholarly difficulty in interpreting the text.

[2] For recent discussion by prominent scholars, see especially the exchanges found in William H. Bellinger, Jr., and William R. Farmer, ed., *Jesus and the Suffering Servant: Isaiah 53 and Christian Origins* (Harrisburg, Penn.: Trinity Press International, 1998). From this volume the following essays are of particular importance: Morna Hooker, "Did the Use of Isaiah 53 to Interpret His Mission Begin with Jesus?", 88-103; Rikki E. Watts, "Jesus' Death, Isaiah 53, and Mark 10:45: A Crux Revisited," 125-51; and N. T. Wright, "The Servant and Jesus: The Relevance of the Colloquy for the Current Quest for Jesus," 281-97. For other references, see also Craig A. Evans, *Mark 8:27-16:20*, Word Biblical Commentary, 34b (Nashville: Thomas Nelson, 2001), 109-125; W. D. Davies, Dale C. Allison, Jr., *A Critical and Exegetical Commentary on the Gospel According to Saint Matthew*, 3 vols., International Critical Commentary, 28 (Edinburgh: T. & T. Clark, 1988, 1991, 1997), 3:94-100; Rikki E. Watts, *Isaiah's New Exodus in Mark*, Wissenschaftliche Untersuchungen zum Neuen Testament. 2, 88 (Tübingen: J. C. B. Mohr [Paul Siebeck], 1997), 270-87; N. T. Wright, *Jesus and the Victory of God* (Minneapolis: Fortress Press, 1996), 579-91; Ben Witherington, *The Christology of Jesus* (Minneapolis: Fortress Press, 1990), 251-56; Volker Hampel, *Menschensohn und historischer Jesus: Ein Rätzelwort als Schlüssel zum messianischen Selbstverständnis Jesu* (Neukirchen-Vluyn: Neukirchener, 1990), 326-33; Peter Stuhlmacher, "Vicariously Giving His Life for Many, Mark 10:45 (Matt 20:28)," in *Reconciliation, Law, and Righteousness* (Philadelphia: Fortress Press, 1986), 16-29; G. R. Beasley-Murray, *Jesus and the Kingdom of God* (Grand Rapids, Mich.: W.B. Eerdmans, 1986), 273-83; Joachim Jeremias, *New Testament Theology I. The Proclamation of Jesus,* trans. John Bowden (New York: SCM, 1971), 292-94; Jeremias, "Das Lösegeld für Viele (Mk 10.45)," in *Abba: Studien zur neutestamentlichen Theologie und Zeitgeschichte* (Göttingen: Vandenhoeck & Ruprecht, 1966), 216-29; Morna Hooker, *Jesus and the Servant: The Influence of the Servant Concept of Deutero-Isaiah in the New Testament* (London: S.P.C.K., 1959); C. K. Barrett, " "The Background of Mark 10:45," in *New Testament Essays*, ed. A. J. B. Higgins (Manchester: Manchester University Press, 1959), 1-18.

While to my mind the arguments favoring an Isaianic background are stronger, the debate continues, and even those scholars who agree that Isaiah lies behind the text are still left with unanswered questions about the exact meaning of Mark 10:45.[3] In this essay, I would like to advance a fresh interpretation of the "ransom for many," not by rehashing arguments about Isaiah, but rather by focusing on those aspects of the wider Old Testament background of the text which are often overlooked but which provide important keys to its meaning.

First, I will argue that the "ransom saying" should be interpreted in light of the Danielic background present throughout Mark 10:35-44, and not isolated from the preceding material.[4] When this is done, it becomes clear that the request of James and John that leads to the ransom saying presupposes the vision of the eschatological kingdom described in Daniel 7, with Jesus as the royal "one like a Son of Man" and themselves as the exalted "saints of the most high." This Danielic background, combined with the role of the Twelve as representatives of the twelve tribes, establishes an initial link to the eschatological restoration of Israel. Second, I will argue that Jesus' ominous response to James and John about having to suffer before being exalted also presupposes the Danielic vision of the kingdom, but focuses on the sufferings of the eschatological tribulation that will precede the exaltation of the "Son of Man." Third, I will suggest that Jesus ties the royal figure of the "Son of Man," who suffers in the tribulation in Daniel 7, to the royal figure of the "Messiah," who dies in the eschatological tribulation in Daniel 9, and that this is the origin of his claim that the Son of Man must "give his life." This point will be crucial to the overall argument, because the purpose of the tribulation in Daniel is to atone for the sins that led Israel into exile and inaugurate the restoration of Israel and the end of the exile.[5] Finally, I will attempt to show that Jesus' words

---

[3] See especially the comments of Davies and Allison, *The Gospel According to Saint Matthew*, 3:100 (cited below).

[4] The tendency to treat Mark 10:45 in isolation from its surrounding context—despite the fact that there is no clear textual justification for doing so—is so widespread that it almost needs no documentation. For a recent example, see James D. G. Dunn, *Jesus Remembered* (Grand Rapids, Mich.: W.B. Eerdmans, 2003), 812-15.

[5] Throughout this essay, I will use the terminology of the "end of the exile," the "restoration of Israel," and the "new exodus" to refer to roughly the same event: the ingathering of the scattered tribes of Israel from among the Gentiles to Zion. For fundamental differences between my understanding of this concept and that of N. T. Wright, see Brant James Pitre, "The Historical Jesus, the Great Tribulation, and the End of the Exile: Restoration Eschatology and the Origin of the Atonement" (Ph.D. diss., University of Notre Dame, 2004), 31-40. As I argue there, whereas Wright speaks of a metaphorical "end" of the Babylonian exile of the Jews (587 B.C.), I am speaking primarily of a real return from exile by all twelve tribes, including those scattered during the Assyrian exile (722 B.C.). In other words, I have in mind the restoration of all Israel in an eschatological kingdom. For a recent treatment of these themes in Acts, see David W. Pao, *Acts and the Isaianic New Exodus* Wissenschaftliche Untersuchungen zum Neuen Testament. 2, 130 (Tübingen: Mohr Siebeck, 2000).

about the "ransom" for "many" fit squarely into this eschatological context by demonstrating that the terminology draws on the widespread Old Testament hope for the restoration of all Israel: that is, the ingathering of the scattered tribes—including the lost ten tribes of the northern kingdom—in a new exodus.

When seen in the light of these points, Jesus' otherwise mysterious words in Mark 10:45 become amazingly clear. He is declaring that the messianic Son of Man will give his life in the eschatological tribulation in order to release ("ransom") the scattered tribes of Israel (the "many") from their exile among the Gentile nations. That is, he will give his life, in a kind of new Passover, in order to bring about a New Exodus: the long-awaited return from exile.

The Exaltation of the Twelve in the Eschatological Kingdom

Mark 10:35-45 is easily demarcated from its surrounding context.[6] Scholarly opinion, however, is divided on whether it constitutes a single unified passage, or should be broken down into two or even three parts. I have argued elsewhere in greater detail that the passage should be treated as a single unit.[7] For reasons of space, I will presuppose these arguments here, and hope that the explanatory power of the exegesis offered herein is itself a convincing argument for the unity of the text.

The unit of Mark 10:35-45 begins with James and John approaching Jesus and asking him: "Give to us that we should sit, one at your right hand and one at your left, in your glory" (Mark 10:37). Although commentators who would break up the text into various pieces often pass remarkably quickly over this text,[8] a proper understanding of the Old Testament background of their request is crucial for grasping the unity and significance of the rest of the dialogue. In short, the request of James and John appears to presuppose the vision of Daniel 7, in which "one like a Son of Man" is exalted in the eschatological kingdom along with the "saints of the Most High." While greater certitude that Daniel is in fact in view will only come through further examination of Jesus' responses to the Twelve,

---

[6] See, e.g., Evans, *Mark 8:27-16:20*, 113-115.

[7] See, Pitre, "The Historical Jesus, the Great Tribulation, and the End of the Exile," 490-497.

[8] See, e.g., D. E. Nineham, *The Gospel of St. Mark*, The Pelican Gospel Commentaries (Harmondsworth: Penguin Books, 1963), 278-279, who fails to discuss the request of James and John in any detail whatsoever.

for now let it suffice to notice the striking convergence of images with Mark 10:35-45 as a whole:

> As I looked, *thrones* were placed,
> and one that was ancient of days took his seat ...
> his throne was fiery flames ...
> the court *sat in judgment*,
> and the books were opened. ...
>
> And to [*the one like a Son of Man*] was given dominion
> and *glory and kingdom*,
> that all peoples, nations, and languages should *serve* him;
> his dominion is an everlasting dominion,
> which shall not pass away,
> and his kingdom one that shall not be destroyed. ...
>
> But *the court shall sit in judgment* ...
> And *the kingdom and the dominion and the greatness*
> of the kingdoms under the whole heaven,
> *shall be given to the people of the saints of the Most High*,
> their kingdom shall be an everlasting kingdom,
> and all dominions shall serve and obey them.
>
> (Dan. 7:9-10, 14, 26-27)[9]

At this point, the parallels are few, but strong: images of the disciples "sitting," presumably on thrones (Mark 10:37), with a "Son of Man" (Mark 10:45) who has been given "glory" (Mark 10:37)—all of these make it reasonable to suggest that James and John appear to view Jesus as the royal "one like a Son of Man" and themselves as the (soon-to-be) exalted "saints of the Most High." Hence, their request establishes a theme of eschatological rule and glorification, and this theme is not completed until Jesus' explicit mention of the Son of Man in Mark 10:45 hearkens back to the thrones and glory of Daniel 7.[10]

If there should be any doubt, however, about the royal and eschatological nature of the brothers' request, two further points might prove helpful. First, although there is no explicit mention of a "kingdom" in

---

[9] All translations of the Old Testament contained herein are, unless otherwise noted, from the Revised Standard Version. All New Testament translations are the author's own.

[10] For arguments favoring the presence of Daniel 7 behind Jesus' words in Mark 10:45, see esp. Morna D. Hooker, *The Son of Man in Mark* (London: S.P.C.K., 1967), 103-47.

Mark 10:37, its terminology is certainly royal. Indeed, the specific image of sitting at Jesus' "right hand" (ἐκ δεξιῶν) and "left hand" (ἐξ ἀριστερῶν; ἐξ εὐωνύμων) (Mark 10:37, 40) is clearly regal in character. Such language is often used in the Old Testament and Second Temple literature to depict sitting at the right and left hand of a king.[11] Moreover, this royal context is confirmed by the specific image of sitting beside Jesus in his "glory" (δόξῃ) (Mark 10:37).

While the terminology of "glory" is used in a vast array of contexts in the Old Testament,[12] it very frequently refers to the royal glory of a king, whether God[13] or a human being.[14] Specifically, it is often used in conjunction with the image of being seated on *thrones* "of glory"—that is, being given positions of royal authority alongside a king.[15] One notable juxtaposition of these images is found in Isaiah's account of Eliakim, who, when raised to the office of "prime minister"[16] in the royal court of King Hezekiah, receives not only "the key of the house of David" and the authority to "open and shut," but also becomes a "throne of glory" (Isa. 22:23). In this instance, to "sit" on a throne of "glory" would be to have the highest office within the Davidic kingdom.[17] Hence, the request of James and John is not simply a friendly request to recline in close proximity to

---

[11] For example, during the reign of Solomon, the "queen mother," Bathsheba, is honored by having a "seat" or "throne" (θρόνος) brought in for her so that "she sat at his [the king's] right hand" (ἐκάθισεν ἐκ δεξιῶν αὐτοῦ), according to the Greek Septuagint translation (LXX) of 1 Kings 2:19. Similarly, the Sons of Korah praise the "throne" (θρόνος) of a newly anointed king, and rejoice that "at your right hand (ἐκ δεξιῶν σου) stands the queen in gold of Ophir" (Ps. 44:7-10 LXX). One of the most famous enthronement psalms begins, "The Lord says to my lord: 'Sit at my right hand' (κάθου ἐκ δεξιῶν μου) till I make your enemies your footstool" (Ps. 110:1 LXX)—clearly a royal setting of honor and glory. For further references, see 1 Kings 22:19; 2 Chron. 18:18; *Testament of Abraham* 12:8; Josephus, *Antiquities of the Jews* 6.235.

[12] For "glory" as dangerous presence of God, see Exod. 16:7; 24:16; 33:18-22; Lev. 9:6, 23; Num. 14:10; 1 Sam. 4:21-22. For "glory" as God coming in "a cloud" or "clouds" (see Daniel 7), see Exod. 16:10; 24:16; 40:34-35; Num. 16:42; Deut. 5:22-24; 1 Kings 8:11; Ezek. 10:4.

[13] Cf. Pss. 24:7-10; 57:5, 11; 72:19; 96:3, 7; 102:15; 108:5; 145:11-12; 1 Chron. 29:11-12; Isa. 6:3; 60:1-3; 66:18-19; Hab. 2:14.

[14] Cf. 2 Chron. 1:12; 17:5; 32:27; Job 19:9; Ps. 8:5; Prov. 25:2.

[15] The Lord sits on a "throne of glory" (Jer. 14:21; 17:12) and can exalt others to this status (1 Sam. 2:8).

[16] The technical term is "over the house" (Isa. 22:15), but this is difficult to render into English.

[17] It is of course precisely this text from Isaiah that forms the background of the account in which Peter as chief of the Twelve is given the "keys of the kingdom" and the power to "bind and loose" in Matthew's gospel (Matt. 16:16-19; cf. also Matt. 18:18). See Davies and Allison, *The Gospel According to Saint Matthew*, 2:640 for further discussion.

Jesus at the "messianic banquet," [18] or merely a plea to be with him at "the parousia."[19] It is a formal and direct request to receive the highest offices and authority (next to that of Jesus himself) in the eschatological kingdom.

The second point is more remote, but still important. In short, one could even argue that this royal imagery is implicitly *Davidic* insofar as the disciples' request presupposes the restoration of the kingdom *to all twelve tribes* (represented by the apostles)—a reality which only existed during the time of the Davidic kingdom under David and Solomon, before the time when the tribes split and the monarchy was divided (see 1 Kings 12).[20] The plausibility of this interpretation is supported by parallel visions of eschatological exaltation found elsewhere in the gospel tradition:

> Truly I say to you, in the new creation, when *the Son of Man shall sit on his throne of glory*, you who have followed me shall also *sit on twelve thrones, judging the twelve tribes of Israel.*
>
> (Matt. 19:28)

> You are those who have continued with me in my trials; *so do I appoint to you—just as my Father appointed to me—a kingdom*, so that you may eat and drink at my table *in my kingdom*, and *sit on thrones judging the twelve tribes of Israel.*
>
> (Luke 22:28-30)

Whatever the differences between these texts, they both, like Mark 10:35-45, presuppose the exaltation of the disciples to royal places of honor alongside Jesus as both king (Luke) and Son of Man (Matthew). And this is all tied to the eschatological restoration of the twelve tribes of Israel and the advent of the kingdom. This link between the request of James and

---

[18] Cf. Hooker, *The Gospel According to Saint Mark*, 246. While regal and convivial imagery are, admittedly, not necessarily mutually exclusive (see Luke 22:28-30), the immediate context does not suggest a banquet. See John Meier, who argues that the terminology of "sitting" (καθίζω; καθῆμαί) is not the usual Greek terminology for "reclining" at table in banquet settings but rather connotes sitting in judgment in a royal setting. John P. Meier, *A Marginal Jew: Rethinking the Historical Jesus*, 3 vols. (Doubleday 1991), 3:218, following S. Légasse, "Approche de l'épisode préévangélique des fils de Zébédée (Marc x.35-40 par.)," *New Testament Studies* 20 (1974): 170-74.

[19] Evans, *Mark 8:27-16:20*, 116, is quite correct to insist that the reference to Jesus' glory does not necessarily refer to "the parousia": "[I]n the setting of the life of Jesus (*Sitz im Leben Jesu*), the question refers to the kingdom of God on earth, that is *the restored Israel* in which the great prophecies (especially of Isaiah) will be fulfilled, when all nations will come to Jerusalem to worship the LORD" (emphasis added). Contrast Vincent Taylor, *The Gospel According to St. Mark*, 2d. ed. (London: Macmillan, 1966), 440.

[20] In this regard, the parallels between the three mighty men of King David and Jesus' three disciples— Peter (the "rock"), and James and John (the "sons of thunder")—are at least suggestive (see 1 Sam. 23:8-12; cf. Mark 2:23-28).

John, the disciples as representatives of the twelve tribes, and the restoration of Israel cannot be allowed to slip from view, for it will prove very important for further exegesis.

The Suffering of the Son of Man in the Tribulation

If any doubt should exist regarding whether or not Daniel 7 lies behind the disciples' request, the suggestion should be confirmed by Jesus' own response. For he counters the brothers' desire for exaltation—which drew on Daniel—with images from the very same text: the example of "great" Gentile rulers who are tyrants (Dan. 7:3-8, 11-12), the language of "serving" rather than being served (see Dan. 7:14, 27), and the promise of suffering for the disciples. For in Daniel, it is quite clear that those who are ultimately exalted, the saints of the Most High, *will first have to suffer during the eschatological tribulation.* They "shall be given over" into the hand of the final eschatological tyrant "for a time, two times, and half a time" (Dan. 7:25).

It is this last point, that the saints in Daniel will have to suffer the tribulation before their exaltation, which explains Jesus' otherwise baffling response to James and John. While the brothers are eager to be exalted alongside their teacher in his glory, they have forgotten that the glorious kingdom spoken of by Daniel will only be established *after* a period of eschatological tribulation. Jesus apparently recognizes their failure to grasp this point, and he reminds them of it by asserting: "You do not know what you are asking. Are you able to drink the cup which I drink or to be baptized with the baptism with which I am baptized?" (Mark 10:38).

These words, although enigmatic, provide an important clue to understanding Mark 10:45. They suggest that the suffering of Jesus, as Son of Man, will take place in the eschatological tribulation. Indeed, as the majority of scholars agree, the image of the cup in Mark 10:38 is a metaphorical "cup" of suffering.[21] Similarly, the image of being "baptized," of being submerged, is also employed in the Old Testament and Second

---

[21] While the image can be used positively to depict the "cup" of blessing (Pss. 23:5; 116:13), it is more often the case that it is used negatively to refer to the "cup" of sorrow and suffering. See, with various shades of meaning, Pss. 75:7-8; 11:5-7; Isa. 51:17-23; Ezek. 23:32-34; Hab. 2:16-17; Jer. 49:12; Lam. 4:21; Jer. 25:16, 27, 29, 31, 33, 34-38. Similar usage of the "cup" of suffering and judgment continues in the Second Temple period. See *Psalms of Solomon* 8:14-15, and the Qumran documents *Pesher on Habbakuk* 11:14; *Prayer of Nabonidus* 4:6. Cf. also Rev. 14:10; 16:19; 18:6; *Ascension of Isaiah* 5:13; *Testament of Abraham* 1:3; Ignatius, *Letter to the Romans* 7:3; *Martyrdom of Polycarp* 14:2. For other references and discussion, see Dunn, *Jesus Remembered*, 803; Meier, *A Marginal Jew* 3:263, n. 50; Evans, *Mark 8:27-16:20*, 117; Rudolf Pesch, *Das Markusevangelium,* 2 vols. Herders theologischer Kommentar zum Neuen Testament (Freiburg: Herder, 1977), 2:156-57.

Temple Judaism as a metaphor for undergoing suffering.[22] What is striking about this second image, however, is that the "baptism" of Jesus is used elsewhere in the gospels with reference to the distress that Jesus will undergo *in the eschatological tribulation*:

> I came to cast fire upon the earth; and how I wish that it were already kindled! *I have a baptism to be baptized with*; and how I am constrained until it is fulfilled!
>
> (Luke 12:49-50)

Regarding these strange verses, many scholars agree that Jesus' language of being "baptized" with a "baptism" refers to nothing less than his own anguish and suffering in the eschatological tribulation.[23] If so, then my suggestion—that Jesus is reminding James and John that the saints in Daniel must first suffer the tribulation before being exalted in the eschatological kingdom—is confirmed.

More important than the fate of James and John, however, is the fate of Jesus as Son of Man. For he again refers to the Danielic tribulation, with far more specificity, when he calls the Twelve together and readjusts their thinking by reminding them they will not be like "the great" among "the Gentiles." Rather, greatness among the Twelve will consist of being a "servant" and "slave" of the others (Mark 10:42-43). The reason: "the Son of Man did not come to be served but to serve and to give his life as a ransom for many" (Mark 10:45).

The first and most important link between these final words of Jesus and the eschatological tribulation is, of course, the presence of the expression "the Son of Man." This term of course points us back to the

---

[22] See, e.g., 2 Sam. 22:4-7, 17-18; Pss. 18:4-6, 16-17; 32:6; 42:7; 69:1-2, 13-17; 124:1-5; 144:7-11; Job 22:11. While I am not sure how much should be made of the point, it is at least intriguing that, given the messianic context of James and John's request and Jesus' response, the imagery of being "baptized" in a flood of suffering, occurs repeatedly in the thanksgiving psalms of *David*. Since Jesus does in fact seem to accept the royal status ascribed to him by James and John (Mark 10:40), he may be countering their vision of royal exaltation by invoking an image used repeatedly in the psalms of David to depict the suffering and distress of the "king," "messiah," and "servant" of the Lord (2 Sam. 22:51; Pss. 69:17; 144:10). For other references to baptism as suffering in the primary sources, see, for example, Dunn, *Jesus Remembered*, 366, n. 129; Meier, *A Marginal Jew*, 3:263-64, n. 51; Dale C. Allison, Jr., *The End of the Ages Has Come: An Early Interpretation of the Passion and Resurrection of Jesus* (Philadelphia: Fortress Press, 1985), 124-28.

[23] See, e.g., Dunn, *Jesus Remembered*, 808-809; Dale C. Allison, Jr., "The Eschatology of Jesus," in *The Origins of Apocalypticism in Judaism and Christianity*, vol. 1 of *The Encyclopedia of Apocalypticism*, ed. John J. Collins (New York: Continuum, 1998), 288-89; Witherington, *The Christology of Jesus*, 123-24; Allison, *The End of the Ages Has Come*, 124-28; Ben F. Meyer, *The Aims of Jesus* (London: SCM, 1979), 213.

visions of Daniel 7 and to the tribulation described therein. But this more obvious connection is also confirmed by other aspects of Jesus' words. In particular, his distinctive mention of "the great" (οἱ μεγάλοι) among "the Gentiles" (τῶν ἐθνῶν) whose rulers "lord it over" (κατακυριεύουσιν) their subjects, is evocative of the Danielic "great (μεγάλα) beasts" who are Gentile kings and who, during the last days, will "lord it over many" (κατακυριεύσει . . . ἐπὶ πολύ) (LXX Dan. 7:3-11; 11:39 in Symm., the Greek translation of Symmachus).

Moreover, Jesus contrasts the Gentile kings' tyranny over "many" with the lordship of the Son of Man, whom he insists "did not come to be served (διακονηθῆναι) but to serve (διακονῆσαι)," and to give his life as a ransom "for many" (ἀντὶ πολλῶν) (Mark 10:45). This is a striking claim in light of the fact that in Daniel 7 the "one like a Son of Man" is given dominion so that "all peoples, nations, and languages should serve (δουλεύσουσιν) him" (Dan. 7:14 Theod.). Indeed, Jesus appears not only to be overturning the expectations of James and John regarding the messianic kingdom, but conclusions that could be drawn straight from the visions of the "one like a son of man" in Daniel itself.[24] In so doing, he is directly tying his (and possibly the disciples') imminent suffering to the eschatological tribulation described in Daniel 7.[25]

This being said, one important issue remains unresolved: while Daniel 7 certainly describes the persecution of the saints/Son of Man, it does not describe their execution, and it is execution (or death of some sort) that is suggested in Mark 10:45.[26] The Son of Man spoken of by Jesus will not only suffer but will also die—he will "give his life" as a ransom "for many."

At this point interpreters often turn to Isaiah 53 to show its influence on Jesus' words.[27] And, although the passage probably did have an influence, I would suggest that another text in Daniel provides the backdrop for the suggestion that the Son of Man would die as a ransom

---

[24] Compare for example, Dunn, *Jesus Remembered*, 814; Stuhlmacher, "Vicariously Giving His Life for Many," 21; Seyoon Kim, *The Son of Man as the Son of God*, Wissenschaftliche Untersuchungen zum Neuen Testament 30 (Tübingen: J. C. B. Mohr [Paul Siebeck], 1983) 39-40; Barrett, "The Background of Mark 10:45," 8-9.

[25] Along these lines, see Hooker, "Did the Use of Isaiah 53 to Interpret His Mission Begin with Jesus?" 100, and *The Gospel According to Saint Mark*, 250; Watts, *Isaiah's New Exodus in Mark*, 260-61; Barrett, "The Background of Mark 10:45," 10-14.

[26] Although in Daniel 7 the Son of Man can be read as suffering via the saints of the Most High, there is certainly no explicit description of his suffering and *death*. The emphasis is entirely on the persecutions of the saints: the Son of Man only comes on the scene for vindication, not tribulation.

[27] See, e.g., Davies and Allison, *The Gospel According to Saint Matthew*, 3:95-96; Watts, "Jesus' Death, Isaiah 53, and Mark 10:45," 136-47; Stuhlmacher, "Vicariously Giving His Life for Others," 19-20; Jeremias, *New Testament Theology*, 292-94.

for many. Indeed, if this text is read as an eschatological prophecy (as a first-century Jew would have done) and not as an apocalyptic allegory of political events of the second century B.C. (as most modern scholars do[28]), it quite clearly describes at least three things: the coming death of the Messiah during a period of eschatological tribulation; the atoning function of the tribulation; and the end of the exile:

> [24]Seventy weeks of years are decreed concerning you people and your holy city, *to finish the transgression, to put an end to sin*, and *to atone for iniquity*, to bring in ever-lasting righteousness, to seal both vision and prophet, and to anoint a most holy one. [25]Know therefore and under-stand that from the going forth of the word to restore and build Jerusalem to the coming of *a Messiah, a prince*, there shall be seven weeks. Then for sixty-two weeks it shall be built again with squares and moat, but in a troubled time. [26] And after sixty-two weeks, *a Messiah shall be cut off*, and shall have nothing; and the people of the prince who is to come shall destroy the city and the sanctuary. *His end shall come with a flood*, and to the end there shall be war; desolations are decreed. [27]And *he shall make a strong covenant with many* for one week; and for half of the week he shall cause sacrifice and offering to cease; and upon the wing an abomination that makes desolate, until the decreed end is poured out on the desolator.
>
> (Dan. 9:24-27)[29]

Several points need to be made about this crucial text. The first is somewhat obvious, but extremely important. In short, while this Old Testament prophecy of a dying Danielic Messiah is often overlooked in discussions of Mark 10:45, the text is quite clear. There shall be a future period of eschatological tribulation in which a royal Messiah will not only come, but will be *killed*.[30] Hence, the death of the coming Messiah shall not take place just anytime, but *during the tribulation*, during the "seventy

---

[28] John J. Collins, *Daniel: A Commentary on the Book of Daniel* (Hermeneia; Minneapolis: Fortress, 1993), 352-60, for his and other modern interpretations.

[29] RSV, slightly modified.

[30] This is the meaning of the Hebrew idiom "he will be cut off" (יכרת). Cf. Gen. 9:11; 41:36; Ps. 37:9; Isa. 11:13; 29:20, etc.

weeks of years" of trouble and war that must take place before the restoration of Jerusalem.[31]

Second, the primary purpose of this tribulation is *to atone for Israel's sin*: "to finish transgression, to put an end to sin, and to atone for iniquity" (Dan. 9:24). This threefold purpose is expressly stated by the angel Gabriel, and reveals that the eschatological suffering described will not only be punitive, but redemptive and restorative, ushering in the time of "everlasting righteousness" and the restoration of Jerusalem.

Third—and this is crucial—the forgiveness of sins that is wrought by the tribulation will mean nothing less than *the end of Israel's exile*. This point, although not explicitly stated in Daniel 9:24-27, is nevertheless quite clear from the surrounding context, which focuses on Jeremiah's prophecy of exile (Dan. 9:2; cf. Jer. 25, 29), the scattering of all Israel to "all the lands to which you [the LORD] have driven them" in the Exile (Dan. 9:7), as well as the Deuteronomic curses of calamity and exile in "the law of Moses" (Dan. 9:11-13; cf. Lev. 26:27-45; Deut. 28:15-68). In other words, the eschatological tribulation described by Gabriel is nothing less than the climax of Israel's exilic sufferings. In this vein, Daniel implores the Lord to bring Israel out of exile just as he had brought them "out of the land of Egypt with a mighty hand" (Dan. 9:15)—that is, in a new exodus. This new exodus will mean a new deliverance from exile, a new return of the twelve tribes to the promised land.

In short, Daniel has just finished praying for the forgiveness of Israel's sins and the restoration of Israel in a new exodus (Dan. 9:7-19). In response, Gabriel promises him a period of tribulation that will atone for iniquity (Dan. 9:24-27). The obvious implication of this exchange is that the sufferings of the tribulation—including one of the most striking afflictions, the death of the Messiah—will not only bring about the forgiveness of sins, but also its biblical corollary: the end of the exile.[32]

---

[31] This single text renders inexplicable statements such as those of Hartmut Stegemann that *nowhere* "in all pre-Rabbinic Judaism is the possibility ever entertained that the coming Messiah can be killed." (*The Library of Qumran: On the Essenes, Qumran, John the Baptist, and Jesus* [Grand Rapids: W.B. Eerdmans, 1998], 104). Daniel 9 not only entertains the possibility, it describes the event in an eschatological prophecy.

[32] As N. T. Wright has brilliantly argued, in the Old Testament, "Forgiveness of sins is another way of saying 'return from exile'" (*Jesus and the Victory of God*, 268-274). While we do not have the space here to defend this suggestion, see his discussion, as well as Lev. 26:33; cf. 26:43; Lam. 4:22; Jer. 31:10-12, 31-34; Ezek. 36:24-34; cf. also 37:15-28; Isa. 40:1-11. I would add also the important text of 1 Kings 8:33-34. In this hypothesis, Wright is followed by Scot McKnight, *A New Vision for Israel: The Teachings of Jesus in National Context* (Grand Rapids, Mich.: W.B. Eerdmans, 1999), 224-27.

The final step in this exegesis of the Old Testament background of Mark 10:35-45 is to recognize that Jesus' statements are not only drawing on both Daniel 7 and 9 but *combining* these two texts into a "composite messianic picture."[33] For Jesus, the royal "one like a Son of Man" who comes during the tribulation (Daniel 7) and the "Messiah, a prince," who also comes during the tribulation (Daniel 9), *are the same eschatological figure.*

This is a crucial point, for it explains why Jesus would even suggest that "the Son of Man" would die in the tribulation when no such death is described in Daniel 7. He recognizes that both Daniel 7 and 9 describe *the same tribulation*, the tribulation of the last days, which will precede the establishment of the "everlasting kingdom" in "everlasting righteousness" (see Dan. 7:27; 9:24). As a result, he is harmonizing the royal and messianic figures of both into one.[34]

Once this point is grasped, several other aspects of Mark 10:35-45 as a whole become clear. For example, Jesus' curious use of the image a "baptism" to refer to his impending suffering in the tribulation can be explained if he is drawing on Daniel's visions of the coming of the Messiah during the final tribulation; for Daniel prophesies that "his end"—that is, the death of the Messiah—would come "with a flood" (Dan. 9:27). Also, the giving of the Son of Man's life for "many" finds a parallel in the "covenant" made by the messianic prince with "many" before the end of the tribulation (Dan. 9:27).

Finally, in both the words of Jesus and in Daniel, the purpose of these events appears to be linked with atonement for sin. In Daniel, the events of the final tribulation—the death of the Messiah, the destruction of

---

[33] The terminology is that of Wright, who argues that Jesus combines the same two Danielic texts elsewhere: "Jesus in Mark 13 has already alluded to Daniel 9; when we find, shortly afterwards, a quotation from Daniel 7, we are fully justified in assuming that this composite messianic picture is in mind. Nor is it simply a general evocation of vague 'messianic' ideas. The picture is very sharp: this Messiah-figure will bear the brunt of gentile-fury, and will be vindicated. When we put this alongside Dan. 9:24-27, the complete picture includes the real end of the exile, the final atonement for sin, the anointing of a most holy place, the arrival of an anointed prince, the 'cutting off' of an anointed one, the cessation of the sacrifices, and the setting up of the 'abomination that desolates'. It looks as though the combination of Daniel 7 and 9 provides part of the major theme of Jesus' Temple-discourse, in the middle of which the clear implication is that the Temple's destruction and Jesus' own vindication, *precisely as Messiah*, somehow belong together" (emphasis original). Wright, *Jesus and the Victory of God*, 515.

[34] Despite the modern hesitancy to view the "one like a Son of Man" in Daniel 7 as a Messiah, it should be noted that the oldest extant Jewish interpretations of the "one like a Son of Man" in Daniel, *1 Enoch* 46 and *4 Ezra* 13, are explicitly messianic (as is admitted by Collins, *Daniel* 306-307). Hence, Jesus' combination of the two figures, although distinctive, would fit quite squarely into early Jewish interpretation of Daniel 7.

the Temple and Jerusalem, and the covenant with "many"—are somehow thought to finish the transgression of Israel and to atone for the sin that brought about the exile (Dan 9:24). In parallel fashion, the words of Jesus in Mark 10:45 suggest that the death of the Son of Man will effect some kind of redemptive atonement—a "ransom"—for some as yet unidentified group, "the many."

The 'Ransom for Many' and the End of the Exile

While recourse to Daniel illuminates Jesus' words about his own "baptism" of suffering and the death of the Son of Man in the tribulation, it does not say anything explicit about this death functioning as a "ransom for many." Indeed, the terminology of "ransom" or release occurs nowhere in either Daniel 7 or 9.

Again, this is often where interpreters of Mark 10:45 leave Daniel aside and turn to Isaiah 53 to show how the servant makes his "life" an "offering for sin" to "bear the sin of many" (Isa. 53:10, 12).[35] And again, these images do suggest a connection between Mark 10:45 and Isaiah 53, even if the former is not explicitly "citing" the latter. Nevertheless, even scholars who accept the Isaianic background do not necessarily achieve total clarity regarding the meaning of Jesus' words. Notable here is the conclusion of W. D. Davies and Dale Allison:

> [A]lmost every question we might ask remains unan-
> swered. What is the condition of 'the many'? Why do they
> need to be ransomed? To whom is the ransom paid—to
> God, to the devil, or to no one at all? Is forgiveness effect-
> ed now or at the last judgment or both? How is its appro-
> priated? . . . We have in the Gospel only an unexplained
> affirmation.[36]

These are important questions, which need to be answered; but to a large extent they have not yet received a satisfactory answer in the scholarly

---

[35] See similar moves regarding Mark 9:12 as the context for Mark 10:45 in Watts, "Jesus' Death, Isaiah 53, and Mark 10:45," 131-36.

[36] Davies and Allison, *The Gospel According to Saint Matthew*, 3:100.

literature.[37] However, I submit that they can be answered by properly placing Jesus' language of a "ransom" for "many" in the context of the Old Testament and Second Temple Judaism and by continuing to keep in mind the eschatological tribulation in the book of Daniel.

When this is done, it becomes clear that in Mark 10:45, Jesus is using the language of the Old Testament prophets to declare that the Son of Man will give his life in order to release ("ransom") the scattered exiles of Israel (the "many"). That is, he will give his life, in a kind of new Passover, in order to bring about a new exodus: the return from exile. Jesus' declaration is a biblically evocative declaration about the new exodus (the "ransom") and the restoration of the lost tribes of Israel (the "many"). This can be demonstrated by a brief survey of both images in the Old Testament and Second Temple Judaism.

In the Greek Old Testament, the terminology of "ransom" (Gk. λυτρόω; λύτρον) can have several dimensions of meaning, but on a very basic level the verbal form, λυτρόω, means to "release by payment of ransom," while the nominal form, λύτρον, refers to "the price of release, ransom."[38] Both forms are most commonly employed to translate the Hebrew terms "ransom" (פדה) and "redeem" (גאל) (and, less frequently, "atone" [כפר]). Whichever of the two primary Hebrew terms is used, the basic meaning of *release* or *deliverance* by way of *payment* is almost always retained, whether the context is one of deliverance from punishment

---

[37] Signs of struggle similar to those found in Davies and Allison regarding what Mark 10:45 actually means are present throughout scholarly literature on the subject. To cite a few examples: Morna Hooker, after all of her work on this passage, can only conclude that "In some mysterious way, which is not spelt out, the sufferings of one man are used by God to bring benefit to others" (*The Gospel According to Saint Mark*, 249). What is the "mysterious way"? And what is the "benefit"? Is this all we can say about this text, after all the wrangling about the Isaianic background? Ben Witherington states quite clearly: "We are not told in Mark 10:45b what the many are freed from" and then goes on to conjecture that "in view of Jesus' exorcisms, he was thinking of freeing them from Satan's grasp; freeing God's people from sin may be in view" (*The Christology of Jesus*, 256). This is a good surmise, but again, the text says nothing about either "Satan" or "sin," nor does its terminology implicitly evoke either of these. George Beasley-Murray concludes that "the Son of Man in Mark 10:45" gives his life as "a freely offered sacrifice, in order that the kingdom of God might be opened for mankind in its totality" (*Jesus and the Kingdom of God*, 283). But does the text say anything at all about "opening" the kingdom of God to "mankind in its totality"? And again, how does this work? Is there anything in early Judaism or the Old Testament to suggest that the kingdom of God could be (or would need to be) "opened" through the death of an individual? These examples could easily be multiplied. What is important to note, however, is that in each case, the exegete is forced to leave the text behind and create (or at least substitute) interpretive categories from some other source that will make some sense out of Jesus' words, but with the effect that they remain ultimately opaque.

[38] See J. Lust et al., *A Greek-English Lexicon of the Septuagint*, 2 vols. (Stuttgart: Deutsche Bibelgesellschaft, 1992, 1996), 2:286.

(human[39] or divine[40]), slavery,[41] debt,[42] guilt or sin,[43] affliction,[44] and even death.[45] For our purposes, what is striking about this terminology is that it is perhaps most prominently used to describe a very particular type of deliverance: deliverance or release *from exile*.

This fact is rarely noted by commentators on Mark 10:45, who almost invariably move quickly from a study of the meaning of the word "ransom" (λύτρον) into the scholarly debate over the Isaianic background of Jesus' words. This debate has distracted exegetes from observing how deeply Jesus' terminology is rooted in the *rest* of the Old Testament, especially the prophets, outside of Isaiah.[46]

---

[39] Num. 35:31, 32.

[40] Exod. 30:12; Hos. 7:13; Sir. 49:10. For many more references, see those listed below on enslavement to Egypt or the nations in exile.

[41] Lev. 19:20; 25:48, 49, 51, 52, 54; Exod. 21:8. This can be applied to the freeing of the land from its labor (Lev. 25:24).

[42] Lev. 25:25; 27:15, 19, 20, 27, 31.

[43] Deut. 21:8; Pss. 25:22; 26:11; 32:7; 103:4; 130:8.

[44] 2 Sam. 4:9; 1 Kings 1:29; Pss. 7:2; 31:5; 34:22 (cf. v. 19); 55:18; 59:1; 69:18; 72:14; 118:34, 154; 144:10; Sir. 48:20.

[45] Exod. 21:30; Num. 35:31, 32; Jer. 15:21; Lam. 3:58; Dan. 6:28; Sir. 51:2, 3; Num. 3:12, 46, 48, 49, 51 (Levites taken in place of first-born sons); Exod. 13:13-15; 34:20; Num. 18:15, 17 (ransoming of first-born sons); Lev. 27:13, 33 (ransom of animal sacrifice by monetary substitute); Pss. 49:7-8, 15; 71:23; 103:4; Hos. 13:14 (deliverance from Sheol).

[46] Examples of this tendency to overlook the clear Old Testament links between "ransom" terminology and deliverance from exile abound. To note a few: Robert Gundry's brief list of ransom texts in the Old Testament not only presents a strong contrast with his usually exhaustive catalogues of biblical parallels, but his concluding remark regarding them is revealing: "The OT passages do not help interpret Mark 10:45" (Gundry, *Mark*, 591). He then moves immediately into a discussion of Isaiah 53. Perhaps even more striking are the comments of Morna Hooker, who actually recognizes that the Old Testament repeatedly "link[s] the notion of redemption with God's saving action in bringing his people up from slavery in Egypt" and even calls it "a common theme in passages where the verb λυτρόω is used" (Hooker, *The Gospel According to Saint Mark*, 248-49). However, she makes no attempt to use this "common" Old Testament theme in her actual exegesis of Mark 10:45, but is deterred, yet again, by the debate over Isaiah. Finally, Barnabas Lindars recognizes that the "ransom" terminology evokes "the Old Testament idea of redemption from slavery," but feels no compunction to apply this meaning to Mark 10:45 and instead rejects the passage as necessarily "later than the time of Jesus, because the idea of self-sacrifice is distinctively Greek" (Lindars, *Jesus Son of Man* [Grand Rapids, Mich.: W.B. Eerdmans, 1983], 77-78). But the text does not use the terminology of "self-sacrifice"—it uses the terminology of "ransom." He need only have examined the Old Testament prophets to find that the expectation that Israel would be "ransomed" from exile is anything but "distinctively Greek."

The fact is that "ransom" (λυτρόω) terminology is used over and over again in the Old Testament to depict two prominent events in salvation history: Israel's past deliverance from exile in Egypt in the exodus, and its future deliverance from exile in the new exodus, the ingathering of the scattered tribes from among the nations.[47]

As for the first exodus, there are several striking texts that use the language of "ransom" (often translated as "redeem") to signify release from exile:

> [God said to Moses:] [6] Say therefore to the people of Israel, 'I am the LORD, and I will bring you out from under the burdens of the Egyptians, and I will deliver you from their bondage, and *I will ransom you*[48] with an outstretched arm and with great acts of judgment, [7] and I will take you for my people, and I will be your God; and you shall know that I am the LORD your God, who has brought you out from under the burdens of the Egyptians. [8] *And I will bring you into the land which I swore to give to Abraham, to Isaac, and to Jacob.*"
>
> (Exod. 6:6-8)[49]

> [42] [Israel] did not keep in mind [the LORD's] power,
> or the day when he *ransomed*[50] them from the foe;
> [43] when he wrought his signs in Egypt,
> and his miracles in the fields of Zoan.
> [44] He turned their rivers to blood, so that they could not drink of their streams . . .
> [49] He let loose on them his fierce anger, wrath, indignation, and distress, a company of destroying angels . . .

---

[47] The major exception to this is of course Watts, "Jesus' Death, Isaiah 53, and Mark 10:45," 141, and *Isaiah's New Exodus in Mark*, 270-84. Remarkably, even N. T. Wright, who is otherwise very adept at spotting themes that run throughout the Old Testament prophets, does not draw this connection.

[48] וגאלתי אתכם in the Hebrew Masoretic Text (MT) LXX λυτρώσομαι ὑμᾶς in the Septuagint translation (LXX).

[49] All translations are from the RSV, with the more traditional translation of "redeem" sometimes being changed to "ransom" in order to properly highlight the biblical echoes present in the λύτρον terminology of Mark 10:45.

[50] MT פדם LXX ἐλυτρώσατο.

[51] He smote all the first-born in Egypt,
the first issue of their strength in the tents of Ham.
[52] Then he led forth his people like sheep,
and guided them in the wilderness like a flock . . .

(Ps. 78:42-55)

For I brought you up from the land of Egypt,
and *ransomed you*[51] from the house of bondage;
and I sent before you Moses, Aaron, and Miriam.

(Mic. 6:4)

These are by no means the only examples of the connection between
"ransom" terminology and return from exile. Indeed, it is striking just how
many times "ransom" or "redemption" terminology is used in the Old
Testament to describe the release from slavery and exile that took place in
the exodus from Egypt.[52]

In light of such an abundance of occurrences, it should come as no
surprise that "ransom" terminology would come to play a key role in
prophecies of the new exodus, when the scattered tribes of Israel would be
restored from among the nations. These occurrences, it is important to note,
are present in some of the most prominent oracles in the prophetic corpus.

For example, in Isaiah 43,[53] the "ransom" of Israel is directly
connected to the people being gathered from "east," "west," "north," and
"south," and their going through a "baptism" of fire and water:

---

[51] MT פְּדִיתִ֔יךָ LXX ἐλυτρωσάμην σε.

[52] See also Exod. 15:13, 16; Deut. 7:8; 9:26; 13:5; 15:15; 24:18; 2 Sam. 7:23; 1 Chron. 17:21; Neh. 1:10;
Esther 4:17 (LXX only); 1 Macc. 4:11; Pss. 74:2; 77:15; 106:10; 136:24; Isa. 51:10-11; 63:9. Again, while
different Hebrew terms such as גאל and פדה lie behind various occurrences of λυτρόω terminology in the
LXX, the basically synonymous nature of these two terms should be clear; see esp. Isa. 51:10-11.

[53] While there is simply not enough space in a brief essay such as this to cite the texts in their entirety,
the reader is strongly encouraged to consult the entire chapter for each example in order to witness the
full force of the parallels.

> But now thus says the LORD, he who created you, O Jacob,
> he who formed you, O Israel:
> *"Fear not, for I have ransomed you*[54]
> I have called you by name, you are mine.
> When you pass through the waters I will be with you;
> and through the rivers, they shall not overwhelm you;
> when you walk through fire you shall not be burned,
> and the flame shall not consume you . . .
>
> (Isa. 43:1-2)

This ingathering of the exiles from among the nations is directly tied to the "new thing" the Lord is doing: namely, the new exodus (see Isa. 43:18-19).[55] In similar fashion, Isaiah 52 links the ransom of Jerusalem with the "good news" of the Lord reigning in Zion and, again, a new exodus in which Israel will come back from the nations, but not in haste, as in the first exodus:

> Shake yourself from the dust, arise, O captive Jerusalem;
> loose the bonds from your neck,
> O captive daughter of Zion.
> For thus says the LORD: "You were sold for nothing,
> and *you shall be ransomed*[56] without money . . ."
>
> (Isa. 52:2-3)

In Jeremiah 31, the famous chapter regarding the "new covenant" that will exceed the covenant made during the first exodus, the "ransom" of Jacob comes about when the "remnant of Israel" is brought in from the ends of the earth as a "great company" and gathered like a scattered flock:

---

[54] MT גְּאַלְתִּיךָ LXX ἐλυτρωσάμην σε.

[55] While I count Isaiah 43 among the many texts that connect "ransom" terminology with the New Exodus, I do not agree with the hypothesis that it is Isa. 43:1-4 rather than chapters 52-53 that is the principle Isaianic background to Jesus' statements in Mark 10:45. See Hampel, *Menschensohn und Historischer Jesus*, 326-333 and Stuhlmacher, "Vicariously Giving His Life for Many," 23-25. For strong critiques, see Watts, "Jesus' Death, Isaiah 53, and Mark 10:45," 144-46, and Gundry, *Mark*, 592.

[56] MT תִּגָּאֵלוּ LXX λυτρωθήσεσθε.

> Hear the word of the LORD, O nations,
> and declare it in the coastlands afar off;
> say, "*He who scattered Israel will gather him,*
> and will keep him as a shepherd keeps his flock."
> *For the LORD has ransomed[57] Jacob,*
> *he has redeemed him from hands to strong for him.*
> They shall come and sing aloud on the height of Zion.
>
> (Jer. 31:10-12)

In language very similar to that found in Jeremiah, Micah 4 conjoins the ingathering of the Gentiles to Zion with the time in "the latter days" when the Lord will "ransom" the scattered remnant of Israel. In this text, however, we find in striking fashion not only the language of redemption and ingathering, but of the "coming" of the "kingdom" of God:

> It shall come to pass in the latter days
> that the mountain of the house of the LORD
> shall be established as the highest of the mountains,
> and shall be raised up above the hills;
> and peoples shall flow to it
> and many nations shall come . . .
> And you, O tower of the flock,
> hill of the daughter of Zion,
> *to you it shall come,*
> the former dominion shall come,
> *the kingdom* of the daughter of Jerusalem . . .
> for now you shall go forth from the city
> and dwell in the open country;
> you shall go to Babylon.
> *There you shall be rescued,*
> *there the LORD will ransom you*[58]
> *from the hand of your enemies.*
>
> (Mic 4:1-2, 8, 10)

Finally, Zechariah 10 describes the return of the "house of Judah" (the Jews deported to Babylon) and the "house of Joseph" (the ten northern tribes of Israel)—hence, all twelve tribes—as their being "ransomed" and gathered in from among the Gentiles in what is clearly a new exodus. He even forecasts that this future ingathering will be preceded by a time of tribulation—which he quite strikingly compares to the first passage through the Red Sea:

---

[57] MT פדה LXX ἐλυτρώσατο.

[58] MT יגאלך LXX λυτρώσεταί σε.

> *I will signal for them and gather them in,*
> *for I have ransomed them,*[59]
> *and they shall be as many as of old.*
> Though I scattered them among the nations,
> yet in far countries they shall remember me,
> and with their children they shall live and return.
> *I will bring them home from the land of Egypt,*
> *and gather them from Assyria;*
> and I will bring them to the land of Gilead and Lebanon,
> till there is no room for them.
> They shall pass through the distress of Egypt,
> and the waves of the sea shall be smitten,
> and all the depths of the Nile dried up.
>
> (Zech 10:8-11)[60]

Redemption as the Restoration of All Israel

From this brief catalogue it should be clear that when Jesus speaks of the Son of Man giving his life as a "ransom," the first thing that would come to mind of an ancient Jewish audience is not simple "atonement" for sins, but rather the *redemption of all Israel from Exile.* This would be specially true if he were to conjoin such terminology with the imagery of *passing through water.* This, of course, is exactly what he does when he speaks of his "baptism" in Mark 10:38. Such imagery would be evocative—as we see in the prophets—of Israel's deliverance from Egypt via its passage through the Red Sea (see Isa 43:2; Zech 10:11).[61]

And, if any question should remain regarding whether "ransom" terminology alone could evoke such a widespread hope, I would submit that when the language of "ransom" is combined with the words "for *many*," as it is in Mark 10:45, little room for doubt is left. The reason: the language and imagery of "many" is also used in the Old Testament and Second Temple Judaism to evoke the hope for the new exodus, the end of the exile, and the restoration of all Israel.

In the Old Testament, the image of "many" or of a multitude being brought back from exile is notably present in texts which look forward to the restoration of the twelve tribes. Remarkably, this imagery is probably

---

[59] MT פְּדִיתִים LXX λυτρώσομαι αὐτούς.

[60] These texts by no means exhaust the use of "ransom" terminology to describe the end of the exile and the ingathering of scattered Israel from among the nations. See further: Isa. 44:21-23; 51:11; 62:12; Jer. 50:33-34; Lam. 5:8; cf. 4:22; Hos. 13:14; cf. 13:4-5, 14:7; Zeph. 3:15 (LXX); cf. 3:19-20; Zech. 3:1 (LXX).

[61] This suggested connection with the Exodus is even stronger if the imagery of the "cup" of suffering can be tied to the sufferings of the Passover trials, as it is, for example in Mark 14. For further discussion, see Pitre, "The Historical Jesus, the Great Tribulation, and the End of the Exile," 623-30.

rooted in the first Exodus itself. For the slavery from which Israel was "ransomed" (Exod. 6:6-8) began when they became too "many" (Exod. 1:9), so that they left Egypt as a "multitude"[62] (Exod. 12:38-39).

This initial link between the "ransom" of "many" and the Passover and exodus continues in Old Testament prophecies of the new exodus. Perhaps the most direct parallel to Jesus' words in Mark 10:45 is Zechariah's prophecy that those whom the Lord "shall ransom"[63] from exile shall be "as many[64] as of old"—that is, as many as in the days of the first exodus (Zech. 10:8). Also noteworthy is Jeremiah's comparison of "Jacob," whom the Lord has "ransomed,"[65] with a "great company"[66] who will be brought back to the land from "the farthest parts of the earth" (Jer. 31:8, 11).

Hosea likewise declares that when "the people of Judah and the people of Israel shall be gathered together"—that is, when all twelve tribes are gathered—"the number of the people of Israel shall be like the sand of the sea, which can be neither measured nor numbered" (Hos. 1:10-11). Even in Isaiah, it is none other than the scattered exiles of Israel who are the "many" astonished at the Servant (Isa. 52:14). They are the "many"[67] who will be "accounted righteous" because of his death (Isa. 53:11); they are the "many"[68] whose "sin" he will bear (Isa. 53:12).[69]

But perhaps the most intriguing use of the language of "many" comes to us from Daniel, where the word is used repeatedly to describe the righteous remnant who undergoes *the eschatological tribulation*. It is these "many"[70] who will make a covenant with the messianic prince during the

---

[62] MT רב LXX πολύς.

[63] MT פדיתים LXX λυτρώσομαι.

[64] MT רבו LXX πολλοί.

[65] MT פדה LXX ἐλυτρώσατο.

[66] MT קהל גדול LXX ὄχλον πολύν.

[67] MT רבים LXX πολλοῖς.

[68] MT רבים LXX πολλούς.

[69] It is not clear to me whether the "many nations" described in Isa. 52:15 should be considered part of this group.

[70] MT רבים LXX πολλούς.

tribulation (Dan. 9:27),[71] and be persecuted during the last days (Dan. 11:33, 34, 39). It is the "many," as Gabriel tells Daniel, who "shall purify themselves, and make themselves white, and be refined" in the sufferings of the last days (Dan. 12:10). Most importantly, it is also these "many" who, after suffering the tribulation, shall ultimately be raised from the dead:

> And there shall be a time of tribulation such as never has been since there was a nation till that time; but at that time your people shall be delivered, every one whose name shall be found written in the book. And *many* of those who sleep in the dust of the earth shall awake, some to ever-lasting life, and some to shame and everlasting contempt. And those who are wise shall shine like the brightness of the firmament; and *those who make righteous the many*,[72] like stars for ever and ever. . . .
>
> (Dan. 12:1-3)[73]

Like all "resurrection" texts in the Old Testament, this text is also a prophecy of the *restoration of Israel from exile*. This connection between resurrection and the restoration of Israel finds its classic expression in Ezekiel's vision of the valley of dry bones, in which bodily resurrection signals the return of the twelve tribes of Israel, the coming of the Davidic Messiah, and the end of the exile (see Ezek. 37).[74]

The end of the exile is also implicitly in view in Daniel. For when Daniel asks Gabriel when the resurrection of "the many" is to take place, the angel answers by referring him back to both the tribulation in Daniel 7 ("a time, two times, and half a time," Dan. 12:7; cf. 7:25) and the tribulation in Daniel 9 (the "abomination of desolation," Dan. 12:11; cf. 9:27). As we saw above, this tribulation represents the climax of Israel's exilic suffering. Hence, "the many" in Daniel are those Israelites who, after

---

[71] The same terminology is employed throughout Daniel in both the MT and the LXX; I will not repeat it here for the sake of clarity.

[72] MT הרבים LXX τῶν πολλῶν.

[73] RSV, slightly modified.

[74] Similar connections between restoration and resurrection are present in Isaiah 26-27 and Hosea 5-6. For a full-scale treatment of the resurrection which recognizes its connection to the restoration of Israel, see esp. N. T. Wright, *The Resurrection of the Son of God* (Minneapolis: Fortress, 2003), 108-128.

enduring the tribulation that will accompany the coming of the "Son of Man," will be made righteous when the exile comes to its end at the resurrection of the dead.[75]

The case for these links between the "many," the exile, and the restoration of Israel, can be clinched by studying use of the image in the Second Temple period. *The Similitudes of Enoch* depicts the end of the exile as "a whole array" of chariots loaded with people coming "from the east and from the west" to worship the Lord of the Spirits (1 En. 57:1). Even more remarkable, the author of the Qumran text, *1Q Rule of the Community*, who most certainly identified his fellow covenanters with the Israelite exiles (see 1QS 8:12-14, 9:18-20), repeatedly speaks of the community in precisely the same terminology as Daniel: they are "the Many" (הרבים).[76] Finally, perhaps the most striking parallels can be found in 4 Ezra and Josephus, both of whom use the image of a *multitude* to *describe the lost ten tribes of Israel*:

> And as for your seeing him [the Son of Man, the Messiah] gather to himself *another multitude (aliam multitudinem* in the Latin) that was peaceable, *these are the ten tribes* which were led away from their own land into captivity in the days of King Hoshea, whom Shalmaneser the king of the Assyrians led captive. . . .
>
> *(4 Ezra 13:39-40)*[77]

> The entire body of Israel remained in that country; wherefore there are but two tribes in Asia and Europe subject to the Romans, while *the ten tribes* are beyond Euphrates until now, and are an *immense multitude*, and not to be estimated by numbers.
>
> *(Antiquities of the Jews* 11.133)[78]

---

[75] See also Marvin C. Pate and Douglas W. Kennard, *Deliverance Now and Not Yet: The New Testament and the Great Tribulation*, Studies in Biblical Literature, 54 (New York: Peter Lang, 2003), 39-41. It should be noted here that some have seen in this language of "the many" in Dan 12:3 an allusion to the "many" who are justified by the Suffering Servant of Isaiah 53. Cf. Collins, *Daniel*, 385. Wright, *Jesus and the Victory of God*, 589, n. 190, also picks up on this, and uses it to strengthen his contention that Jesus has Isaiah 40-55 in mind in both his words and deeds.

[76] The term occurs some 27 times in 1QS 6-9. See Martin G. Abegg, Jr., "Exile and the Dead Sea Scrolls," in ed. James M. Scott, *Exile: Old Testament, Jewish, and Christian Conceptions*, Supplements to the Journal for the Study of Judaism, 56 (Leiden: Brill, 1997), 112-25 (esp. 122).

[77] Trans. Bruce Metzger, in *The Old Testament Pseudepigrapha*, ed. James H. Charlesworth (New York: Doubleday, 1983, 1985).

[78] William Whiston, trans., *The Works of Josephus: Complete and Unabridged*, rev. ed. (Peabody, Mass.: Hendrickson, 1987).

These texts clearly show that the ancient hope for the restoration of *all* Israel—including the lost ten tribes—from the time of Daniel to the time of *4 Ezra*, was often expressed by means of the image of "the many" or a "multitude." This is easily explained: for it was the *greater part* of Israel, ten of the twelve tribes, who had been scattered to the four winds by Assyria and remained in exile even unto Josephus' day.

The upshot of all this is simple: Jesus' words about a "ransom" for "many" in Mark 10:45 are directly evocative of the exodus, the exile, and the restoration of the twelve tribes of Israel. To one steeped in the promises of the Israelite prophets or informed by early Jewish eschatology, any prophet speaking of the Son of Man giving his life as "a ransom for many" would call to mind one thing: the still unfulfilled promise of the Lord to "atone for iniquity" and to ransom the lost ten tribes from among the nations, bringing them home to the promised land in a new exodus.

The New Exodus, the Forgiveness of Sins, and the Suffering Servant

It is this link between the New Exodus and atonement for sin that finally brings us back to the issue around which so much scholarly debate on Mark 10:45 has revolved: the Suffering Servant of Isaiah 53. While we certainly do not have the space to enter into the debate in any detail, our distinctive focus on the Old Testament background of the death of the Messiah, the atoning tribulation, and the restoration of Israel, may lend indirect support to the position that Jesus is in fact drawing on the Isaianic servant figure in "the ransom saying." The reason: in Isaiah, the figure of the Servant, like that of the messianic Son of Man, is not only tied to atonement for sin; he also inaugurates a *new exodus* and *the restoration of the tribes of Israel.* Given everything we have seen so far, reread these two key texts regarding the servant:

> And now the LORD says,
> who formed me from the womb to be *his servant,*
> *to bring Jacob back to him,*
> and that Israel might be gathered to him. . . .
> "It is too light a thing *that you should be my servant*
> *to raise up the tribes of Jacob*
> *and to restore the survivors of Israel;*
> I will give you as a light to the nations,
> that my salvation may reach to the ends of the earth."
>
> (Isa. 49:5-6)

Surely he has borne our griefs
and carried our sorrows;
yet we esteemed him stricken,
smitten by God, and afflicted.
But he was wounded for our transgressions,
he was bruised for our iniquities;
upon him was the chastisement that made us whole,
and with his stripes we are healed. . . .
All we like sheep have gone astray;
we have turned every one to his own way,
and the LORD has laid on him the iniquity of us all. . . .
He poured out his soul to death,
and was number with the transgressors,
yet *he bore the sin of many,*
and made intercession for transgressors.

(Isa. 53:4-6, 12)

The juxtaposition of these two texts should make quite clear: the servant of Isaiah takes upon himself the iniquities and sins of exiled Israel—the "many" scattered "sheep" who have "gone astray"—in order to "raise up the tribe of Jacob and to restore the survivors of Israel." That is, he makes his life an "offering for sin"—the sin of Israel that led to its exile, in order to bring about the restoration of all Israel in a new exodus. Moreover, this new exodus, unlike the first, will somehow be universal in scope, for it will include the ingathering not only of Israel, but of the Gentile nations (see Isa. 66).[79]

In short, Jesus' words about the "ransom for many" in the end appear to be a *combination* of figures from Daniel and Isaiah that draws on their common hope for a new exodus and the restoration of Israel. In both, the exile is only brought to an end by a climactic period of tribulation or affliction in which a key figure, the Messiah/Son of Man, or the servant, dies, and thereby atones for the sins of Israel that have led her into exile in the first place.

---

[79] Many other texts in Isaiah 40-55 point to the important connections between the forgiveness of sins and the end of the exile. For example, when Israel's "iniquity" is forgiven, a new exodus will occur (Isa. 42:1-5). When the Lord blots out Israel's "transgressions" and does not "remember" its "sins," they will be "ransomed" and gathered "from the end of the earth" (Isa. 43:1-28). When Jacob's "transgressions" are swept away "like a cloud," and they are "ransomed," they will return to Jerusalem and rebuild the city (Isa. 44:21-28). Israel was sold into exile because of its "iniquities" and "transgressions," when they are "ransomed," the Lord will dry up the sea to clear a path for their return (Isa. 50:1-3). See also Wright, *Jesus and the Victory of God*, 268-74.

Indeed, in light of this exegesis, all of Mark 10:35-45 makes a great deal of sense. James and John, presupposing the messianic identity of Jesus, make a request to sit at his right and left hand in the glory of his kingdom. Jesus responds with a question: are they able to drink the cup of tribulation and be baptized in the waters of suffering which he as (Danielic) Messiah will have to undergo? Their answer, in the affirmative, not only leads Jesus to explain that it is not his place to grant them places of authority, but also to emphasize that in the (again Danielic) eschatological "kingdom," the Son of Man will not lord it over his subjects like the Gentile tyrants but rather will suffer and die for them as a "servant." As both the Servant of Isaiah and the Messiah of Daniel, the Son of Man will suffer and die at the climax of Israel's exile, and will thereby effect an atonement for sin (the "ransom") for the scattered multitude of the lost sheep of the house of Israel (the "many"). In so doing, his death, along with the other sufferings of the time of trial, will bring about the end of the exile.

This, I would humbly suggest, is the solution to the notorious crux of Mark 10:45. This is its most plausible interpretation. Jesus is saying that the Son of Man as Messiah will perish in the tribulation, the climax of the exile, and that his life will function as a "ransom" for the "many" who have been scattered. His death will atone for sin and will restore the tribes of Jacob and raise up the survivors of Israel, bringing them back to Zion in the long-awaited return from exile, the new exodus.

Conclusions and Implications

The implications of the interpretation offered herein have a potentially significant impact on our understanding of the text at the levels of exegesis, history, and theology. By way of conclusion, I will briefly note some of these.

First, at the level of exegesis, the link between the ransom for many and the restoration of Israel from exile allows us to provide a solution to a famous *crux interpretum*. As noted above, despite the intense focus which has been paid this text, it continues to present serious difficulties to modern exegetes and to leave many questions unanswered. In particular, the questions of "Who are the many?" and "From what are they ransomed?"—which continue to baffle exegetes—can now be answered quite clearly: the many are the scattered tribes, the exiles of Israel, who are to be ransomed from among the Gentile nations.[80]

---

[80] Contrast this specificity with the vagueness and difficulty present in the proffered answered cited in the footnote above.

The strength of this solution lies not only in its clarity, but also in the fact that it employs the language and imagery of the Old Testament itself, and not just a single text, but a host of texts which converge around the central Old Testament hope for the new exodus and the restoration Israel from among the Gentiles.

Second, at the level of history, this interpretation raises serious questions about the widespread scholarly doubt that the "ransom saying" originated with the historical Jesus. While we did not have the space to properly engage this question in this essay, I have taken it up elsewhere in some detail.[81] Here I would simply point out a curious paradox in Jesus research: namely, although recent historical Jesus scholarship has produced a veritable flood of literature placing Jesus quite squarely in the context of *early Jewish restoration eschatology*, it has at the same time either totally *ignored* Mark 10:45 or declared it inauthentic (the former often functioning as a tacit approval of the latter).[82]

For example, E. P. Sanders, perhaps the foremost proponent of Jesus as a prophet of restoration eschatology, dismisses the suggestion that Jesus could have intended his death to have sacrificial and redemptive efficacy as "weird."[83] As we have seen in this exploration, nothing could be further from the truth. Instead, the "ransom saying" is remarkably congruent with the Old Testament hope for the restoration of Israel and fits quite squarely into the reconstruction of Jesus a Jewish eschatological prophet. In light of this fact, I would challenge Jesus researchers to take up the important question of its authenticity anew and fill the gaping scholarly hole surrounding a saying which could tell us a great deal about how the prophet from Nazareth might have understood his own mission to Israel.

Third and finally, at the level of theology, the link between the ransom saying and the restoration of Israel has the potential to open new doors in contemporary discussion of soteriology in general and the doctrine of the atonement in particular. It is widely known that the towering figure of St. Anselm and his influential formulation of the theory of substitutionary atonement in *Cur Deus Homo* has been strongly criticized

---

[81] See Pitre, "The Historical Jesus, the Great Tribulation, and the End of the Exile," 534-83.

[82] For references, see Pitre, "The Historical Jesus, the Great Tribulation, and the End of the Exile," 536.

[83] E. P. Sanders, *Jesus and Judaism* (Minneapolis: Fortress Press, 1985), 333.

for some time; yet many questions remain regarding how to understand this most central of Christian doctrines.[84]

In light of this situation, what may be needed now is a fresh reformulation of the discussion, one which draws directly on biblical language and imagery, so that the "sacred page" might truly be "the soul of sacred theology."[85] This study has used the biblical concepts of the eschatological tribulation, the exile and restoration of Israel, and the new exodus, to throw new light on Jesus' concept of his atoning death. My hope is that theologians interested in this fundamental soteriological issue might also find these biblical categories helpful and illuminating for future discussion and reflection.

---

[84] For recent surveys with bibliography, see esp. Charles E. Hill and Frank A. James III, *The Glory of the Atonement: Biblical, Historical, and Practical Perspectives: Essays in Honor of Roger Nicole* (Downers Grove, Ill.: InterVarsity, 2004), and Michael Winter, *The Atonement* (Collegeville, Minn.: Liturgical Press, 1995). See also Gustaf Aulén, Christus Victor: *An Historical Study of the Three Main Types of the Idea of Atonement*, trans. A. G. Herbert (New York: Macmillan, 1969).

[85] Second Vatican Council, Dogmatic Constitution on Divine Revelation, *Dei Verbum* (November 18, 1965), 24.

Letter & Spirit 1 (2005): 69-86

MEMORIAL AND TYPOLOGY IN JEWISH AND CHRISTIAN LITURGY

• Sofia Cavalletti •

Buon Pastore Montessori Catechetical Center, Rome

We can see an ideological connection between the synagogue and the church: the essential element in the world of the synagogue is the proclamation of the Word of God, and the first part of the Mass is called the Liturgy of the Word. Nevertheless, it is essential to remember that when Jews speak about "redemption" either they are referring to the liberation from Egypt or to the eschatological redemption. Christians believe that redemption has already reached its climax in the person of Jesus the Nazarene and are expecting its completion at the end of history, when "God will be all in all" (1 Cor. 15:28). This means that we are looking together at the same moment in the future, but from different points of view.

The synagogue originated in the exile. The Jews, deprived of the Temple, sought for a means of replacing the animal sacrifices offered there. The Lord had associated his presence in a very special way with the Temple, and after its destruction he himself was, in a sense, in exile. Yet he continued to speak to his people through his Law (*Torah*). This was the principal means of communicating with him and of answering his presence among them.

But the origins of the synagogue were not merely contingent and due to historical situations; when the Jews returned to the land of their fathers and reconstructed the Temple, the use of the synagogue increased rather than diminished, thus proving its vitality. It was rooted in a religious need which became deeper and more widespread as time went on, a desire that religion should penetrate more deeply into daily life and that the non-priestly classes should have a more lively participation in its activities.

During the earthly life of Jesus, the synagogue for the Jew was perhaps the truest expression of spirituality. Jesus himself and his apostles frequently chose to teach in the synagogue. "Jesus went about teaching in their synagogues," says Matthew (6:23). He was often in the synagogues of Capernaum and Nazareth (Matt. 12:9, 13, 54; Mark 1:21, etc.). He himself, summarizing his life's work, says before the Sanhedrin: "I have spoken openly to the world; I have always taught in your synagogues and in the Temple" (John 18:20).

Jesus' Teaching in the Synagogue

Jesus spoke his own word during the synagogue worship. He had a reason for this and, in our opinion, his reason must be sought in the spirit of the synagogue's worship itself, which was totally centered on the Word of God. This Word was solemnly proclaimed to the people and they responded by prayer.

The nucleus of synagogue worship was the Pentateuch, which the Jews consider to be in a special way *Torah*, hence, the teaching of God. By the time of Jesus the first reading was complemented by and joined to a second from the prophetical books. The oldest available information on the arrangement of these readings comes from texts slightly posterior to the time of Jesus. However, as religious traditions are in general conservative, we can think that this information applies also to the synagogue practice of the time of Christ. The prophetic text often explains and interprets the passage of the Torah. Sometimes it helps to place a feast in its historical context, at others it is a spiritual or homiletic comment on the chosen passage. Finally, the prophetic reading is messianic, in that it describes a vision of the future or a liberator who will come "on that day" to bestow God's Spirit of comfort, salvation, and plenitude upon his people.

The prophetic reading placed the Torah in its future perspective— the expectation of an event still to come, the coming of a long-awaited person. It can be said that in such instances as these, the liturgy of the synagogue seemed as if straining towards a fulfillment yet to come. Thus, at the end of the readings, the worshippers praised God who had just spoken his word to them, and in a prayer that is essentially eschatological, they asked him to hasten this fulfillment.

> Magnified and sanctified be his great name in the world which he hath created according to his will. May he estab- lish his kingdom during your life and during your days, and during the life of all the house of Israel, even speedily and at a near time.[1]

This prayer, the *Kaddish*, for many centuries has concluded the synagogue readings; it probably did so also at the time of Jesus. Hearing the promises of God aroused the desire of their speedy realization, and the *Kaddish* was the most natural response. The similarity of the *Kaddish* with the *Our Father* is obvious—they are both eschatologically oriented. It would seem that Jesus found in this future-orientated worship, and in those who shared it, the material and moral setting for the proclamation of his own word.

Many of the episodes in the life of Jesus can be fully understood only if they are seen in this light, for example the multiplication of the loaves as narrated by John (6:1-15).[2] This miracle explains the later

---

[1] *The Authorized Prayer Book*, rev. ed., commentary and notes by Joseph H. Hertz (New York: Bloch, 1948), 423.

[2] See Aileen Guilding, T*he Fourth Gospel and Jewish Worship* (Oxford: Clarendon Press, 1960); R. Houston Smith, "Exodus Typology in the Fourth Gospel," *Journal de litterature biblique* (1962): 329ff.

discourses of Jesus in which he calls himself "the bread of life" (John 6:22). Between the pericope of the miracle, which occurred at some undetermined place on the banks of Lake Tiberias, and Jesus' discourse in the synagogue at Capernaum, comes the account of the walking on the waters when the boat of the apostles almost floundered in the storm. This miracle must have been performed between Jesus' leaving the place where he multiplied the loaves and his journey to Capernaum. In this context the evangelist states precisely: "It was shortly before the Jewish festival of Passover" (John 6:4), adding that "there was plenty of grass there" (John 6:10)—thus stressing the fact that the season was spring.

These details are given by the evangelist so as to place his narrative in its proper setting: the liturgical solemnity of the Passover. We know that the central point of the paschal liturgy for the Jews is the Exodus, and that the Canticle of the Red Sea is read in the synagogue, a canticle which celebrates God's manifestation of his power in bringing his people through the Red Sea. What must have been the effect of this passage on the apostles who had just witnessed the extraordinary power of Jesus over the waters! They, and all those to whom the miracle was known, could not have failed to make this connection. They would have heard in the synagogue how "the LORD drove back the sea with a strong easterly wind all night, and he made dry land of the sea. The waters parted . . . " (Exod. 14:21), and they could scarcely have failed to remember that while a strong wind was blowing Jesus had walked dry-footed across the sea of Tiberias, almost as though a path had been opened for him.

The prophets, referring to the Exodus, had said that "on that day" (that is, the messianic times) a new way would be opened over the waters. Is there, perhaps, a connection between the words of the prophets and the miraculous event on the waters of the lake? The people of Israel had passed through the Red Sea, Jesus over Lake Tiberias; and Jesus was the one that some had begun to acknowledge as the Messiah.

During the Passover the account of the sending of the manna to satisfy the hunger of the Israelites in the desert is also read from Numbers 11. The discourse on the bread of life which takes up the greater part of Chapter 6 in John's Gospel is an answer to the question: "What miracle will you show us that we should believe in you? What work will you do? Our fathers ate manna in the desert, as Scripture says, 'He gave them bread from heaven to eat' " (6:31). The gospel text makes no reference to the Passover liturgy; St. John evidently considered the previous reference to the feast to be clear enough.

To we who read these texts so long after they were compiled it is less clear why the crowd recalled the manna, which Jesus took as the theme of his discourse and of the subsequent discussion. But as soon as we realize that the account of the manna had probably just been read in the synagogue, the connection becomes clearer. Jesus uses the question to show how the Scripture can be read also as hinting at himself. The manna had saved the Hebrews from temporal death; he had come down from heaven to save men from eternal death. "Your fathers ate the manna in the desert and they are dead. . . . I am the living bread which has come down from heaven. Anyone who eats this bread will live for ever."

The parable of the Good Shepherd is found only in John 10, and it is completed by that of the lost sheep in Luke 15. John ends his narrative by saying that it was winter, on the Feast of the Dedication. This feast commemorated the purification of the Temple by Judah Maccabee after it had been profaned by Antiochus Epiphanes, and during the liturgy for this feast the patriarch Joseph's instructions to his brothers—that it should be made clear to Pharaoh that they and their fathers before them had always been shepherds—is read (Gen. 46:28-47:12).

The account of David's seeking permission from Saul to fight Goliath is also read. David describes himself as an intrepid shepherd, constantly attentive to his father's flock (1 Sam. 17:34-36). The prophetic reading for the feast (Ezek. 34), shows the shepherd David in a different light—he is the "one shepherd" to whom God will entrust his sheep and to whom he is bound by the "covenant of peace." David's relationship with God is difficult to establish because, in the same passage, the prophet explains that *God himself* will gather his flock together "on that day." He will seek out the dispersed sheep to bring them back so that he can heal their wounds and cure their sickness.

The entire liturgy of the Dedication, centered on the theme of the "shepherd," gave Jesus the opportunity of presenting himself as the "Good Shepherd" who, in contrast to those shepherds who "fed themselves" (see Ezek. 34), defends his sheep like David, giving his life for them—the "one shepherd" who, like the Lord himself in Ezekiel, goes in search of his sheep when they are lost. Seen in the light of the liturgical setting of Jesus' words, the parable of the Good Shepherd can be read as an explicit declaration by Jesus that he is the Messiah. And the identification of the Shepherd with the Lord himself (see Ezekiel) can lead to a very profound understanding of the nature of Jesus as Messiah.

The great autumn festivals are also reflected in the teaching of Jesus. The liturgy was performed in the Temple with certain "popular" elements introduced by the Pharisees, chief among these being the libation on the altar. This took place towards the end of the festival: water was drawn from a spring outside the walls of Jerusalem, carried into the city through a gate which is still called the Water Gate, and poured out on the altar in supplication for rain. The entire rite is given a messianic interpretation through the prophetic reading which follows it.

> When that day comes,
> running waters will issue from Jerusalem,
> half of them to the eastern sea,
> half of them to the western sea;
> they will flow summer and winter.
> And the LORD will be king of the whole world.
> When that day comes, the LORD will be unique.
> (Zech. 14:8-9)

These words of Zechariah urge the people to dwell no longer on the present, but to see in the water poured out on the altar, the eternal "living water" which "on that day" will make the earth fruitful. Ezekiel speaks again of the marvelous fertilizing power of this water (Ezek. 47). According to a rabbinical interpretation, this marvelous fertility will renew the earth in such a way that, no longer contaminated by man's sin, it will be restored to its pristine fruitfulness.

Moreover, according to this interpretation, between the earth's origin and its messianic renovation there is in salvation history the essential event of the exodus when Israel drank from miraculous springs in the desert.[3] This must not be forgotten. Thus, when the Jews participated in this Temple liturgy, they looked back to the origin of the world, saw it already being renewed at a crucial moment of Israel's history, and at the same time looked forward to the time when all their hopes would be realized.

It is against this liturgical background that Jesus cries: "If any man is thirsty let him come to me" (John 7:37). With these words Jesus hints in an implicit way—as was usual in his teaching—that he is the source of living water.

From the beginning of his ministry, Jesus consistently placed his teaching in the context of synagogue worship. Luke tells of his preaching in the synagogue at Nazareth and places it in the first year of his public life, shortly after the miracle at Cana. News of that miracle would soon have reached Nazareth, which is close to Cana. This perhaps accounts for the fact that on the following Sabbath Jesus was called upon to read in the synagogue of Nazareth, where he was known only as "the son of Joseph."

The story is familiar: how he was given the scroll of the prophet Isaiah, read the passage (Isa. 61:1-2), and then rolled up the scroll, handed it back to the assistant and sat down. "And," Luke's account continues, "all eyes in the synagogue were fixed on him" (Luke 4:16).

The hope of the people was not to be disappointed. On that day in the synagogue they listened to an explanation of Scripture such as they had never before heard. This was why Jesus said: "This text is being fulfilled today, even as you listen."

The very presence of Jesus in the synagogue meant that the Word of God, revealed by the prophets and patriarchs, had found a new answer; a new step in history had been reached. In Jesus' lips "today" means that, in his person, salvation had reached its climax, and now we have to wait for its completion in the whole world.

Out of the Synagogue: The Liturgy of the Word

The apostles, like Jesus, preached their good news in the synagogue. Even Paul, "the apostle of the Gentiles," is recorded as preaching in the

---

[3] Exod. 15:22-27; 17:1-7. *Tosefta Sukkah*, 3.3-18.

synagogues at Antioch (Acts 13:14-43), at Philippi (Acts 16:13), at Thessalonika, where he preached for three successive sabbaths (Acts 17:2-3), and finally at Corinth (Acts 18:4).

And the Liturgy of the Word that the Church developed grew out of the synagogue worship the early Jewish Christians were so familiar with. The Christian Liturgy of the Word is still marked by the synagogue from which it originated. If we compare the Sabbath services with the oldest forms of the Christian liturgy, we cannot fail to notice some similarities of structure. In the words of Righetti, "a true and exact continuity of worship was intentionally allowed by the first Christians."[4]

Justin Martyr, in his *First Apology*, has left us a very ancient description of the Mass. In the introductory part are to be found, although in a different order, almost all the elements of the synagogue service:

> . . . And on the day which is called Sunday, there is an assembly in the same place of all who live in cities, or in country districts; and the records of the apostles, or the writings of the prophets, are read as long as we have time. Then the reader concludes: and the president verbally instructs and exhorts us to the imitation of these excellent things: then, we all together rise and offer up our prayers. . . .[5]

A description of the Eucharist follows, and the service ends with a collection for the poor. In Justin's account, there is no mention of the profession of faith (*Shema*) which is part of the synagogue service, nor of the blessing which closes it. But all the other elements are common to both synagogue and church.

The "prayers" mentioned by Justin could be what Christians today call the "prayers of the faithful." Like those of the synagogue, they conclude the Liturgy of the Word by presenting to God the needs of all men. They resemble the greatly venerated "Eighteen Blessings," which traditionally contain three parts—the first devoted to praise, the last to thanksgiving, and a central portion that changes according to the feast and contained prayers of petition suited to different occasions. It is also quite possible that when Justin speaks of "prayers," he also includes praying of the psalms. Selections from these were recited in the synagogue before the Scripture readings. In both church and synagogue the readings are followed by a sermon, and at the end of both services a collection is made for the poor.

---

[4] Mario Righetti, *Manuale di storia liturgica*, 4 vols. (Milan: Ancora 1959-66), 3:62.

[5] Justin's description is quoted at length in the *Catechism of the Catholic Church*, no. 1345.

On the basis of the data given by Justin, the following "order of worship" scheme can be drawn up:

> *Christian Liturgy of the Word*
> — ?
> — Prayers of Intercession
> — Psalms (?)
> — Readings (Law, Prophets, Gospel)
> — Sermon
> — ?
> — Collection for the Poor
>
> *Synagogue Service*
> — Profession of Faith
> — Prayer of the "Eighteen Blessings"
> — Psalms
> — Readings (Law and Prophets)
> — Sermon
> — Priestly Blessing
> — Collection for the Poor

The resemblance between these two structures is still more striking when we compare the Jewish with the more recent Christian form in which the people respond to the proclamation of the Word of God by a profession of faith, thus introducing into the Christian cult an element of Jewish worship which was not present at the time when Justin wrote.

From Passover Meal to Eucharist

It is still more significant to see how the Eucharist, the most important act of Christian worship, originated in the context of Jewish worship. Without entering into the question of the paschal character of the Last Supper, we would like to draw attention to the similarity of structure which exists between it and the Jewish Passover meal. Scholars continue to discuss whether or not the Last Supper has to be envisaged against the background of a Jewish paschal celebration; but it is certain that at a very early date Christians attributed a paschal character to the Eucharist.

There are no available texts of the Passover meal dating from the time of Jesus, but in the corpus of civil and religious rules called the Mishna, particularly the treatise on Passover (*Pesahim*), the additions to this treatise (*Tosefta*), and an interpretative text (*Sifrei*), there exists an outline of the Passover meal. These documents date to the second century A.D. and can therefore be trusted to give an accurate description of the Passover ritual as observed by Jesus and his apostles.

According to the Mishna, the Passover meal (which the Jews call *seder*) was celebrated at the beginning of the Christian era in much the same way as it is celebrated today: after the blessing of the day had been recited over the first cup of wine, all the requisite foods are brought to the chief of the seder. Among these foods was, of course, the unleavened bread (*matzoh*). According to a well-documented custom of a later date, the unleavened bread is presented to the chief of the meal. He divides one of them in two, covering one part with a small napkin and placing the other with the uncut portions. Over them all he then recites the customary and already ancient formula for the blessing of bread: "Blessed art thou, O LORD our God, who bringest forth bread from the earth."[6]

The divided matzoh seems to have a special importance because a second blessing is pronounced over it immediately after the first: "Blessed art thou, O LORD our God, who hast sanctified us with thy commandments and commanded us concerning the eating of unleavened bread." After this blessing the chief of the seder eats a piece of the matzoh and distributes it to those at table.[7] The portion which had been placed under the napkins is brought out at the end of the meal and consumed without a blessing. The final blessing over the rest of the food follows. It must be kept in mind that these details are found only in a relatively late text; but, given the scarcity of earlier liturgical documents we cannot exclude the possibility of their referring to a much earlier practice.

At this point the youngest child present must question as to the particular significance of the Passover night, how it differs from all other nights. Why is the bread unleavened, why are the herbs bitter, why is the meat roasted and not boiled? These questions prompt the chief to explain the meaning of the celebration, which he does according to the precepts of the Mishnah, "beginning with the humiliation and ending with the glory."[8] In other words, he has to comment on the passage from Deuteronomy (26:5-10): "My father was a wandering Aramean. He went down into Egypt . . . there he became a nation, great, mighty and strong. The Egyptians ill-treated us, and the LORD brought us out of Egypt with mighty hand and outstretched arm. . . ." He also has to comment on the text of Joshua (24:2-13)[9]: " 'In ancient days your ancestors lived beyond the

---

[6] *Berakhot,* 39b.46.

[7] *Mahzor Vitry,* 94, 96. See Enrico Mazza, *La celebrazione eucaristica: genesi del rito e sviluppo dell'interpretazione* (San Paolo: Cinisello Balsamo 1996), 29, 59.

[8] *Pesahim,* 10.4.

[9] Jerusalem Talmud, *Pesahim,* 10.4.37d.

River [Euphrates] . . . then I brought your father Abraham from beyond the river and led him through all the land of Canaan. . . . Then I sent Moses and Aaron. . . . So I brought you out of (Egypt). . . . I gave you a land where you never toiled, you live in towns you never built; you eat now from vineyards and olive groves you never planted."

These are two very ancient outlines of salvation history. They stress the Lord's call to the fathers of the Israelites to leave an idolatrous country in order to take possession of the promised land that he would give to them, his people, and the liberation from enslavement to the Egyptians when Israel truly became the free people of God. This brief summary of the history of Israel provides the chief of the seder with a particularly suitable context in which to explain the reasons for eating roast lamb, unleavened bread, and bitter herbs. In the Passover rite during which the eating of the foods is prescribed, every Jew can relive his historic past, actualized in the celebration. The paschal lamb (*pesah*) recalls how the Lord had "passed over" (*pasah*) the houses of the Israelites at the very moment when the first-born of the Egyptians were dying. The unleavened bread is a reminder that because they had to leave Egypt in haste there was not time for the bread to rise. The bitter herbs recall the bitterness of their sufferings in bondage.

Yet this history is never really past, since it is reenacted in the person of every Jew who participates in the Passover rite.[10] According to the Mishnah, every Jew must "consider himself as having come forth from Egypt." The Passover rite enables all Jews to become conscious of this liberation and to share in it. Therefore, every Jew is bound to

> thank, praise, laud, glorify, exalt, honor, bless, extol, and adore him who performed all these miracles for our fathers and for us. He has brought us forth from slavery to freedom, from sorrow to joy, from mourning to holiday, from darkness to great light, and from bondage to redemption. Let us then recite before him a new song: Hallelujah.[11]

These words mark the beginning of the recitation of the first part of the Psalms of Praise (*Hallel*), Psalms 113 and 114. These psalms must end with a mention of redemption, to which mention Rabbi Akiba (50-135 A.D.) gave a clearly messianic character:

---

[10] Gerhard von Rad, *Theologie de l'Ancien Testament* (Geneve, 1963), 112 ff.

[11] Nahum N. Glatzer ed., *The Passover Haggadah,* rev. ed. (New York: Schocken, 1969), 51.

> So, O LORD our God and God of our fathers, bring us to other festivals and holy days that come toward us in peace, happy in the building of thy city and joyous in thy service. And there may we eat of the sacrifices and the paschal offerings. . . . Blessed art thou, O LORD, redeemer of Israel.[12]

The history recalled by the chief of the seder is being continued in the person of every Jew who participates in the Passover rite, while at the same time it looks forward to that future foretold by the prophet, when Jerusalem will be rebuilt and unending worship will be celebrated there. At this point a second cup of wine is blessed and the meal begins. It is truly a ritual meal preceded and followed by readings and prayers. It is this celebration that makes it possible for the Jew in every age to share in the liberation wrought by God for his people.

The blessing "over the food" follows, in thanksgiving for the meal. A third cup of wine is then blessed, after which comes a blessing for the earth and another blessing that begins, "To him who restores Jerusalem."[13]

The thanksgiving is completed by the blessing of a fourth cup of wine. This is the most solemn of all the blessings and the tradition says that David alone would be worthy to bless this cup, thus clearly attributing to the cup a messianic character. The blessing is followed by the other Psalms of Praise beginning with Psalm 115 ("Not to us, O LORD, not to us, but to thy name give glory") and ending with Psalm 118.

There follows another prayer, of which the Mishnah gives only the name: "Benediction over the Song." However, Rabbi Johanan knew already in the third century[14] that this prayer concluded the Psalms of Praise in almost every rite, and hence those of the Passover meal:

> The breath of every living thing shall bless thy name, O LORD our God, and the spirit of all flesh shall glorify and exalt thy memory, our king, for ever. From the eternity of the beginning to the eternity of the end, thou art God, and except for thee we have no redeeming and saving king, liberating and delivering, and provident and compassionate in every time of trouble and distress. We have no king but thee, O God of the first things and the last, God of all creatures, the LORD of all generations, who is lauded with many songs of praise, who conducts his universe with mercy and his creatures with compassion.

---

[12] Glatzer, *The Passover Haggadah,* 53, 55. The formula of Rabbi Akiba has been preserved practically unchanged throughout the centuries. See Moses Maimonides, *Mishna Torah* (New York: Feldheim, 1971).

[13] *Berakhot,* 48a.

[14] *Pesahim,* 118a. See Rabbenu Shlomo bar Yitzhak in *Mahzor Vitry,* 282.

The L<small>ORD</small> slumbers not nor sleeps. It is he who awakens the sleeping, and rouses the slumbering, and makes the dumb converse, and loosens the bound, and steadies the falling, and straightens the bent. To thee alone do we give thanks. Though our mouths were full of song like the sea, and our tongue of rejoicing like the multitude of its waves, and our lips of praise like the breadth of the horizon, and our eyes were shining like the sun and the moon, and our hands were spread like the eagles of the sky, and our feet light as the hinds—we should never thank thee enough, O L<small>ORD</small> our God and God of our fathers, and to bless thy name, for one of the thousands of thousands and myriads of myriads of the good thou hast done with our fathers and us.

From Egypt thou hast redeemed us, O L<small>ORD</small> our God, and from the house of slaves ransomed us, in famine fed us, and in plenty provided us, from the sword saved us, and from the pest delivered us, and from evil and serious illnesses lifted us. Till now thy compassions have helped us and thy mercies have not deserted us; and may thou never, O L<small>ORD</small> our God, desert us. Therefore, the limbs that thou hast distributed among us, and the spirit and breath that thou hast blown into our nostrils, and the tongue which thou hast placed in our mouths—they shall give thanks, and bless, and extol, and glorify, and exalt, and reverence, and sanctify and crown thy name, our king.

For every mouth shall give thanks to thee, and every tongue shall swear to thee, and every knee shall kneel to thee, and every stature bow down before thee, and all hearts shall fear thee, the inward parts and reins shall sing to thy name. As it is written: "All my bones shall say: 'L<small>ORD</small>, who is like unto thee, / Who deliverest the poor from him that is too strong for him, / Yea, the poor and the needy from him that spoileth him?'" (Ps. 35:10). Who is like thee, and who is equal to thee, and who is comparable to thee, the God who is great, mighty, and awesome, God Most High, master of heaven and earth? We shall praise thee, and laud thee, and glorify thee, and bless thy holy name. As it is said: "Bless the L<small>ORD</small>, O my soul; / And all that is within me, bless his holy name" (Ps. 103:1).[15]

---

[15] *The Passover Haggadah,* 79, 81.

A medieval legend attributed this prayer to Peter. In the absence of data it is not possible to verify such an attribution, but it is easy to imagine that Peter, the only apostle to whom the Father had revealed the true nature of the Messiah (Matt. 16:16), would have grasped the significance of the Last Supper more clearly than the other apostles. In consequence, he might have formulated a prayer in which he recognizes that the incapacity of man to praise God adequately was the best expression of his own inward consciousness.

At this point in the Passover celebration another tradition (*Tosefta*) prescribes that it must end with the following verse from one of the Psalms of Praise: "Blessed is he who comes in the name of the LORD." This conclusion anticipates both by invocation and implied desire the coming of the Messiah and his salvation. It is followed by a final hymn to God, redeemer of his people.

There have been various attempts to specify at what point during the Passover meal Jesus could have pronounced the words of consecration, words which nobody before him had ever pronounced: "Take and eat of this, for it is my Body," and "Take and drink of this, for it is my Blood." The words of consecration over the bread transcend Jewish ritual tradition, but is it possible that they were introduced by the formula already quoted, which is still used by every observant Jew when he breaks bread: "Blessed art thou, O LORD our God, who bringest forth bread from the earth." The Last Supper was a meal overshadowed by the presentiment of death, and the apostles, even if they did not fully understand, surely felt something of this presentiment.

In such a context the above blessing must have assumed the tone and the importance of a prophecy of the resurrection. Jesus identified the bread with his body, so the implication was clear: just as the Lord brought forth bread from the earth so would he bring forth from the grave that body of his son soon to be buried. Moreover, Jewish mysticism later speculated that the bread and wine represent both Israel and the Messiah.[16]

Is it possible also to see in the broken matzoh, which is blessed twice during the Passover meal and hence is particularly sacred, the bread which Jesus consecrated and gave to his apostles? In Jewish tradition the unleavened bread had to be eaten with the lamb, and in time it recalled the lamb.[17] This leads to the supposition that all the prescriptions relating to

---

[16] E. R. Goodenough, *Jewish Symbols in the Greco-Roman Period*, vol. 6 (New York: Princeton University, 1953-1968), 182.

[17] Rashi, *Ad Pesahim*, 119b

the lamb were applied to the bread.[18] Hence this would be the bread over which Jesus—whom John the Baptist called "the Lamb of God"—would have pronounced the consecratory words. All this is just a supposition.

As for the cup, this matter too requires conjecture. Paul would seem to suggest that it was the cup of blessing (see 1 Cor. 10:16). Luke, however, expressly states that the wine was consecrated after the meal, which would correspond with the traditional fourth cup of the Passover celebration. Based on Luke, it seems possible to identify the cup consecrated by Jesus with that cup which was and still is blessed with particular solemnity at the close of the ritual meal. It has already been said that a messianic character was attributed to this blessing and that the Jews expect King David, prototype of the Messiah, to come himself to bless the cup. The Psalms of Praise seem particularly suitable to the experience the apostles were just then living; indeed parts of these psalms seem difficult to understand outside of the particular context:

> . . . Death's cords were tightening round me,
> the nooses of Sheol;
> distress and anguish gripped me,
> I invoked the name of the LORD: "LORD, rescue me!" . . .
> What return can I make to the LORD
> for all his goodness to me?
> I will offer libations to my savior,
> invoking the name of the LORD.
>
> (Ps. 116:3-13)

In this psalm the agony of death alternates with a sense of security in the Lord's help, with a faith which we can define as faith in the resurrection. Perhaps Jesus alone understood the full meaning of these words. The apostles had heard them in an atmosphere of impending tragedy; this, and their uneasiness at the prophecy of Jesus' betrayal, had perhaps rendered them incapable of perceiving the hope and promise inherent in the psalm.

The Last Supper ended with the recitation of the "hymn" mentioned by the evangelists (Matt. 26:30; Mark 14:26) , in which we can recognize the Psalms of Praise that close the Passover meal. Thus was concluded the rite of Jesus which, like his interpretation of the Scriptures in the synagogue, is both old and new.

By means of the blessed wine and matzoh the Jew was able to reactualize in each generation the redemption of Israel and anticipate in petition and desire the completion of the redemption to be wrought by the

---

[18] *Enciclopedia Talmudith*, I, 134.5.

Messiah. That night the apostles could apply to one person the invocation which had for so long expressed the yearning of the Jews: "Blessed is he who comes in the name of the LORD."

As we have said, since that moment both Christians and Jews look together at the same point in the future: the coming of the Messiah or his coming back. For Christians, the Messiah has come, is coming, and *will* come. For the Jews, he *will* come.

At the Last Supper, Jesus once again performed an action in the context of Jewish liturgy. At Nazareth he had wanted the synagogue to be the background of his proclamation that the salvation foretold by the prophets was present, in a very particular way, in his own person. And again, at the crucial moment of his earthly life, when he was about to celebrate his own sacrifice under the veil of the liturgical signs, he chose the context of Jewish worship.

In the brief summary of the history of salvation which the chief of the seder makes for his guests, he mentions its beginning and the determining event of the exodus. Prophets had foreseen that this history would be completed in the messianic age. In the Christian faith vision, a new stage in salvation history has been reached in Jesus; and this stage is a point of arrival and at the same time a point of departure.

If the similarities between the Passover meal and the Last Supper we have pointed out were merely accidental, they would have been limited. On the contrary, these similarities seem to point out that Jewish roots are found in the Christian liturgy of the Eucharist. This being the case, we cannot avoid thinking that both the Jewish and Christian traditions might be linked at the deep level of liturgical life.

Typology and Memorial[19]

So far we have tried to find points of contact between the Jewish tradition and the Christian tradition, focusing mostly on details, even if important ones. But we have also to explore these points of contact at a more general and deeper level.

It is necessary to make some preliminary remarks. The history told in the Bible begins with creation and, passing through many events, reaches a climactic point.[20] For the Jews, this point is the liberation from Egypt. For Christians, this point is found in the coming of Jesus. The climax of biblical history is a point of arrival but at the same time also a point of departure,

---

[19] Sofia Cavalletti, *Il giudaismo intertestamentario* (Brescia: Queriniana, 1991), 104.

[20] The Jewish terminology differs from the Christian one: the Jews call "revelation" the central point of history (exodus); the eschatological completion is called "redemption." See Franz Rosenzweig, *Star of Redemption*, trans. W. Hallo (Notre Dame, Ind.: Notre Dame Press, 1985). The Christian tradition speaks of "creation," "redemption," and "parousia."

because the prophets, above all, drive us to look forward to the completion or fulfillment of the redemption in eschatological time.

Therefore, biblical history is not only recounted. It is also eagerly awaited and hoped for. It extends beyond the boundaries of history in the usual sense of the term. In the Bible it is not so much the span of time— past, present and future—that is primary, but what Augustine calls the "golden thread" that connects the events together. For the people of God there is a plan of God, and this plan weaves together events as they are realized in history. Single events are considered individually, of course, but they are also viewed in terms of the "global picture" in which God is manifesting his plan in the history of mankind. In other words, according to the biblical reading of history, God is the Lord of time, and the Lord of history.

The people of God live with acute awareness that the constant presence of God in history bestows upon history its unity. This means that history can be understood and lived only in the light of the monotheism of Jewish-Christian tradition. The belief that God is *one* (see Deut. 6:4) leads to an understanding that history is one—and that the book that records this history, the Bible, is also one.[21]

One God. One History. One Book. A contemporary Jewish scholar, Stefano Levi della Torre, has described the Jewish people as "an ancient heart turned toward the future."[22] All this must be kept in mind when we try to penetrate into how the biblical message is listened to and lived by the two branches of the people of God, Jews and Christians.[23]

To understand the sacred history recorded in the Bible, Christians use the method called *typology*. The word typology comes from Greek (*tupto*, to beat) and refers to the imprint carved by a matrix. The typological approach to Scripture looks into resemblances and differences between the events of the history of salvation, and into how they impress an imprint, the one into the other.

This approach is found also in the Jewish tradition; in fact it goes back to the prophets. When Isaiah speaks about the eschatological renewal of Israel, he uses the same terms used in the biblical account of creation, in effect looking for a "new creation" (Isa. 65:17). When he speaks about the future liberation, he refers to the exodus, anticipating again what could be

---

[21] Sofia Cavalletti, *Remember the Lord your God: A History of the Jewish People* (Chicago: Liturgical Training Publications, 2003), 1.

[22] *Essere fuori luogo* (To be out of place) (Rome: Donzelli, 1995), 32.

[23] Pope John Paul II has spoken of the Christian people as "the budding, two thousand years ago, of a new branch from the common root" of Jewish faith and history. See "Address to Experts Gathered by the Pontifical Commission for Religious Relations with the Jews" (March 6, 1982).

described as a "new exodus" (Isa. 42:16). The same typological approach is found also in the New Testament, where attention is paid above all to the person of Jesus Christ. And typology continues to be a living part of the Jewish and Christian traditions.

To make proper use of this approach requires considering the entire span of history from the beginning to its ultimate completion. In a Vatican document, we read: "Our aim should be to show the unity of biblical revelation (Old Testament and New Testament) and of the divine plan, before speaking of each historical event, so as to stress that particular events have meaning when seen in history as a whole—from creation to fulfillment."[24] The Second Vatican Council's *Dei Verbum*, also pointed to the "content and unity of the whole of Scripture" as the hermeneutical method of reading.[25]

The typological approach guides us to see each event in history as linked to what preceded it and at the same time projected toward completion—"when God will be all in all" (1 Cor. 15:28). Only such a reading respects the weight of the divine mystery in history. In order to see this mystery in its richness, we must not neglect the eschatological expectation inherent in the Jewish and Christian approach to history. A typology has to be considered in its three stages—beginning, redemption, and parousia—otherwise it would be a typology deprived of hope and would thereby mutilate the plan of God.

Neglect of this point has resulted—to it must be said the shame of we Christians—in what has been called the *theology of substitution*. This theology wrongly declares: once there was Israel, now there is the Christian Church. The tragic consequences and sufferings this approach brought about are still living in the body of many in the Jewish community. And it is still heavy on humanity's conscience. We hope such consequences will teach us to reject this theology forever.

We return now to what was said about the Jewish passover and the Eucharistic celebrations. Both celebrations make us live past events in the present, orienting us to eschatology; this is evident for everybody who is familiar with these celebrations. Every liturgical event condenses time in some way, making us live in the present events that, without the celebration, would be lost forever, and projecting them towards the *eschaton*, thus preparing the completion of history.

---

[24] Commission for Religious Relations with the Jews, *Notes on the Correct Way to Present the Jews and Judaism in Preaching and Catechesis in the Roman Catholic Church* (1985): II, 1.

[25] Second Vatican Council, Dogmatic Constitution on Divine Revelation, *Dei Verbum* (November 18, 1965), no. 12.

This approach to liturgy, common to both branches of the people of God, is called "memorial." When we speak about "memorial" in the liturgy, we find ourselves using the same terms we used when speaking about typology with regards to the reading of Scripture. Memorial and typology each annul the distance between historical events, causing them to converge into the "eternal present" of a manifestation of salvation and of God's love which encompasses the whole of history. Typology makes the listening to the Word today capable of creating a link with past history and what is still the object of hope, trying to discover the "golden thread" of the plan of God which unites events into a single history. The memorial makes it possible to live today the salvation already realized in the events of the past and projected towards the eschatological completion, awaited now in hope and prayer.

What is the deep connection, the link that unites typology and memorial? The Second Vatican Council's *Sacrosanctum Concilium* speaks about the "table" of the Word and of the Body of Christ, using the same term for both.[26] Therefore, it is in the uniqueness of the table, which both are referred to, that they find the reason of their similitude. Such a similitude is born from the very depth of both, issuing from the unique source from which they derive.

Typology and memorial are linked at the level of the reality which both help us to reach—the infinite mystery of God. The mystery expresses himself and acts; we can reach him through listening and sacramental celebration. When the mystery expresses himself and we listen, our listening follows the typological approach; when we celebrate the mystery in a sacrament, our participation is realized according to the memorial.

When we listen or when we celebrate the mystery, the reality we try to reach is always the same: the one "table" of the Word and of the Body of the Lord. If the "table" is one, also the "rules" of the table must be the same. In order to receive the divine message and live it, it is necessary to follow the same rules which help us to grasp its totality; that is to say, we always have to live history as if it is concentrated in the present, in its dual dimension of past and future.

We must say that typology and memorial are *the methods* connatural to the mystery of God revealing himself in history. It is not possible to really pry into the mystery (and not simply study the Bible) without typology. And it is not possible to celebrate the same mystery apart from memorial.

---

[26] Second Vatican Council, Constitution on the Sacred Liturgy, *Sacrosanctum Concilium* (December 4, 1963), nos. 48, 51.

The fact that throughout the whole development of their traditions, Jews and Christians have shared the same approach, at such a depth of religious life, even if from different points of view, is something that must be pondered with the greatest attention.

Letter & Spirit 1 (2005): 87–100

THE WORD OF GOD IN THE LITURGY OF THE NEW COVENANT

• Jeremy Driscoll, O.S.B. •

Mount Angel Seminary, Oregon
Pontifical Athenaeum of St. Anselm, Rome

In this paper I want to unfold and explore the dynamic of the Word of God in the liturgy of the new covenant—in the Mass in particular. I mean not only the Word as narrative proclamation, but the Word as memorial and invocation, remembrance and salvific encounter, in which the believer participates in the mystery of the Trinity, the mystery of God's life revealed in Scripture and accomplished and actualized in the liturgy.

It is in the liturgy that we see that Scripture is not so much a book as a living Word from God, a Word which, when announced in the assembly, defines the very event that is underway. It is God's intervention and offer of salvation in the here and now of a particular gathering of believers.

The Word of God has a dynamic toward sacrament; that is, its proclamation in an assembly of believers becomes a communication of salvation for those who hear it, an event of salvation. This event is not simply so many words pronounced and heard—the words find expression in signs and gestures and actions, all of which reveal the deepest mystery which the words contain.

Proclaimed in the Eucharistic liturgy, the Scriptures reveal their deepest mystery in bread and wine exchanged by people who play different roles in the assembly, such that it becomes manifest that the whole cosmos and the whole of history are destined for transformation in the Spirit of the risen Lord. This transformation, which makes present the risen Lord's paschal sacrifice, and the communion which offers the participants a share in it, are a very concrete, ecclesial locus of revelation. Here do we have that of which *Dei Verbum* speaks: we participate in the divine nature, having access to the Father through the Son and the Holy Spirit.[1]

Han Urs von Balthasar observed that as the life of Jesus progresses two things stand out: The Word becomes more and more flesh, and the flesh becomes more and more Word.[2] By the first, he means that to the abstract nature of the commands of the Law and the prophets Jesus

---

[1] Second Vatican Council, Dogmatic Constitution on Divine Revelation, *Dei Verbum* (November 18, 1965), no. 2.

[2] H. Urs von Balthasar, "The Word, Scripture and Tradition," in *Explorations in Theology*, I: *The Word Made Flesh*, trans. A.V. Littledate and A. Dru (San Francisco: Ignatius, 1989), 13.

imparts a divine, factual presence. By the second, he is noting that Jesus increasingly unifies the scriptural words in himself, making his earthly life the perfect expression of all the earlier revelations of God.

This idea can be extended in terms less immediately scriptural, that is, ontologically: The eternal Word, entirely in all that he is, becomes more and more flesh. And all that is flesh is transformed more and more into all that the Word is. I want to suggest that this is the very dynamic that the liturgy reveals, the very dynamic in which the liturgy consists. If Word becoming flesh and flesh becoming Word is what may be called the form or shape of salvation in history, it may also be said that the liturgy takes that same form or shape.

The 'Sacramentality' of Revelation

Salvatore Marsili made a similar observation in his reflections on the "sacramentality of revelation."[3] This sacramentality is discovered by reflecting on the shape and scope of revelation. Sacramentality emerges as a necessary dimension because God's revelation is communication with human, embodied beings. It is *participation* and this cannot be realized except through a sacramental economy. This claim can be made because liturgy is actualization of the Word in the very assembly where it is proclaimed. Yet this Word cannot be actualized unless it achieves its sacramental dimensions. The Word—as word—proclaims all that Christ was and did in his earthly existence.

That Word is seen as a sacramental phenomenon when the event which the words proclaim converges with the sacramental rite that represents it. Thus the Word becomes the event of salvation in the midst of the celebrating assembly.

It is useful to connect what Marsili is saying here with *Dei Verbum's* by now classic statement concerning the relationship between the actual words of the scriptural text and the events of salvation history: "This economy of revelation is realized by deeds and words, which are intrinsically bound up with each other. As a result, the works performed by God in the history of salvation show forth and bear out the doctrine and realities signified by the words; the words, for their part, proclaim the works, and bring to light the mystery they contain."[4]

---

[3] S. Marsili, "Teologia liturgica," in *Nuovo Dizionario di Liturgia*, eds. D. Sartore and A. M. Triacca (Rome: Paoline, 1984), 1508-1525.

[4] *Dei Verbum*, no. 2.

A similar dynamic and one rooted in this, is at work in the liturgy. The words of the Scripture not only proclaim the *events* of salvation history and the mystery contained in these.[5] When these words are proclaimed in the liturgy, they also proclaim the *event* of the sacramental celebration, which is that same *event* of salvation history, actualized here and now. Put more simply perhaps: what Scripture proclaims becomes sacrament.

In fact, when we look at the shape of the Eucharistic liturgy, it is this very form that can be discerned. We are accustomed to this. We speak of the Liturgy of the Word and the Liturgy of the Eucharist. But now it becomes clear that this is not an arbitrary arrangement. It is liturgy in the same detailed form of salvation itself: words becoming sacrament, words rooted in events. And the reason why liturgy is in this form is because it is nothing less than the same thing. It is salvation history—that is, it is Word becoming sacrament.[6]

In the Liturgy of the Word, the Scriptures are read in a certain order, an order that follows the order of salvation history. That is, the liturgy begins with a text from the Old Testament and moves toward the climax of the proclamation of the gospel. This is the order of the Liturgy of the Word, because the gospel is the climax and center of the Scripture; or put more comprehensively: because Christ himself is the fulfillment of the history of Israel. Thus, for a Christian, only from the perspective of the gospel is the Old Testament text understood in its fullness, or again: only in Christ is the history of Israel understood. Some reading from the writings of the apostles forms a link between gospel and Old Testament, a contemplative insight, a theological insight that helps bind the event of the gospel to the event of the Old Testament.[7]

---

[5] The Latin here uses *mysterium*. Doing so, the document makes use of the more ample understanding of mysterium, which in patristic usage referred first to the deepest sense of the Scriptures and thus by extension to the liturgical celebrations of baptism and Eucharist. The sacramental dimensions of this word may not have been intentional in the mind of the Council Fathers of Vatican II, but the use of the word here is fortuitous, for it allows us to extend the thought to liturgical celebrations, as would have been natural in patristic thought.

[6] In what follows I am much indebted to a number of studies which have influenced me in a general way and which, for this reason, it will not be possible to cite specifically, except occasionally. In addition to S. Marsili and H.U. von Balthasar, cited above, I rely here on the following: Rino Fisichella and R. Latourelle, eds., *Dictionary of Fundamental Theology* (New York: Crossroad, 1994); Ghislain Lafont, *God, Time and Being*, trans. L. Maluf (Petersham: St. Bede's, 1992); J. Corbon, *The Wellspring of Worship* (New York: Paulist, 1988); P. McPartlan, *The Eucharist Makes the Church, Henri de Lubac and John Zizioulas in Dialogue* (Edinburgh: T&T Clark, 1995); J. Zizioulas, *Being as Communion* (Crestwood: St. Vladimir's Seminary, 1985).

[7] I am not speaking here necessarily of specific sets of texts as found in the Lectionary for the celebration of a given day, where this connection is sometimes more, sometimes less clear, as the case may be. The point is a general one about this structure in the liturgy. However, once the theological significance of this structure is grasped, as well as the sacramental (hear *mystery*) economy to which it is referring, profound and unexpected connections can emerge between the texts that will not appear when the texts are simply read side by side as texts.

Why is the gospel the center of this part of the liturgy? How can this claim be made? On a most basic level, exegesis itself leads us to make such a claim. When one has finished with all the exercises that divide the Scriptures up into various pericopes and redactions, and if there still remains some energy to try to put them back together again, it is not difficult to see that the Scriptures as a whole lead to a center.

There is a center already to the Old Testament, even though it represents a host of theological traditions developed during well over a thousand years. Everything is organized around the exodus, the wandering in the desert, the coming into the promised land. All things either lead to that, recount that, or look back to that. The whole of revelation for Israel is focused in what God manifested himself to be in these events. Every subsequent generation remembered and celebrated them, defined its present dealings with God in reference to them.

The New Testament functions within this thought world. It continues the sort of reading of the Scriptures that was already well established there, and it discerns in them—in the exodus, the desert, the promised land—the foreshadowing and indeed some hint of explanation for the wonderful events that unfolded in the life of Jesus of Nazareth. Jesus becomes a new center for such readers, and the texts of the New Testament are the written evidence of their way of reading the Old.

Jesus may be said to be a new center of the history of Israel. But his own life also has a center. The gospels, especially, lead us toward this center. A German exegete in the first part of the twentieth century said the gospels are passion narratives with long introductions.[8] This is well said.

If we look at the kerygma of the primitive Church as represented in somebody like St. Paul, we can see a situation that did not yet feel the need of something like the gospel genre. Paul preached only the death and resurrection of Jesus, and he managed to preach the gospel without reference to the many words, parables, and miracles of Jesus, not to mention the details of his birth. In other circumstances and as the years passed, communities felt the need for a more extended narrative of the life of Jesus. In the case of Matthew and Luke this need reaches back to the very origins and birth of Jesus.

But in every case whatever was narrated about Jesus—be it the marvelous details surrounding his birth, be it the words and deeds of his active ministry—had as its purpose placing the mystery of his passion in its fuller context, a center which a preacher like Paul could never let us lose sight of. The four gospels all lead clearly to this center, to the passion. The other writings of the New Testament unfold the consequences of such a

---

[8]   Martin Kähler, *The So-Called Historical Jesus and the Historic, Biblical Christ* (1896; reprint, Philadelphia: Fortress Press, 1964), 80, n. 11.

center, showing in various ways that the believer is summoned to share in the Lord's passion and so in his victory.

The 'Event' of Christ

The liturgical celebration of the Word reveals something deeper about this center of revelation that we find in the New Testament. The "event" of Christ —in whom all the other events of Israel and indeed of all the world find their center and fulfillment—is revealed as "an hour which does not pass away."[9] Thus the Scripture which proclaims Christ, is doing nothing less than announcing and manifesting this hour (more specifically, some detail, some particular scene in this hour) as being the very hour of the liturgy itself.

Marsili stresses the event character of liturgy. Liturgy is an event in the same sense as all other events in the economy of salvation—the intervention of the living God in human history, which, precisely because it is God's doing, cannot slip into the past. In a given liturgy, specific words from the Scripture are proclaimed, as *Dei Verbum* states: "the words, for their part, proclaim the works, and bring to light the mystery they contain."[10]

The expression "the mystery they contain" deserves close attention. This mystery includes the power of the Word of God in every moment to be received anew as an actual communication of salvation. Every proclamation of the Word in the liturgy is a moment irreducibly new: the event of Christ (all the events of Scripture are the event of Christ) becomes the event of the Church. That is to say, the Word-event of Christ becomes the event of the assembly that here and now hears this Word. The Word proclaimed in liturgy is not some pale reflection or residue of the event proclaimed there. It is the whole reality to which the words bear testimony made present.

The most complete example of what is being claimed here is found in the Liturgy of the Word at the Easter Vigil. Seven long readings of the Old Testament climax in the gospel which announces Christ risen. The liturgy is the actualization of these words for the particular assembly that hears them. This is to say: The event of that liturgy is everything that the Scriptures proclaim—creation, exodus, exile, and restoration—culminating in Christ's resurrection in that assembly.[11] The particular assembly is the place, the time, the people, the moment in history in which Christ is risen.

---

[9] On this expression, see the precise and compact formulation in the *Catechism of the Catholic Church*, no. 1085.

[10] *Dei Verbum*, no. 2.

[11] Such a context, created by the proclamation of the Word, is the context for the celebration of Baptism and the Eucharist that follows, that is, in the expression of von Balthasar—the Word becoming more and more flesh. Baptism and Eucharist as celebrated at the Easter Vigil offer a separate opportunity for the kind of discussion we are conducting here. I do not pursue it at this point so as not to lose the thread of this more general discussion of Word and Eucharist.

None of these claims about the power of the Word could be made were it not for the action of the Holy Spirit, whose gift and creation the Scriptures are and whose inspiration is needed to understand them aright.[12] Put another way, the risen Lord himself must open our minds in the Spirit to the understanding of those words. When he does, our minds grasp nothing less than the wonderful reality that this moment of listening becomes in the very hearing an event of salvation, the same event that the words proclaim.

The exodus of Israel out of Egypt is the "exodus" of Jesus from this world to his Father, and every believer discovers in penetrating the meaning of the Scriptures that he or she too is living this one and only exodus. The many events of the Scriptures are parts of one event: Jesus Christ, and him crucified and risen in his Church, in each believer.[13] This is the one and only center of the Scriptures. It is an hour which does not pass. The reading of the Word in the liturgy manifests this reality in the midst of the believing assembly, in the depths of our hearts.

Between Remembrance and Invocation

In the Eucharistic liturgy, the Spirit who writes the Scriptures now brings those Scriptures forward to become flesh, to become Sacrament. To explore this dimension of the liturgy, I want to focus on the elements of *anamnesis* and *epiclesis*. These are technical terms which in their strictest application name parts of the *anaphora*, or Eucharistic Prayer.

Anamnesis is a celebrative narration and remembering of the events of Christ's paschal mystery—his death, resurrection, ascension, his coming again in glory—and an offering of these to the Father. But a dimension of anamnesis pervades the whole celebration: It is all remembering, and in the festive setting the remembered past is rendered present in mystery and becomes the event which the assembly enacts and participates in.

Within the liturgy, epiclesis is the invocation of the Father that he send the Holy Spirit upon the gifts for their transformation and that the Spirit fill those who receive the gifts. None of what is believed to happen during the rite would be possible without the action of the Holy Spirit. If in anamnesis concrete events from the past are recalled in a festive narration,

---

[12] On the intimate relation between Christ the Word and the Scriptures as Word of the Spirit, see von Balthasar, "The Word, Scripture, and Tradition," 15-16.

[13] Herein lies the pattern and the task for the homily, an indispensable dimension of the Liturgy of the Word. One of the ordained, who by his ordination functions in that moment as a sacrament of the apostolic tradition apart from which the Scriptures cannot be understood, must make these connections explicit for the particular assembly in its concrete circumstances: exodus of Israel, exodus of Jesus, exodus of us all.

in the epiclesis the view moves beyond the limits of a strict chronology and understands the event of the liturgy also as a visit from the future. The risen Christ already stands in that definitive future in which he is established by his glorification, and through him the Spirit descends from that future in a new Pentecost upon the worshipping assembly and makes it to be one Body, one Spirit, in him.

Anamnesis and epiclesis are most fruitfully understood together, as distinguishable and yet inextricably intertwined. They are the fundamental ritual shapes in which the believing community encounters the God who reveals himself. The Christian understanding of anamnesis is rooted in the Old Testament notion of a *memorial*, captured in the verse from the Psalm, "The Lord has made a memorial for his wonders" (Ps. 111:4).

The great events of Israel's history, when narrated in a feast, become contemporary to the hearers, to those celebrating the feast. Other cultures believed that by the festive narration of primordial origins they could thereby be brought again within the realm of cosmic purity and power. It was Israel's unique belief that something similar could happen regarding actual events from its history.

This belief flows from Israel's understanding that the very events of her history were a word of God to her, and as such, that word could not grow old or stale or weaker or lose its effect. "The Word of the LORD remains forever" (see Isa. 40: 8). Thus, it was enough to repeat the words which narrated the events to bring each new generation of Israelites into participation with the originating events of the community.[14]

This is especially clear in the celebration of Passover. We see in the Passover that when we say "narrate events" we mean far more than a thin monotone of words pronounced aloud. We mean a narrative in which words are surrounded by gestures and signs and indeed an entire elaborate meal in a particular place and with particular people. And in the context of that narrative, recounted in this precise way on this particular night, the question inevitably arises: "Why is this night different from all other nights?" The answer can be given that by remembering Israel's Passover from Egypt those who remember thereby "pass over" from Egypt with her. Indeed, this defines an Israelite—one becomes such by celebrating the feast.[15]

This (and the other feasts commemorating other events recorded in the Old Testament) are the memorial of the Lord's wonders that he has given Israel. And it is significant that this *is given by the Lord*. It is he who has worked the wonderful deeds, and it is he who makes it possible to celebrate them in such a feast. The primordial events which found the community and in which each subsequent generation shares by participation

---

[14] This unique Old Testament understanding of the nature of a feast is classically described in G. von Rad, *Theologie des alten Testaments*, 2 vols. (Munich: C. Kaiser, 1958-1966), 2:108-133.

[15] See Exod. 12:26-27; 13:8, 14-15; Deut. 6:20-25; and the contemporary ritual of the Jewish Passover.

are not events produced and generated by the community's ingenuity, any more than the memorial feast is such. Both are received realities, which the community gratefully accepts as gifts from God.

Jesus, the Jew, draws on all these notions the night before he dies when, in the context of the Passover meal[16] he consciously and intentionally summarizes or recapitulates all of Israel's history in himself. In the signs of the meal which he selects, he is conscious that he holds all of Israel and all her history in his hands as he takes up the bread and wine. He identifies that whole history with himself and with the death he will undergo on the morrow, saying over these elements: "This is my body, this is my blood."

The Fulfillment of Israel's History

This moment, this action, is unfathomably profound. This is not some vague identification of Israel's history with the story of Jesus. It is a sign unmistakable in its significance: Israel's history finds its fulfillment in the body that will hang on the cross, in the blood that will be shed there. This blood opens a new covenant, "the new covenant in my blood." And it is precisely in the context of these signs and their transformation that we receive Jesus' command, "Do this in memory (anamnesis) of me" (see Luke 22:19-20; 1 Cor. 11:25).

With this command the psalm verse, "The LORD has made a memorial for his wonders," shifts into its definitive christological key. And indeed, the Church slowly came to realize that the riches contained for her by being obedient to this command would be boundless. For this meal, repeated as received—again, not as invented by the ingenuity of the community—in each subsequent generation, would be the context in which the Lord's promise about the Holy Spirit would be fulfilled: "He will lead you into all the truth" (John 16:13).

We learn something here about truth and how it is received: For Christians, truth is not a proposition, a *gnosis*. It is a somebody, a person: Jesus Christ. And it is not he in some static form but he in the action of his dying and rising. This is truth and this is life (John 14:6). And how do we know so? It is revealed to us by the experience of Eucharist, by repeating what the Lord himself gave us to do.

---

[16] We can prescind from the debates among exegetes, arising from the difference between the synoptics and John on this point, about whether or not the historical Last Supper was actually a Passover celebration. The tradition represented in the relevant New Testament texts and the tradition of reading those texts all closely associate Jesus' Last Supper with the theological meaning of Passover. This is the relevant point here.

The Eucharist is a memorial of the supper on the night before Jesus died, but this supper pointed to the meaning of the cross, whose meaning is finally revealed in the resurrection and the rest of the unfolding of the paschal mystery. Thus to remember the supper, which by foreshadowing his death already was swept up in its hour (into the "ontology" of that hour), is our way of remembering his death. For the supper now "reshadows" for us that hour and is thereby swept up into it. Henceforth, all memorial, all anamnesis refers to this central event of salvation history. All remembering is ultimately a remembering of this.

The risen presence of the Crucified One is the eternally present fact of the new creation, the new covenant. In his resurrection all death—and so all the past—is swallowed up. The "technique" of memorial splices us into this *fact*.[17] This fact is also a future, for the resurrection contains as part of its very logic not only the defeat of past death but likewise of all death and all time subsequent to the historical moment of the death and resurrection of Jesus. Thus, celebrating the meal as a memorial is a remembering oriented toward the future.

Although the Lord's command at the Last Supper rivets the Church's attention on the Eucharistic dimensions of anamnesis, it is not difficult to see in a general way the anamnetic dimensions of all liturgy. To call the liturgical proclamation of the Word of God "anamnesis," as the *Catechism of the Catholic Church* does,[18] is to claim that this proclamation inserts us into those primordial and originating events. But since the Word always has its dynamic drive toward sacrament, the sacramental action itself also is expressive—and more densely so—of this same anamnetic element.[19]

---

[17] J. Zizioulas, *Eucaristia e Regno di Dio* (Magnano: Quiquajon, 1996), 15, helpfully reminds us that the Eucharistic meal not only has its historical roots in the Last Supper but also in those resurrection appearances during the forty days when the Lord ate and drank with his disciples. This is especially clear in Luke 24:30-31, but also John 21:13. That is, the risen Lord is showing himself in the signs that he made to refer to his death, most notably, in his wounds. See John 20:20,27; Luke 24:40. That this memory of the death of the Lord is not merely backward looking but in itself has an eschatological thrust is shown by Paul: "For as often as you eat this bread and drink the cup, you proclaim the death of the Lord *until he comes*" (1 Cor. 11:26).

[18] *Catechism,* no. 1103.

[19] All that I have said so far is well summarized in a particularly dense paragraph of the *Catechism*, no. 1085. It is too long to cite in full here, but "In the liturgy of the Church, it is principally his own paschal mystery that Christ signifies and makes present. . . . His paschal mystery is a real event that occurred in our history, but it is unique: all other historical events happen once, and then they pass away, swallowed up in the past. The paschal mystery of Christ, by contrast, cannot remain only in the past, because by his death he destroyed death. . . . The event of the cross and resurrection abides and draws everything toward life."

The most exquisite anamnesis which the Church performs is the Eucharistic narrative, and in its most narrow technical and liturgical sense the word "anamnesis" refers to that prayer which immediately follows the words of institution wherein all the dimensions of the paschal mystery are remembered. But the whole anaphora is permeated with a narrative structure, grounding the "hour" of the liturgical celebration in the "hour" of Jesus' paschal mystery, which does not pass away.

The 'Today' of the Sacraments

Around the Eucharist cluster the other sacraments and indeed all the liturgy of the Church. In addition to the other sacraments we should highlight in a special way the Liturgy of the Hours and the calendar of the liturgical year. All this is memorial. All this is the *hodie*, the "today" of the feast.[20] Only in this *hodie* is the content of Revelation fully revealed, a content which we are easily inclined to identify too thinly simply with the Bible taken as a book. The book is a means to an end—the presence of the living Word in the midst of the believing assembly, accomplishing and extending to that assembly what has been accomplished in concrete historical events. When we celebrate a memorial of those events, those events become the event of that liturgical hour.

None of these magnificent claims of the worshipping Church would be possible without the action of the Holy Spirit, who accompanies the Son in every stage of his own work in the economy. Epiclesis is the liturgical manifestation of this indispensable role of the Holy Spirit in the economy of salvation.

By way of basic definition: epiclesis is an invocation of the Father that he send the Holy Spirit to transform the gifts which the Church brings before him. This liturgical practice is also best understood by searching for its roots in the whole history of salvation. If there is an intimate and inextricable relation between anamnesis and epiclesis in the liturgy, it is because there is an intimate and inextricable relation between the mission of the Son and the mission of the Holy Spirit in the history of salvation.

Just as Christian anamnesis is rooted in the Old Testament notion of memorial, Christian epiclesis is rooted in the Holy Spirit's role in the shaping of the scriptural word of the Old Testament and, more foundationally, the shaping of the events to which that word testifies. It is all this that Christians profess, in what seems at first glance a somewhat laconic expression, in the line from the creed which concerns the Spirit: "He spoke through the prophets."

---

[20] See B. de Soos, *Le mystere liturgique d'apres Saint Leon le Grand* (Munster: Aschendorf, 1958), 22-27.

The Holy Spirit shapes all the events of Israel's history—and before that the very creation itself—in such a way that they are all "types" of Christ. The events themselves and the words that bear testimony to those events in the inspired scriptures are all mysteriously shaped so that they find fulfillment in the Son's incarnation, in his death and resurrection. They have already foreshadowed it. They have accustomed a nation to its patterns. The history of Israel illumines and clarifies these; the history of Israel is the *context* (in the fullest sense of that word) in which the eternal Word (the eternal "text") is uttered in the flesh.

As salvation history comes to the "fullness of time," it is the "work" of the Holy Spirit to form out of one particular human life a vessel capable of expressing the total being of God through the person of the Son. Thus, the Spirit overshadows Mary and forms the Father's Son in her womb (Luke 1:35).

And the Spirit accompanies the earthly life of Jesus through each of its phases, appearing in visible form at his Baptism (Matt. 3:16; Mark 1:10; Luke 3:22; John 1:32), driving him into the desert to be tempted (Matt. 4:1; Mark 1:12; Luke 4:l), anointing him as he inaugurates his ministry in Nazareth (Luke 4:18), enveloping him in the cloud of the transfiguration (Matt. 17:5; Mark 9:7; Luke 9:34), being breathed forth from Jesus in his death on the cross (John 19:30), raising him from the dead (Rom. 8:11), and being breathed on the apostles from his risen body (John 20:22).

When Jesus took bread and wine into his hands the night before he died, as we described it above, the moment and its possibilities had been long in preparation by the work of the Holy Spirit. "He spoke through the prophets," that is, the whole of Israel's history had been formed in such a way that it could all converge in this moment and its meaning. The Exodus, around which Israel's entire history centers both before and after, was accomplished fact. Words of the Spirit-formed Scriptures bore testimony to it. A memorial feast given by the Lord brought each new generation of Israelites under its force. Jesus himself had celebrated the feast many times during the course of his life, as had his disciples. A history, a language, a vocabulary, a set of rituals were all in place for Jesus' use in that moment.

He takes into his hands what the Spirit had prepared for him, and over it pronounces words which the Spirit with whom he is anointed moves him to speak: "This is my body, this is my blood." Thus, together with the Spirit, does he express his own understanding of his mission, which brings the history of Israel to fulfillment.

Thus, together with the Spirit, does he express his own willingness to pour out his life for the sake of the many. What the meal shows so magnificently and in so many layered ways—echoing with words and gestures and food thousands of years of history and the very creation of the cosmos —will be shown in the events that begin to unfold at the end of this very meal: Jesus' arrest, his death, resurrection, ascension, and the Pentecost of the Spirit. All this the Spirit shapes into the events that are the perfectly articulated Word of the Father to sinful humanity, the life-giving Word of the Father.

The form and dynamic movements of the rites in liturgy echo the form and dynamic movement of salvation history itself, which in its own turn ultimately echoes the very form and dynamic movement of divine trinitarian love. We have seen that in its Eucharistic liturgy the Church has been faithful in the celebration of a rite given by Jesus himself in the course of his earthly existence. To be sure, such a rite did not contain an epiclesis, even if the Holy Spirit was very much involved, as we have noted. But very soon in the course of the practice of Eucharist in the various churches, some ritual expression of the Holy Spirit's indispensable action inevitably came to the fore.

We have said that the epiclesis is an invocation that the Father send the Holy Spirit to transform the gifts of the Church, in the case of the Eucharist, gifts of bread and wine. In the meal that Jesus gave to be celebrated in his memory he identified the bread and wine with himself, more specifically with the death that he would undergo on the morrow. The bread broken is his body broken on the cross. The wine poured out is his blood poured out.

These signs are meant to show that his death becomes a kind of nourishment for us. But in and of itself death cannot be a nourishment. It must be transformed, and such transformation is the work of the Holy Spirit. A prayer before communion in the Latin liturgy puts this very well: "Lord Jesus Christ, by the will of the Father and the work of the Holy Spirit your death brought life to the world."

This transformation of death into life-giving nourishment for the Church is nothing less than the resurrection itself. It is the Spirit who raises Jesus from the dead (see Rom. 8:11). The eternal Spirit is henceforth and forever Spirit of the risen Lord poured out on all mankind, and it is as Spirit that the risen Lord is present everywhere. The "technique" of epiclesis is a ritual means of splicing into the realm of this Spirit, not some vague Spirit but the Spirit who accomplishes for the Church in the Eucharist what was worked in the resurrection itself. "If the Spirit of him who raised Jesus from the dead dwells in you, then he who raised Christ from the dead will bring your mortal bodies to life also, through his Spirit dwelling in you" (Rom. 8:11).

The Spirit who molded a body for the Word in the womb of the Virgin Mary, the Spirit who raised the body of Jesus from the dead—this same Spirit now fills the gifts which the Church has brought and makes them to be one and the same thing: the body formed from Mary's body, the body raised from the dead. It is precisely here in the Eucharist that the

Church is constituted as the body of Christ. The body taken from Mary, the body raised from the dead, the Church as body of Christ—these are not different or separate bodies. They are one and the same. And it is not a static body. It is the body crucified and risen, which, standing at the right hand of the Father, forever offers itself to him in an hour which does not pass away. In the Spirit, death disappears, and the body of Christ, formed from the whole cosmos and the whole of history, rises alive from the tomb and passes over to the right hand of the Father.

If talk about anamnesis inevitably has about it a certain pull to the past, to a memory of the deeds of Jesus in history, then talk about epiclesis and the work of the Spirit clearly shows that "remembering Jesus" includes the paradox of remembering a future. Indeed, the Spirit pulls the weight of memory as much, if not more so, toward the future as toward the past. For there is only one way to remember Jesus crucified and to encounter him or—as the Latin tradition has long loved to consider the Eucharist—only one way to have the sacrifice of Calvary present on the altar: Jesus crucified is none other than the now risen Lord, present to us in the Spirit.

And the risen Lord, freed from the bondage of time and space, even while being present in all time and space, is already living the future which is the recapitulation of all things in himself (see Eph. 1:10). It is this Lord—"And the Lord is the Spirit!" (2 Cor. 3:17)—who is present to the Church which celebrates his memorial. If the sacrifice of Calvary can be present anywhere beyond the historical Calvary, it is because where the risen Lord is present—"And the Lord is the Spirit!"—he is present as the one once crucified there.

The epiclesis of the Eucharistic liturgy, then, is the culminating work of the Holy Spirit in the whole life of the Church. It is nonetheless important to be mindful that the other sacramental rites also have an epiclesis that is vital to understanding what each sacrament accomplishes.[21] Likewise, although there is no explicit epiclesis in the Liturgy of the Hours or in the liturgical calendar of feasts, these have their power and force precisely through the work of the Holy Spirit. Each of the sacraments is variously ordered toward the Eucharist. In each, through the invocation of the Holy Spirit and the particular way in which that rite expresses its anamnetic or memorial dimension, there is accomplished what the sacrament intends.

What do all the other sacraments intend? Among other things, bringing the Church together for the celebration of the Eucharist. In each sacramental epiclesis there can be discerned its preparation in "the Holy Spirit speaking through the prophets." In each, too, there is some pattern

---

[21] J. Corbon speaks usefully of each of the sacraments from the point of view of their epiclesis in *The Wellspring of Worship*, 108-122.

which echoes the Spirit's accompanying Jesus through the course of his earthly existence. The rite is in these same forms and patterns, which, as we have said, ultimately is patterned by the form and dynamic movement of divine trinitarian love.

Here we see in the liturgy, the final accomplishment and actualization of God's will for the world, the meaning of salvation history—that we have access to the Father through the Son in the Holy Spirit, that we share in the trinitarian life, in the divine life of the Blessed Trinity. This is the purpose of the divine action in the history of salvation, a divine action that continues in the dynamic of the Word toward sacrament in the liturgy. God invites all people to share in the communion that God is—in the communion of the Father, Son, and Holy Spirit—and by this sharing to live in a new communion with one another.

Letter & Spirit 1 (2005): 101-136

WORSHIP IN THE WORD
Toward a Liturgical Hermeneutic

• Scott W. Hahn •

St. Paul Center for Biblical Theology

Twentieth-century biblical scholarship was dominated by historical and critical theories and methodologies. This development marked the full flowering of seeds sown in Europe more than three centuries earlier, in the aftermath of the wars of religion and the rise of the Enlightenment project.[1]

As a result of this movement in scholarship, today in large segments of the academy and even the Christian community, the Bible tends no longer to be read and studied as *Scripture*—a "word" spoken by God to a community that acknowledges this word as authoritative and normative for its life and worship. Instead it is read as a "text," a literary and historical artifact bearing no more or less meaning or legitimacy than any other product of ancient civilization.

The consequences of this shift in biblical understanding and interpretation have been felt in every area of Catholic and Protestant faith and life—from doctrinal formulations and organizational structures to disciplines and worship. Much has been written in recent years on the implications of historical-critical methods and the philosophical assumptions that underwrite them. That broader conversation, which aims at reforming the use of these methods, is crucial and must be continued.

However, I want to focus in this paper on what I believe to be the most significant achievement of historical and literary scholarship—namely, the recovery of the *liturgical sense of sacred Scripture*. By this I mean the living relationship between *Scripture*, the inclusive canon of the apostolic churches, east and west, and *liturgy*, the ritual public worship of God's covenant people, especially the eucharistic and sacramental liturgies of the Church. The recovery of this liturgical sense of Scripture is now only beginning to be recognized. I hope in this paper to make some small contribution to our appreciation of the significance of this recovery and the potential it holds for biblical scholarship in the century ahead.

---

[1] See generally, Hans Frei, *The Eclipse of Biblical Narrative: A Study of Eighteenth and Nineteenth Century Hermeneutics* (New Haven: Yale University Press, 1974); Hans Reventlow, *The Authority of the Bible and the Rise of the Modern World* (London: SCM Press, 1985); Klaus Scholder, *The Birth of Modern Critical Theology: Origins and Problems of Biblical Criticism in the Seventeenth Century* (Philadelphia: Trinity International Press, 1990); Richard John Neuhaus, ed. *Biblical Interpretation in Crisis: The Ratzinger Conference on Bible and Church* (Grand Rapids, Mich.: Wm. B. Eerdmans Publishers, 1989); Jon D. Levenson, *The Hebrew Bible, the Old Testament and Historical Criticism* (Louisville: Westminster/John Knox, 1993), especially Chapter 3: "Historical Criticism and the Fate of the Enlightenment Project"; William T. Cavanaugh, " 'A Fire Strong Enough to Consume the House': The Wars of Religion and the Rise of the State," *Modern Theology* 11 (1995): 397-420.

I will begin by first discussing the *liturgical content and context* of the Scriptures, which modern scholarship has helped us to see. I will discuss this in terms of what I call the material and formal unity of Scripture and liturgy. This unity, I argue, invites us to make a *liturgical reading* of the entire canonical text. The heart of this paper will outline this approach to a canonical reading, focusing on what I describe as the Bible's liturgical *trajectory* and *teleology*. Finally, I will discuss three exegetical principles that emerge from this liturgical reading of the canonical text—the notions of divine economy, typology, and mystagogy. My aim is to advance the consideration of a new, *liturgical hermeneutic*. I contend that such a hermeneutic has superior interpretive and explanatory power and is capable of integrating the contributions of historical and literary research while at the same time respecting the traditional meanings given to the Bible by the faith community from which it originates.

Scripture's Liturgical Content and Context

The recovery of Scripture's liturgical sense is the product of two critical findings of modern biblical scholarship: First, the recognition of the final canonical shape of Scripture as essential for determining the meaning and purpose of individual passages and books of Scripture; and secondly, the identification of the covenant as Scripture's keynote narrative theme. Together, these findings have helped us to see a unity between Scripture and liturgy that may be described as both formal and material. Their unity is *formal* in that Scripture was canonized for the sake of liturgy, and the canon itself derived from liturgical tradition. Their unity is *material* in that the content of Scripture is heavily liturgical.

Details about the origins of the *canon* as a definitive collection of sacred writings expressing the faith, worship, and instruction of the believing community remain elusive and are still debated among scholars.[2] However, there is general recognition that the motives for establishing the canon were largely liturgical and that liturgical use was an important factor in determining which Scriptures were to be included in the canon. Put simply, the canon was drawn up to establish which books would be read

---

[2] See, generally, Lee M. McDonald and James Sanders, eds., *The Canon Debate* (Peabody, Mass.: Hendrickson Publishers, 2002); Brevard S. Childs, *The New Testament as Canon: An Introduction* (Philadelphia: Fortress Press, 1984); Lee M. McDonald, *The Formation of the Christian Biblical Canon*, rev. ed. (Peabody, Mass.: Hendrickson Publishers, 1995). For a review of the most recent literature and its significance, see Brevard S. Childs, "The Canon in Recent Biblical Studies: Reflections on an Era," *Pro Ecclesia* 14 (2005): 26-45.

when the community gathered for worship, and the books included in the canon were those that were already being read in the Church's liturgy.[3]

The scriptural canon, then, was enacted primarily as a "rule" for the liturgy (the Greek word κανών, meaning rule or measuring stick; see Gal. 6:14-16).[4] But textual analysis and form criticism have helped us see the profound shaping influence of liturgical use on the composition and final form of individual texts. In some cases—certain psalms, for instance—this is self-evident. And we know from internal evidence that many New Testament texts, especially the epistles and the Book of Revelation, were composed for the express purpose of being read in the eucharistic liturgy (see Rev. 1:3; 1 Tim. 4:13).[5] But close literary analysis has also enabled us now to see that the final form of the gospels reflects their use in the eucharistic worship of the early community. Some have even argued that the gospels' final form was shaped by a kind of ongoing dialogue with the Jewish texts being read in the synagogue, especially for Israel's great feasts.[6]

---

[3] James A. Sanders has written: "That which is canon comes to us from ancient communities of faith, not just from individuals . . . the whole of the Bible, the sum as well as all its parts, comes to us out of the liturgical and instructional life of early believing communities." *From Sacred Story to Sacred Text* (Philadelphia: Fortress, 1987), 162; Everett Ferguson has observed: "Distinctive worship practices . . . served as preconditions for a canon of Scripture. The Eucharist involved the remembrance of the passion of Christ and particularly the institution narrative." "Factors Leading to the Selection and Closure of the New Testament Canon," in *The Canon Debate*, 296. The liturgical motivations for the canon are widely acknowledged. Carroll Stuhlmueller, C.P., describes the Scriptures as "the . . . liturgical documents of Old and New Testament times." *Thirsting for the Lord: Essays in Biblical Spirituality* (Staten Island, N.Y.: Alba House, 1977), 102. Gerard Sloyan has observed, "The Scripture came into existence as part of the life of a worshipping community. . . . There can be no doubt whatever that liturgical influences were strong in the formation and even the actual writing of large sections of both testaments." See "The Liturgical Proclamation of the Word of God," in *Bible, Life, and Worship: Twenty-Second North American Liturgical Week* (Washington, D.C.: The Liturgical Conference, 1961), 9.

[4] See Paul M. Blowers, "The *Regula Fidei* and the Narrative Character of Early Christian Faith," *Pro Ecclesia* 6 (1997): 199-228.

[5] Raymond Orlett, "An Influence of the Liturgy Upon the Emmaus Account," *Catholic Biblical Quarterly* 21 (1960): 212-219; Andrew Brian McGowan, " 'Is There a Liturgical Text in This Gospel?' The Institutional Narratives and their Early Interpretive Communities," *Journal of Biblical Literature* 118 (1999): 73-87; Ugo Vanni, "Liturgical Dialogue as a Literary Form in the Book of Revelation," *New Testament Studies* 37 (1991): 348-372; Hakan Ulfgard, *Feast and Future: Revelation 7:9-17 and the Feast of Tabernacles*, Coniectanea Biblica., New Testament Series 22 (Stockholm: Almqvist & Wiksell International, 1989); W. Hultitt Gloer, "Worship God! Liturgical Elements in the Apocalypse," *Review and Expositor* 98 (Winter 2001): 35-57; David Aune, "The Apocalypse of John and the Problem of Genre," *Semeia* 36 (1986): 89; David Barr, "The Apocalypse of John as Oral Enactment," *Interpretation* 40 (1986): 243-256.

[6] M. D. Goulder, *The Evangelists' Calendar: A Lectionary Explanation of the Development of Scripture* (London: SPCK, 1978); Willard M. Swartley, *Israel's Scripture Traditions and the Synoptic Gospels: Story Shaping Story* (Peabody, Mass.: Hendrickson Publishers, 1994); David Daube, "The Earliest Structure of the Gospels," *New Testament Studies* 5 (1958): 174-187; E.H. Van Olst, *The Bible and Liturgy,* trans. J. Vriend (Grand Rapids, Mich.: Wm. B. Eerdmans Publishers, 1991), 45-50.

We see then an original unity between the liturgy and the Bible. What establishes and constitutes that bond is God's new covenant made in the blood of Jesus (Luke 22:20). The canon of Scripture—Old and New Testaments—was for the early Church what the "book of the covenant" was for Israel (see Exod. 24:7; 2 Chron. 34:30). Indeed, it is instructive that κανών was not originally the word applied to the list of biblical books. Eusebius, writing in the early fourth century, rather spoke of the Scriptures as "encovenanted" or "contained in the covenant" (ἐνδιαθηκος).[7]

It is not surprising that many scholars have recognized the "covenant" as the recurrent and theologically significant theme in the canonical text. The vast literature on this topic cannot be rehearsed here.[8] What has not been as well recognized is the crucial unity of both Scripture and liturgy in the establishment, renewal, and maintenance of God's covenant relationship with his people.[9] It is nonetheless true that the books of the new and old covenants are heavily liturgical in content. This is what I mean in describing a *material unity* between Scripture and liturgy—the Bible in many ways is *about* liturgy.

Much of the Pentateuch is concerned with ritual and sacrificial regulations; significant portions of the wisdom, historical, and prophetic books take up questions of ritual and worship. The New Testament, too, is filled with material related to the sacramental liturgy. The Gospel of John, for instance, unfolds as a kind of "sacramentary" in the context of the Jewish lectionary calendar; the Letter to the Hebrews and the Book of Revelation contain sustained meditations on the meaning of the Christian liturgy, and

---

[7] See McDonald and Sanders, *The Canon Debate*, 295-320; 432.

[8] For a review of the relevant themes and literature, see Scott W. Hahn, "Kinship by Covenant: A Biblical Theological Study of Covenant Types and Texts in the Old and New Testaments" (Ph.D. diss., Marquette University, 1995) and Scott W. Hahn, "Covenant in the Old and New Testaments: Some Current Research (1994–2004)," *Currents in Biblical Research* 3 (2005): 263-292. See also, F. M. Cross, "Kinship and Covenant in Ancient Israel," in *From Epic to Canon: History and Literature in Ancient Israel* (Baltimore: Johns Hopkins University Press, 1998); M. G. Kline, *By Oath Consigned: A Reinterpretation of the Covenant Signs of Circumcision and Baptism* (Grand Rapids, Mich.: Wm. B. Eerdmans Publishers, 1968). Yves Congar, O.P., summarized the constant teaching of Christ, the apostles, and the Church fathers: "The content and meaning of Scripture was God's covenant plan, finally realized in Jesus Christ (in his *transitus*) and in the Church." *Tradition and Traditions: An Historical and a Theological Essay* (London: Burns and Oates, 1966), 68-69.

[9] Very few commentators have recognized what Albert Vanhoye has identified as the essential relationship between liturgical cult and covenant in the Bible: "The value of a covenant depends directly on the act of worship which establishes it. A defective liturgy cannot bring about a valid covenant. . . . The reason for this is easily understood. The establishment of a covenant between two parties who are distant from each other can only be accomplished by an act of mediation and, when it is a question of mankind and God, the mediation has of necessity to be conducted through the cult." *Old Testament Priests and the New Priest According to the New Testament* (Petersham, Mass.: St. Bede's Publications, 1986), 181-182.

the letters of Paul and Peter are animated by liturgical and cultic concerns. From Genesis to Revelation, it can be argued, Scripture is, by and large, *about* liturgy—about the proper way to worship God and receive his blessings.[10] Often it is liturgy, or the culpable neglect of liturgy, that drives the biblical drama. Also, though this topic has not been well-studied, liturgy appears at the most significant junctures of the salvation history recorded in the canonical Scriptures.

Modern biblical scholarship, then, has helped us to discover not only the *liturgical content* of the Bible but the *liturgical context* in which the Scriptures were first written, transmitted, and canonized. With the acknowledgment of this material and formal unity between Scripture and the liturgy, we are now in the position to take these advances in biblical scholarship to their next logical and even necessary conclusion—to begin to undertake a "liturgical reading" of the canon of Scripture. My contention is this: Insofar as the canon of Scripture was established for use in the liturgy, and inasmuch as its content is "about" liturgy, it follows that we must engage Scripture *liturgically* if we are to interpret these texts according to the original authors' intentions and the life-situation of the believing community in which these texts were handed on.

In what follows I want to begin this process of engagement. Through canonical analysis, I want to offer a reading of the "meta-narrative" of Scripture focusing on liturgy—what it is and how it functions in the Bible's grand "story."[11] If I can be forgiven my use of overly long quotations in the notes, I intend here to be in dialogue with some of today's most important biblical exegetes. I want to demonstrate how much of the best work being done in the field is leading us to see the liturgical sense of Scripture. At the same time, I hope to suggest ways in which a liturgical reading can unify and provide even greater explanatory and interpretive power to their insights and findings.

Such a sketch must necessarily be broad brush. But by focusing on the central moments in the canonical narrative—creation, the exodus, the

---

[10] For this argument and a review of the relevant literature, see Scott Hahn, *Letter and Spirit: From Written Text to Living Word in the Liturgy* (New York: Doubleday, 2005), especially Chapter 3: "The Unities of Scripture and Liturgy."

[11] My method, while not explicitly spelled out or defended below, proceeds from within a confessional framework that is Catholic yet ecumenical. My method is broadly informed by certain presumptions of canonical criticism: that the final or canonical form of the text represents the primary object of study; that individual texts should be understood in light of their canonical context, as books within a bi-covenantal corpus; and that there is an underlying unity to the canon, such that all the texts of the canon are allowed to speak synchronically on a given subject. My method is also informed by speech-act theory as it has been applied to the divine "discourse of the covenant" reflected in the Old and New Testaments and in the Church's liturgical tradition. See generally on these methodological questions: Rolf Rendtorff, "Canonical Interpretation: A New Approach to Biblical Texts," *Pro Ecclesia* 3 (1994): 141-151; Craig G. Bartholomew and Michael W. Goheen, *The Drama of Scripture: Finding Our Place in the Biblical Story* (Grand Rapids, Mich.: Baker Academic, 2004); Kevin J. Vanhoozer, *First Theology: God, Scripture, and Hermeneutics* (Downers Grove, Ill.: InterVarsity Press, 2002).

Davidic monarchy, and the new covenant—I believe we will see the familiar biblical outlines in a new light. Further, from this liturgical reading, certain hermeneutical implications will emerge. These we will consider at the conclusion of this paper.

Reading the Canon 'Liturgically'

I must begin by anticipating my conclusion: A liturgical reading of the canonical text discloses the Bible's *liturgical trajectory* and *liturgical teleology*. As we will see, this is the unspoken conclusion that much of today's best exegesis points us toward. Put another way: as presented in the canonical narrative, there is a liturgical reason and purpose for the creation of the world and the human person, and there is a liturgical "destiny" for creation and the human person. Man, as presented in the canonical text, is *homo liturgicus*, liturgical man, created to glorify God through service, expressed as a sacrifice of praise.

This is seen in the Bible's very first pages. Commentators have long observed the royal and cultic language and the liturgical rhythms in the creation narrative. It is likely that the text's final form has been shaped by its constant use in the liturgy of ancient Israel.[12] Genesis 1, in fact, reads like a liturgical hymn. Creation unfolds in a series of sevenfold movements, beginning with the first verse which is exactly seven words long in Hebrew, and proceeding with seven clearly defined creative speech acts of God ("Let there be. . .").

Intertextual analysis has helped us to see the linguistic and thematic parallels between the account of the primordial seven days and the later building of the tabernacle (Exod. 25-40).[13] This in turn has helped us to understand the author's intention in Genesis 1: to depict creation as the fashioning of a cosmic temple, a house of God which, like the later tabernacle and Temple, would be a meeting place for God and the human person made in his image and likeness.

In the second creation account in Genesis 2-3, the garden of Eden is described in highly symbolic terms as an earthly sanctuary—again with evident literary parallels to later sanctuaries, especially the inner sanctum

---

[12] Claus Westermann speaks of Genesis 1 as describing ". . . a heavenly liturgy. With a severe and solemn rhythm the same expressions occur again and again throughout the whole chapter like a litany." See his *Der Schopfungsbericht vom Anfang der Bibel* (Stuttgart, 1960), 10, quoted in Eugene H. Maly, "Israel— God's Liturgical People," in *Liturgy for the People: Essays in Honor of Gerhard Ellard, S.J., 1894-1963* (Milwaukee: Bruce Publishing, 1963), 10-20, at 13.

[13] For background on the idea of the cosmos as temple, see Jon D. Levenson, "The Temple and the World," *Journal of Religion* 64 (1984): 275-298; Barnabas M. Ahern, C.P., "Interpreting the Bible Typologically: The Exodus," in *Voice Crying Out in the Desert*, ed. Carroll Stuhlmueller (Collegeville, Minn.: Liturgical Press, 1996), 46-63; Rikki E. Watts, "On the Edge of the Millennium: Making Sense of Genesis 1," in *Living in the Lamblight: Contemporary Challenges to the Gospel*, ed. Hans Boersma (Vancouver: Regent College Publishing, 2001), 129-151.

of the Temple.[14] For our liturgical reading, the most important parallels are those that describe the terms of the relationship between God and man in the garden and in the sanctuary.

God is described "walking up and down" or "to and fro" (הלך) in the garden (Gen. 3:8). The same Hebrew verb is used to characterize God's presence in the tabernacle (Lev. 26:12; Deut. 23:15; 2 Sam. 7:6-7). The first man is described as placed in the garden to "serve" (עבד) and to "keep" or "guard" (שׁמר) it. These verbs are only found together again in the Pentateuch to describe the liturgical service of the priests and Levites in the sanctuary (Num. 3:7-8; 8:26; 18:5-6).[15] These literary clues suggest the biblical authors' intent to describe creation as a royal temple building by a heavenly king. The human person in these pages is intentionally portrayed as a kind of priest-king set to rule as vice-regent over the temple-kingdom of creation.[16]

The Priestly King of Genesis

This reading of Genesis is confirmed intertextually in the Old Testament and throughout the intertestamental and rabbinic literature.[17] Perhaps the clearest inner-biblical reflection on the nature of the primal human is found

---

[14] See, for instance, Gordan J. Wenham, "Sanctuary Symbolism in the Garden of Eden Story," in *Proceedings of the Ninth Congress of Jewish Studies* (Jerusalem: World Union of Jewish Studies, 1986), 19-25; Lawrence E. Stager, "Jerusalem and the Garden of Eden," in *Eretz-Israel: Archaeological, Historical and Geographical Studies* 26, eds. Baruch A. Levine et al. (Jerusalem: Israel Exploration Society/Hebrew Union College, 1999), 183-194.

[15] "If Eden is seen then as an ideal sanctuary, then perhaps Adam should be described as an archetypal Levite." Wenham, "Sanctuary Symbolism in the Garden of Eden Story," 21.

[16] The language of "image and likeness" suggests both filial relationship and a royal delegation of responsibilities. Compare Genesis 1:26; 5:1 and the kingly and filial imagery in Psalm 8. The command to rule over creation is "an important aspect of the image and likeness." Dexter E. Callender, Jr., *Adam in Myth and History: Ancient Israelite Perspectives on the Primal Human*, Harvard Semitic Studies 48 (Winona Lake, Ind.: Eisenbrauns, 2000), 29.

[17] See J. Oberholzer, "What is Man...?" in *De Fructu Oris Sui: Essays in Honour of Adrianus van Selms*, eds. I. H. Eybers, F. C. Fensham, C. J. Labuschagne (Leiden: Brill, 1971), 141-151; C.J. Louis, *The Theology of Psalm 8: A Study of the Traditions of the Text and the Theological Import* (Washington, D.C.: Catholic University of America, 1946). The Psalter, the wisdom literature, and the prophets all give us the picture of creation as a cosmic or heavenly sanctuary and the Temple as a microcosm (Pss. 52:8; 78:69; 92:13-15; Lam. 2:6; Isa. 60:13,21). The Chronicler understands the task of the Levitical priesthood in terms of the serving, guarding, and gatekeeping imagery in Genesis (1 Chron. 9:17-27; 2 Chron. 23:19; Neh. 11:19). "The garden of Eden was the holy of holies and the dwelling of the Lord," we read in the intertestamental *Book of Jubilees* (8:9). A midrash on Genesis describes Adam's primordial task as that of offering priestly sacrifices (Rabbah Gen. 16:5). In a Targum, Adam is described as having been formed from dust at the precise site where the Temple sanctuary would later be built (*Targum Psuedo-Jonathon Gen. 2:7*). The Qumran community apparently saw itself as the "Temple of Adam" (4Q174 1:6). For a good review of these themes, see G. K. Beale, *The Temple and the Church's Mission: A Biblical Theology of the Dwelling Place of God* (Downers Grove: InterVarsity Press, 2004). Also, Robin Scroggs, *The Last Adam: A Study in Pauline Anthropology* (Philadelphia: Fortress Press, 1966).

in Ezekiel's famous lament over the King of Tyre (Ezek. 28:1-19), though its precise meaning remains the subject of scholarly debate.

Ezekiel describes the king as created in Eden, which is depicted as "the garden of God" and the "holy mountain of God," that is, as a symbol of the site of the Temple (vv. 13,14,16). He "walks among (הִהְלֵּך) the stones of fire" or burning coals (v. 14), which elsewhere are associated with the divine presence (Ezek. 1:3; Ps. 18:13). He is stamped with a "signet" of "perfection" or "resemblance" (v. 12)—a symbol elsewhere associated with royal likeness and authority (Gen. 41:42; Hag. 2:23; Jer. 22:24-25). And the king is clothed in the same precious stones worn on the breastplate of Israel's high priest, the same type of stones also found in Havilah, one of the lands watered by the river flowing from Eden (compare Ezek. 28:13; Exod. 28:17-20; Gen. 2:12).

As the king's creation is described in Adamic and priestly terms, so his sin is characterized as a form of sacrilege and profanation punished by exile and "deconsecration." The king's sin, like Adam's, is grasping after divinity—wanting to be "like a god." This becomes the refrain of Ezekiel's indictment (compare Gen. 3:5,22; Ezek. 28:2,6,9). Driven by cherubim, he is cast from God's presence as a "profane thing" who has desecrated God's sanctuaries (Ezek. 28:16,18; compare Gen. 3:23-24). There may even be an allusion to the curse of Adam in the king's being "turned . . . to ashes upon the earth" (compare Ezek. 28:18; Gen. 3:19; 18:27; Sir. 17:32).[18]

This passage of Ezekiel suggests that already within the Old Testament there was a traditional understanding of the human person as created in relationship with God and endowed with an identity that is at once royal and priestly, filial and liturgical.[19]

The terms of the human relationship with God are ordered by the covenant of the sabbath established on the seventh day.[20] This becomes clear

---

[18] Callender concludes his insightful treatment of Ezekiel's lament: "The image is suggestive of the expelled primal human as an ex-communicated priest." *Adam in Myth and History*, 89.

[19] "It is quite evident that the tradition upon which Ezekiel bases his lamentation in 28:11-19 understands the primal human in priestly terms, or, perhaps better put, in 'intermediary' terms. The imagery he employs is consonant with that of the sacral king, endowed for service as vice-regent of God and mediator between human and divine." Callender, *Adam in Myth and History*, 132.

[20] The term "covenant," of course, is not used in the creation account. However, that creation is ordered to the covenant is everywhere implied. See Robert Murray, *The Cosmic Covenant* (London: Sheed & Ward, 1992), 2-13. In the rabbinic and intertestamental literature, the sabbath was seen as a sign of God's covenant oath with the first man and woman. See, for instance, the midrashic *Sifre Deuteronomy; the Book of Jubilees* (36:7), and 1 *Enoch* 69:15-27. See also Roland de Vaux, *Ancient Israel: Its Life and Institutions* (New York: McGraw-Hill Co., 1961), 2:481: "Creation is the first action in this history of salvation; once it was over, God stopped work, and he was then able to make a covenant with his creature. . . . The 'sign' of the covenant made at the dawn of creation is the observance of the sabbath by man (Ezek. 20:12,20)." Recent Catholic magisterial documents have referred to the sabbath of creation as "the first covenant." See Pope John Paul II, *Dies Domini*, Apostolic Letter on Keeping the Lord's Day Holy (July 5, 1998), no. 8; see also *Catechism of the Catholic Church*, no. 288.

further on in the Pentateuch with Moses' building of the tabernacle and God's giving of the sabbath ordinances. The literary parallels with the creation account suggest a close connection between sabbath, creation, covenant, and the dwelling that Israel is instructed to build.[21] The plans for the dwelling are given by God immediately after the liturgical ratification of the Sinai covenant in Exodus 24. Moses' time on the mountain can be seen as a kind of "new creation"—the cloud of divine presence covers the mountain for six days and on the seventh Moses is called to enter the cloud and receive the divine blueprint for the dwelling. God's instructions consist of a series of seven commands that continue for seven chapters and conclude with the ordinances for the seventh day, the sabbath (Exod. 31:12-17).

The making of the priestly vestments and the building of the tabernacle again recall the creation narrative. In both, the work is also done in seven stages, each punctuated with the words, "as the LORD commanded Moses." As God did, Moses beholds his handiwork, and blesses it (Exod. 39:43). As God "finished his work," so Moses "finished the work" (Gen. 2:1-2; Exod. 40:34). And as God rested on the seventh day, blessing and hallowing it, when Moses finished his work, the divine presence filled the tabernacle (Exod. 40:34).

In the Israelites' work to build the tabernacle we glimpse what the royal and priestly service of the human person was meant to be about: God's sons were to rule in his name, according to his commands. Through their work they were to bring creation to its fulfillment, to complete God's work by making the world a home in which they dwell with him and live as his people.[22]

All of creation is ordered to the covenant, the familial dwelling of God with his people. The sabbath, as the sign of God's "perpetual covenant" (Exod. 31:16), is meant to be a living memorial of the original perfection and intention of God's creation—his desire to "rest" in communion with creation. The sabbath orders human work to worship, labor to liturgy.[23] The royal calling to subdue the earth finds its expression in the liturgical consecration

---

[21] For these parallels, see Samuel E. Balentine, *The Torah's Vision of Worship*, (Minneapolis: Fortress Press, 1999), 136-141; Gary A. Anderson, *The Genesis of Perfection: Adam and Eve in Jewish and Christian Imagination* (Louisville: Westminster/John Knox Press, 2001), 200-202.

[22] See Anderson, *Genesis of Perfection*, 201-202.

[23] "On this day man must recognize the enthroned Lord of hosts who, having completed his work, awaits in the attitude of majestic repose, the liturgical response of his creature." Maly, "Israel—God's Liturgical People," 14.

of the earth's fruits to God. Through their worship on the sabbath, God bestows his blessings on his people and makes them holy (Exod. 31:13).[24]

The Priestly People of the Exodus

These creation themes—man as made for worship in a covenant relationship as God's royal and priestly firstborn—are made explicit in the canonical account of the Exodus. As Adam was made in God's image and likeness, God identifies Israel as "my own people" (Exod. 3:7,10,12; 5:1; 6:5,7) and "my son, my firstborn" (Exod. 4:22-23). And as Adam was made to worship, God's chosen people are liberated expressly for worship.

The early chapters of Exodus involve a play on the word עבד, ("serve" or "work"), the word that described the primeval vocation given to man (Gen. 2:15). The word is used four times to stress the cruel slavery ("hard service") inflicted upon the Israelites by the new Pharaoh (Exod. 1:13-14; see also 5:18; 14:5,12). But the same word is also used to describe what God wants of the Israelites (Exod. 3:12; 4:22; 7:16; 9:1,13; 10:3, 24-26). They are to serve, not as slave laborers but as a people that serves him in prayer.[25] They are to "offer sacrifice" (זבח Exod. 3:18, 5:3). Moses and Aaron are instructed to tell Pharaoh that God wants Israel to hold a religious "feast" or "festival" (חג Exod. 5:1; compare Exod. 12:14; 23:16; 34:25).

Israel's vocation is most clearly stated in the preamble to the covenant at Sinai. There God vows that if Israel keeps his covenant, they will

---

[24] "The sabbath is the sign of the covenant between God and man; it sums up the inward essence of the covenant. . . . [C]reation exists to be a place for the covenant that God wants to make with man. The goal of creation is the covenant, the love story of God and man. . . . If creation is meant to be a space for the covenant, the place where God and man meet one another, then it must be thought of as a space for worship. . . . Now if worship, rightly understood, is the soul of the covenant, then it not only saves mankind but is also meant to draw the whole of reality into communion with God." Joseph Ratzinger, *The Spirit of the Liturgy*, trans. John Saward (San Francisco: Ignatius Press, 2000), 26-27. See also, Jean Danielou, S.J.: "In the cosmic Temple, man is not living primarily in his own house but in the house of God. . . . But at the same time, man is part of creation and has his role to play in it. God has in some way left creation unfinished, and man's mission is to bring it to fulfillment. . . . Man is thus the mediator through whom the visible universe is gathered together and offered up, the priest of that virginal creation over which God lovingly watches." *The Presence of God*, trans. Walter Roberts (London: A.R. Mowbray Co., 1958), 11-12.

[25] Note the use of עבד to describe the priestly liturgical service offered to God in the tabernacle (Num. 3:7-8; 4:23; 7:5; 16:9).

be "my own treasured possession (סְגֻלָּה) among all the nations . . . a kingdom of priests (מַמְלֶכֶת כֹּהֲנִים) and a holy nation (גּוֹי קָדוֹשׁ)" (Exod. 19:5-6).[26] As God's "treasured possession," Israel is the crown jewel of humanity.[27] As a holy nation and a kingdom of priests, Israel is to be corporately what Adam was created to be individually—the firstborn of a new humanity, a liturgical people that will dwell with God in a relationship of filial obedience and worship.

Given a priestly purpose and identity, the Israelites are freed from their service to Pharaoh in a sort of liturgy of liberation. This liturgy begins with the celebration of the Passover ritual instituted by God and prescribed in minute detail (Exod. 12). In a ritual exit procession, the Israelites depart "company by company" led by God (Exod. 12:42, 51; 13:21-22). The event concludes with the singing of a thanksgiving hymn, accompanied by tambourines and dancing (Exod. 15:1-21).

The covenant at Sinai is ratified by liturgical actions—the reading of the book of the Law, the profession of fidelity sworn by the people, the offering of sacrifices, the sprinkling of "the blood of the covenant," and the meal eaten in the presence of God (see Exod. 24:1-9). Much of the Law, in fact, consists of regulations regarding how God is to be rightly worshipped—the design of the tabernacle and furniture, the priestly vestments, the liturgical calendar of festivals, and the ceremonial rubrics of the sacrificial system.

In their worship, the Israelites celebrated their birth as a people of God and rededicated themselves to their royal and priestly vocation (Deut. 6:4-5).[28] Moreover, in Israel's liturgical celebrations, God "remembered" his covenant, making it anew with each generation (Deut. 5:1-4) and extending his blessings to his people through his priests (Num. 6:22-27).

As Israel is given an "Adamic" vocation, it experiences an Adamic fall from grace. And as the primeval fall results in exile and deconsecration

---

[26] "In this nutshell we find a *summary* of the purpose of the covenant, presented from the mouth of Yhwh himself. Here is given the goal of Israel's future." Jo Bailey Wells, *God's Holy People: A Theme in Biblical Theology*, Journal for the Study of the Old Testament Supplement Series 305 (Sheffield: Sheffield Academic Press, 2000), 34-35. See also Roland J. Fahey, *The Kingdom of Priests* (Rome: Pontifical Atheneum Angelicum, 1960).

[27] Following Wells, who sees סְגֻלָּה as connoting "treasure such as...the jewel in a crown belonging to a king." See 1 Chron. 29:3; Eccl. 2:8; Deut. 7:6; 14:2; 26:18; Ps. 135:4; Mal. 3:17. *God's Holy People*, 48.

[28] As Jon D. Levenson concludes, "The renewal of covenant was a central aspect of Israel's worship in biblical times." *Sinai and Zion: An Entry into the Jewish Bible* (San Francisco: HarperCollins, 1985), 80-81. Of the exodus, Louis Bouyer writes, ". . . the legislation and the religious history of Israel are all permeated with the memory of the great event, so too is its liturgy. . . ." *The Meaning of Sacred Scripture* (South Bend, Ind.: University of Notre Dame Press, 1958), 35,37.

of the royal priestly figure, so too does Israel's worship of the golden calf.[29]
God disowns his people, telling Moses pointedly that they are "your people,
whom you brought out of the land of Egypt" (Exod. 32:7; 33:1).[30] God calls the
people "corrupted," using a Hebrew term (שׁחת) found elsewhere to describe
an animal too blemished to sacrifice or a priest unfit for service.[31] In defiling
itself through ritual rebellion, Israel, like Adam, is rendered unfit for its
divine vocation. It is interesting that the royal-priestly title of Exodus 19:6 is
never again used to describe Israel in the Old Testament.

According to the biblical narrative, the apostasy results in the
Levitical priesthood becoming the locus of the holiness that God intended for
all Israel.[32] God's presence remains among the people, but access is highly
restricted and must be mediated by the Levites. A complex array of cultic
laws were introduced for apparently penitential and pedagogical purposes—
as mechanisms that will enable Israel to atone for its inevitable sins against
the covenant and to teach them the true meaning of worship.

This turn of events gives narrative shape to the canonical
presentation of the Law, especially in the sources identified as "Priestly." The
goal of the worship and Law of Israel becomes that of atonement
(Lev. 16:30)—bridging the gap between God's holiness and Israel's sinfulness

---

[29] For a detailed look at the golden-calf apostasy, see Scott W. Hahn, "Kinship by Covenant," 226-253.

[30] Here too we may have an expression of an ancient biblical tradition regarding the priestly identity and vocation of the human person. John A. Davies sees this tradition behind Hosea's later condemnation of Israel's corrupt priesthood and covenant violations (4:4-9; 6:6-7). The passage is fraught with difficulties, but he makes a solid case that Hosea is drawing on a shared understanding of Adam as "the archetypal priest-king in the primal paradise-garden." Davies concludes: "If Hosea has as part of his shared presupposition pool with his readers the story of Genesis 2, with Adam as the idyllic priest-king (see Ezek. 28:12-15; Jub. 4:23-26), together with the notion that Israel at Sinai was constituted as the new humanity, the true successors to Adam (see 4 Ezra 3:3-36; 6:53-59; 2 Bar. 14:17-19), then it makes sense to compare the breach of the Sinai covenant (see Hos. 4:1,2) with the rebellion in the garden (Gen. 3; compare Ezek. 28:16-17)." *A Royal Priesthood: Literary and Intertextual Perspectives on an Image of Israel in Exodus* 19:6, Journal for the Study of the Old Testament Supplement Series 395 (London: T & T Clark International, 2004), 202.

[31] See Lev. 22:25, Mal. 1:14; 2:8. "The point to notice here is that the people of Israel as a whole now have a moral defect that separates them from God. They cannot come to the sanctuary for they have rejected God, and thus have become like a defective animal or a disqualified priest, unable to come into God's presence." A. M. Rodriguez, "Sanctuary Theology in Exodus," *Andrews University Seminary Studies* 24 (1986): 127-145, at 139.

[32] John M. Scholer, *Proleptic Priests: Priesthood in the Epistle to the Hebrews*, Journal for the Study of the New Testament Supplement Series 49 (Sheffield: Sheffield Academic Press, 1991), 13-22.

through a "substitutionary offering of blood."[33] It is beyond the scope of this article to look any more closely at the priesthood or the system of ritual sacrifices. The point is that even in its fallen condition Israel is called to respond as a priestly people. Their distance from God, their desire for "at-one-ment," is to be expressed—and effected—through the liturgical means of sacrifice.

The Priestly Kingdom of David

With the Davidic kingdom we see the fullest expression of the Bible's liturgical anthropology and teleology. In the dynasty established by his covenant with David, God restates his divine will for the human person—to be a son of God, a priest, and a king. The formula of God's original calling for Israel (Exod. 19:6) is conspicuously left unspoken. But there is no doubt that the kingdom established under David and later Solomon is to be a royal and priestly people.[34]

The royal-priestly primogeniture granted to David's seed (2 Sam. 7:14; Pss. 110:4; 89:26-27) is linked to the royal priesthood intended for Israel (Exod. 3:6-17: 4:22; 19:5-6).[35] David is portrayed as a "new Melchizedek"—a priest and king who serves the most high God from his capital in Salem, that is, Jerusalem (compare Gen. 14:18; Pss. 76:2; 110). Throughout the canonical narrative, David is shown taking actions that are at once cultic and political, military and liturgical. His first act after establishing Jerusalem

---

[33] See the important contributions of Hartmut Gese on "The Law" and "The Atonement" in his *Essays on Biblical Theology*, (Minneapolis: Augsburg Publishing House, 1981), 60-116. "The goal of Torah is holiness, which can be symbolically achieved in the cult. This occurs properly through atonement. The act of dedication to God, by which the distance from what is holy is symbolically bridged by the substitutionary offering of blood, is so central for the cult of the Priestly Document, that not only is the great day of atonement the highest holy day, but also every sacrifice takes on the nature of atonement, for it is only atonement, not offering a gift, that can express the meaning of the cult" (at 74).

[34] See the discussion in Hahn, "Kinship by Covenant," 359-360. For God's original promise, see 2 Sam. 7:8-16; 1 Chron. 17:1-15. For the interpretation of this covenant, see Isa. 55:3; Jer. 33:21-22; 2 Chron. 13:5; 2 Sam. 23:5; Pss. 89; 132. Heinz Kruse, "David's Covenant," *Vetus Testamentum* 35 (1985): 139-164; Jon Levenson, "The Davidic Covenant and its Modern Interpreters," *Catholic Biblical Quarterly* 41 (1979): 205-219.

[35] R. E. Clements, *Abraham and David: Genesis XV and Its Meaning for Israelite Tradition* (Naperville, Ill.: A.R. Allenson, 1967). "The Davidic covenant in Chronicles is . . . closely related to the earlier Sinaitic and Abrahamic covenants. Obedience to the law of Moses is basic to the life of the community (1 Chron. 22;13; 28;7; 2 Chron. 6:16; 7:17; 23:18; 33:8) and is implicit in its restoration to God (see 2 Chron. 17:7-9; 19:4-11; 30:15-16; 35:6,12). The Abrahamic covenant with its grant of land finds its fulfillment in the establishment of the Temple (2 Chron. 20:7-8; 1 Chron. 16:15-18)." Brian E. Kelly, "'Retribution' Revisited: Covenant, Grace and Restoration," in *The Chronicler as Theologian: Essays in Honor of Ralph W. Klein*, ed. M. P. Graham, S. L. McKenzie and G. N. Knoppers, Journal for the Study of the Old Testament Supplement Series 371 (London: T&T Clark International, 2003), 215 n. 29.

as capital of his kingdom,[36] is to restore the Ark of the Covenant—the defining symbol of Israel's election and the site of God's living presence among the people during the wilderness period (Exod. 25:8-22; Josh. 3:8-11). David's great concern for the Ark is central to the early drama of his reign, and the Ark's installation in the Temple marks the culmination of the Chronicler's account.[37]

The Ark's restoration is depicted as a grand religious pilgrimage. It is preceded by the ritual purification of the Levites (1 Chron. 15:11), who alone are permitted to transport the Ark under the Mosaic law that David reinstitutes (Deut. 10:8; 1 Chron. 15:2). The procession is a joyous religious feast, complete with liturgical dancing and song led by David and the priests (1 Chron. 15:1-16:3; 2 Sam. 6:11-19).[38] David wears a priest's ephod and there is a sabbatical tone to the event, highlighted by the sacrifices of the priests—seven bulls and seven rams (1 Chron. 15:25) and the joyous praise of God as creator of the world and maker of covenants (1 Chron. 16:14-18,26).

As the Ark is installed, David leads the priests in offering holocausts and peace offerings. Then he blesses the people in the name of the Lord and shares bread, meat, and a cake with every Israelite. What we witness here is Israel's king performing high-priestly acts—leading worship, offering sacrifices, imparting the Lord's blessings.[39] David's actions reestablish the presence of God among the people (1 Chron. 23:25). To ensure the purity of Israel's worship he organizes Aaron's descendants to be "officers of the sanctuary and officers of God" (1 Chron. 24:3,5,19), and installs the Levitical priests "to minister before the Ark of the LORD, to invoke, to thank, and to praise the LORD" every morning and evening and also on feast days (1 Chron. 16:4; 23:25-32).

Restoration of the Ark and the reassertion of the priestly hierarchy (Deut. 10:8) are among the signs that the Chronicler sees David as a new Moses figure, possibly the "prophet like me" that Moses himself had promised (Deut. 18:15).[40] Like Moses, David glories in God's presence in the Ark (Exod. 25:21-22; 30:6,36; Num. 7:89; 17:19). He restores Moses' cultic and worship prescriptions (1 Chron. 15; 21:29; 22:13) and advises Solomon that this liturgical order is crucial to the monarchy's character and success

---

[36] 1 Chron. 28:5; 29:23; 2 Chron. 6:5-6; 13:8; 2 Sam. 5:7,9; 6:10,11.

[37] See Christopher Begg, "The Ark in Chronicles," in *The Chronicler as Theologian*, 133-145.

[38] Endres, "Theology of Worship in Chronicles," 168.

[39] See Hahn, "Kinship By Covenant," 347-349.

[40] On David as heir of Moses' liturgical leadership and restorer of the "divinely ordained" liturgical life of Israel, see William Riley, *King and Cultus in Chronicles: Worship and the Reinterpretation of History*, Journal for the Study of the Old Testament Supplement Series 160 (Sheffield: Sheffield Academic Press, 1993), 163.

(1 Chron. 22:12-13). Why should the king be so concerned about worship? Because the Chronicler believed that God's blessings flowed to the people through the proper celebration of the sacrifices and other liturgies.[41]

The Liturgy of the Temple

The exodus was ordered to the establishment of Israel as a priestly nation. The Sinai covenant was expressed architecturally in the tabernacle. Similarly, the conquest of the land was ordered to the establishment of Israel as a kingdom of priests. The architectural expression of the Davidic Kingdom was not a royal palace, but the Temple.

David, like Moses, is given a divine "pattern" or "plan" (תבנית) for the Temple that will house the Ark permanently (1 Chron. 28:19; Exod. 25:9), and in which God will dwell for all time with his people.[42] The building of the Temple is presented as a new creation. As creation takes seven days, the Temple takes seven years to build (1 Kings 6:38; Gen. 2:2). It is dedicated during the seven-day Feast of Tabernacles (1 Kings 8:2) by a solemn prayer of Solomon structured around seven petitions (1 Kings 8:31-53). God capped creation by "resting" on the seventh day. Built by a "man of rest" (אישׁ מנוחה) 1 Chron. 22:9), the Temple was to be the "house of rest" (בית מנוחה 1 Chron. 28:2) or "resting place" for the Ark and for the LORD (2 Chron. 6:41; Ps. 132:8, 13-14; Isa. 66:1).[43]

---

[41] "The reason for this interest in the divine institution of the sacrificial cult is clear. Worship was effective and beneficial only as long as it was performed in accordance with divine law. *In fact, its divine institution empowered it, so that, by its enactment, the Lord himself received his people*, like a king his petitioners, and acted in their favor." John W. Kleinig, *The Lord's Song: The Basis, Function, and Significance of Choral Music in Chronicles*, Journal for the Study of the Old Testament Supplement Series 156 (Sheffield: Sheffield Academic Press, 1993), 31, emphasis supplied. Reward and retribution, a theme identified so often among scholars of Chronicles, when looked at closely is very often a function of right cultic performance. The Lord is with those who worship him as he wants to be worshipped (2 Chron. 13:10-12). Those who do this will be blessed (1 Chron. 22:13; 28:8; 2 Chron. 13:21; 33:8). Wrong worship will lead God to the destruction of the Temple (2 Chron. 7:19-22). This pattern can be seen too in the story of the Ark. The wrath of the Lord blazes when the Ark is not handled as Moses prescribed—with deadly consequences for Uzzah (1 Chron. 15:13; 2 Samuel 6:6-10).

[42] Levenson, *Sinai and Zion*, 141.

[43] On "rest" and Solomon's election to build the Temple, see Sara Japhet, *I and II Chronicles: A Commentary* (Louisville, Ky.: Westminster/John Knox Press, 1993), 221; Gerhard von Rad, "There Remains Still a Rest for the People of God," in *The Problem of the Hexateuch and Other Essays* (New York: McGraw-Hill, 1966), 94-102; Steven L. McKenzie, "Why Didn't David Build the Temple?: The History of a Biblical Tradition," in *Worship and the Hebrew Bible: Essays in Honour of John T. Willis*, eds. M. P. Graham, R. R. Marrs and S. L. McKenzie, Journal for the Study of the Old Testament Supplement Series 284 (Sheffield: Sheffield Academic Press, 1999), 204-224, at 220-221; Levenson, *Sinai and Zion*, 144-145.

In the Temple worship, the precise sacrificial system of the Mosaic cult continues, but there are new elements and accents. The most apparent innovations are the development of liturgical music and sacred song, both of which are traditionally attributed to David, the divinely inspired, "sweet psalmist of Israel" (2 Sam. 23:1). The kingdom's corporate worship takes the form of praise and thanksgiving.

Many commentators have identified the centrality of songs of praise (תהלה) and songs of thanksgiving (תודה) in the Temple liturgy. Many of the psalms of praise appear to have been written to accompany the offering of sacrifices in the Temple (Pss. 27:6; 54:6,8 141:2). This is true also for the psalms of thanksgiving. In the post-exilic works, we see examples of the Levites organizing "the thanksgiving songs" of the Temple liturgy (Neh. 11:17; 12:8,31).

David's own thanksgiving hymn (1 Chron. 16:7-36) is presented as a kind of paradigm for Israel's prayer. It is, in essence, a celebration of God's covenant in liturgical form. It begins and ends with exhortations to give thanks to God. It glorifies God's holy name and his majesty as the creator of heaven and earth. The focus of praise and remembrance is Israel's status as God's elect. The exodus and Israel's wandering among the nations is remembered. There is, too, a missionary quality about the prayer, as Israel is enjoined to declare God's salvation to all the nations.[44]

Scholars have pointed out that David's hymn includes portions of Psalms 96, 105, and 106. And this hymn sets the tone and provides the content for the acts of worship and the theology of worship we find in the Psalter. God is praised and thanked in remembrance of his mighty works in creation and for his saving words and deeds in the life of Israel—the defining experience being that of the exodus and the covenant. Praise and thanksgiving, accompanied by sacrifice, is understood to be the only appropriate response to the God who has created Israel to be his own and rescued them from death.[45] In calling on the name of the Lord—an injunction heard in David's hymn and throughout the Psalter—the Israelites believed

---

[44] Note the similarities between David's hymn and the prayer Solomon delivers during the Temple dedication liturgy (2 Chron. 6:12-21). "Both divine addresses are concerned with the meaning of the Davidic covenant as the foundation of God's relationship with Israel. In the Chronicler's understanding, this covenant does nothing less than constitute Israel as the earthly manifestation of Yahweh's kingdom, a reality with a twofold expression in the interrelated institutions of the Davidic dynasty and the Solomonic temple." Endres, "Theology of Worship in Chronicles," 175.

[45] See J. Kenneth Kuntz, "Grounds for Praise: The Nature and Function of the Motive Clause in the Hymns of the Hebrew Psalter," in *Worship and the Hebrew Bible*, 149-183, especially 182-183.

themselves to be truly in God's presence as heirs of the blessings of the covenant wrought by his saving deeds.[46]

The Sacrifice of Praise

Prayer in the Psalter moves inexorably in the direction of sacrifice. This is seen most evocatively in the *todah* (תודה) or thanksgiving psalms (for example, Pss. 18; 30; 32; 41; 66; 116; 118; 138). Composed to accompany the offering of a sacrificial meal of bread and meat in the Temple (Lev. 7:1-21), these are some of the highest expressions of the Old Testament's liturgical anthropology.[47]

In the *todah* psalms the experience of the individual believer is almost typologically compared to that of Israel's captivity and exodus experience. Typically these psalms begin with a confession of faith and a vow of praise and self-offering. There follows a lament concerning some life-threatening distress that had befallen the believer. Then the believer describes how God delivered him from death or Sheol (the netherworld) and brought him to sing God's praises in the Temple.[48] In these psalms, "life" is equated with worship and sacrifice in the presence of God in his Temple; "death" is seen as a sort of exile or captivity, to be cut off from God's presence, outside of his Temple.[49]

---

[46] See 1 Chron. 16:10. See also Kleinig, *The Lord's Song*, 146-147: "This proclamation of the Lord's name was a performative enactment. It did not merely impart information about the Lord but actually effected his presence, for wherever his name was proclaimed, he was present with his people, as he had promised in Exod. 20:24. Through their performance of praise, the singers introduced the Lord to his people and announced his presence among them. The people could therefore seek him, since he was present with them there (1 Chron. 16:10-11)." On the presence of God in the ritual remembrance of Israel, see D.P. Niles, "The Name of God in Israel's Worship: The Theological Importance of the Name 'Yahweh'" (Ph.D. diss., Princeton University, 1974), 193-196; T. N. D. Mettinger, *In Search of God: The Meaning and Message of the Everlasting Names*, trans. F. H. Cryer (Philadelphia: Fortress Press, 1988), 8-9; R. J. Tournay, *Seeing and Hearing God with the Psalms: The Prophetic Liturgy of the Second Temple in Jerusalem*, trans. J. E. Crowley, Journal for the Study of the Old Testament Supplement Series 118 (Sheffield: Sheffield Academic Press, 1991).

[47] "It can be said that the thank offering constituted the cultic basis for the main bulk of the psalms. It not only represents the high point of human life, but in it life itself can be seen as overcoming the basic issue of death by God's deliverance into life." Gese, *Essays on Biblical Theology*, 131.

[48] See Hermann Gunkel, *An Introduction to the Psalms* (Macon, Ga.: Mercer University Press, 1988), 199-221.

[49] See the fine treatment of Gary A. Anderson, "The Praise of God as a Cultic Event," in *Priesthood and Cult in Ancient Israel*, ed. G. A. Anderson and S. M. Olyan, Journal for the Study of the Old Testament Supplement Series 125 (Sheffield: Sheffield Academic Press, 1991), 15-33, at 28: "[J]ust as 'life' was experienced in the cult as being before the presence of God in the (heavenly) Temple, so 'death' was experienced in the cult as being cut off from that presence outside the Temple. Both descent to Sheol and ascent to the Temple had ritual accoutrements."

We see in these psalms and in the prophetic literature a new and deepening understanding of the liturgical vocation of man. In the prophets, this recognition of the inner truth of sacrifice often takes the form of denouncing the corruption of Israel's cult and worship (for example, Isa. 1:10-13; 66:2-4; Jer. 7:21-24; Amos 4:4-5,6b; Mic. 6:6-8; Hos. 6:6; Mal. 1:10,13-14). Positively, worship comes to be seen as a sacrificial offering in thanksgiving for redemption, for deliverance from death. Praise is revealed as the sacrifice by which men and women are to glorify God (Pss. 50:14,33; 141:2). God is portrayed as desiring that Israel serve him, not with the blood of animals but with their whole hearts, aligning their will with his, making their whole lives a sacrifice of praise and thanksgiving (Pss. 40:6-8; 51:16-17).

With this profound understanding that they are called to a pure worship of the heart comes the recognition that no amount of ethical striving or moral reform can make them holy enough to serve their God. The psalmist's cry, "Create in me a clean heart, O God . . ." (Ps. 51:7,10-12), finds its answer in the promises of the prophets. A new covenant is promised as a new exodus and a new creation in which there will be a forgiveness of sins and a divine transformation of the heart—God himself will inscribe his law on the heart (Jer. 31:31-34; 32:40; Ezek. 36:24-28).

Ezekiel foretells the new coming of God's royal and priestly servant David, who will shepherd God's people and establish God's Temple sanctuary and dwelling among his people forever (Ezek. 34:23-25; 37:24-28). In this restoration, the prophet says, all the nations will know that God is the one who makes Israel holy. What is being promised is a new sabbath rest, a new dwelling of God with his people. But what was once given to Israel as a sign of its election will now be a sign to all nations (compare Exod. 31:12; Ezek. 37:28).

Indeed, in the vision of the prophets, the new exodus will mark a renewal of Israel's vocation as the firstborn and teacher of the nations. Isaiah sees Israel fulfilling its ancient vocation as "priests of the LORD" (Isa. 61:6), and the instrument of God's blessings for the nations (Isa. 19:24). In the Servant of the Lord, the prophet Isaiah imagines an ideal "new man" whose life has a paschal or sacrificial dimension—who is able to give his life like a sacrificial lamb, as an offering for the sins of his people (Isa. 53). This servant is to be a "covenant to the people . . . a light to the nations." He will make God's salvation known, not only to Israel but to all nations. And the result will be a glorious new liturgical song of praise that will be heard from the ends of the earth (Isa. 42:1-10; 49:1-6; 60:6).

Isaiah foresees nations streaming to Zion to worship the Lord (Isa. 2; see also Jer. 3:16-17). But he also foresees Egypt, the archetypal oppressor of Israel, serving (עָבַד) God, offering sacrifices and burnt offerings on altars erected within its own borders. The dreaded Assyria is also seen joining Egypt in the worship (עָבַד) of Israel's God. These foreign nations will be made heirs to God's covenant with Israel. He will call them what he once called only Israel: "my people" and the "work of my hands" (Isa. 19:16-25 compare Isa. 60:21; 64:7-8; Exod. 5:1; 6:7). In his final vision, Isaiah sees foreigners being made priests, and envisions a new sabbath in which "all flesh shall come to worship" before God (Isa. 66:21-23).[50]

We see then, on the threshold of the New Testament, the promise that man's primal vocation will be renewed, that Israel will be gathered together with all nations at Zion to offer acceptable sacrifice to the God of Israel.

The New Genesis and the New Adam

As more than a generation of scholarship has helped us see, in the New Testament Jesus and his Church are presented as the fulfillment of the promises and institutions of the old covenant. Our understanding has been particularly enhanced by the many fine studies of the use and interpretation of Old Testament texts in the New Testament writings.[51] I cannot hope here to do justice to the findings and insights of these studies. But I would like to illustrate how a liturgical reading of the canonical text can help us to see a unified and integrated pattern to the use of Old Testament types and themes in the New.

The story of the incarnation is told as a new creation. The first words of the New Testament canon—βίβλος γενέσεως—can stand as a kind of title for the whole, "the book of the new genesis." Christ's coming into the world is nothing less than a recapitulation of God's intentions "in the beginning." In Jesus there is a new beginning for the human race. He is explicitly called the new Adam (Rom. 5:12-20; 1 Cor. 15:45-49). And in the early chapters of the Letter to the Hebrews—especially in the opening catena of seven Old Testament quotations—Jesus is described in terms of Adam's original

---

[50] Christopher T. Begg, "The Peoples and the Worship of Yahweh in the Book of Isaiah," *Worship and the Hebrew Bible*, 35-55; G. I. Davies, "The Destiny of the Nations in the Book of Isaiah," in *The Book of Isaiah / Le Livre d'Ilsaie*, ed. J. Vermeylen, (Leuven: Leuven University Press, 1989), 93-120; R. E. Clements, "A Light to the Nations: A Central Theme of the book of Isaiah," in *Forming Prophetic Literature: Essays on Isaiah and the Twelve in Honor of John D.W. Watts*, Journal for the Study of the Old Testament Supplement Series, 235, eds. J. W. Watts and P. R. House, (Sheffield: Sheffield Academic Press, 1996), 58-69. See also, Robert Martin-Achard, *A Light to the Nations: A Study of the Old Testament Conception of Israel's Mission to the World*, trans. J. P. Smith, (Edinburgh: Oliver and Boyd, 1962). See also Walter Vogels, *God's Universal Covenant: A Biblical Study* (Ottawa: University of Ottawa Press, 1986).

[51] See generally, R. B. Hays, *The Echoes of Scripture in the Letters of Paul* (New Haven: Yale University Press, 1989); D. Juel, *Messianic Exegesis: Christological Interpretation of the Old Testament in Early Christianity* (Philadelphia: Fortress Press, 1988). For extensive bibliographies, see Steve Moyise, *The Old Testament in the New* (New York: Continuum, 2001).

royal, filial, and priestly vocation.[52] Here and throughout the Pauline corpus, it is understood that the human vocation was frustrated at the outset by Adam's sin.

It is impossible to put forward here a biblical-theological argument concerning the specific nature of Adam's sin.[53] However, I would suggest that Adam's disobedience was understood inner-biblically as having something to do with a failure to offer himself—what we might call a failure of worship. The fall appears to be more than the transgression of God's legislative commands concerning a fruit tree. That transgression betrays a broader abdication of Adam's task of priestly service in the temple of creation.[54]

In this sense, the story of the fall is truly the first chapter of the Bible, preparing the reader for Israel's history. That history unfolds according to the pattern of Eden—divine benediction is offered and accepted only to be followed quite immediately by human profanation, resulting in punishment by exile from the land of God's presence.[55] In fact, from the

---

[52] For a close reading of the text, see William L. Lane, *Hebrews 1-8*, Word Biblical Commentary 47a (Nashville: Thomas Nelson Publishers, 1991), 46-50: "In Jesus we see exhibited humanity's true vocation. In an extraordinary way he fulfills God's design for all creation and displays what had always been intended for all humankind, according to Psalm 8. He is the one in whom primal glory and sovereignty are restored." Also, James D. Dunn, *Christology in the Making* (Philadelphia: Westminster, 1980), 109-111: "[I]t is *Jesus* who fulfills God's original intention for man—Jesus exalted after death. The risen Jesus is crowned with the glory that Adam failed to reach by virtue of his sin."

[53] For recent entries on the subject, see James Barr, *The Garden of Eden and the Hope of Immortality* (Minneapolis: Augsburg-Fortress Press, 1992), 1-20; S. Towner, "Interpretations and Reinterpretations of the Fall," in *Modern Biblical Scholarship: Its Impact on Theology and Proclamation*, ed. F. Eigo (Villanova, Penn.: Villanova University, 1984), 53-85; R. W. L. Moberly, "Did the Serpent Get it Right?" *Journal of Theological Studies* 39 (1988), 1-27; Robert A. DiVito, "The Demarcation of Divine and Human Realms in Gen. 2-11," in *Creation in the Biblical Traditions*, ed. R. Clifford and J. Collins (Washington: Catholic Biblical Association, 1992), 39-56.

[54] Beale finds in the ancient interpretive literature an understanding of Adam's sin as a failure to guard the garden sanctuary and protect it from defilement and profanation by the serpent. *The Temple and the Church's Mission*, 69-70.

[55] See the important work of Gary A. Anderson, who has shown that "the story of Adam and Eve in the J [Yahwhist] source shows a striking parallel to Israel's larger national story. We might say that the entire narrative of the Torah is in tersely summarized form . . . Adam and Eve fall at the first and only command given to them. And like the nation Israel, the consequences of their disobedience is exile from a land of blessing." *The Genesis of Perfection*, 207-208. See also, Anderson, "Necessarium Adae Peccatum: An Essay on Original Sin," *Pro Ecclesia* 8 (1999): 319-337; Joel Kaminsky, "Paradise Regained: Rabbinic Reflections on Israel at Sinai," in *Jews, Christians and the Theology of the Hebrew Scriptures*, eds. A. Bellis and J. Kaminsky (Atlanta, Ga.: Society of Biblical Literature, 2000), 15-44. Although much work needs to be done in this area, I would argue that the same pattern that Anderson and the rabbis see in the Eden narrative and in the Pentateuch—"the theme of Israel sinning immediately upon reception of a benediction" (Anderson)—can be traced into the period of the judges and on through the divided monarchy. Indeed, Anderson seems to be moving in this direction when he suggests that "this pattern defines not only the narrative of Israel's election but also other founding moments in the Hebrew Scriptures." *Genesis of Perfection*, 206.

unacceptable offering of Cain to the golden calf affair and the strange fire of Nadab and Abihu (Lev. 10:1-3), human sin and disobedience frequently manifests itself as false worship or idolatry. Even the social injustices decried by the prophets often go hand-in-hand with a refusal to offer right worship (Amos 8:4-6).

Again, my purpose here is not to propose any exhaustive explanation of what later tradition came to call "original sin." Nor do I want to reduce the history of sin in the Bible to a story of cultic failure. I do want to suggest that a liturgical reading of Scripture enables us to better understand why Christ's "obedience" is so often cast in cultic, sacrificial, and priestly terms. As animals' blood was used in the liturgical worship of Israel, the New Testament writers describe Christ's blood, offered in sacrifice on the cross, as the agent of atonement for the sin of Adam and Israel. This identification of Christ's redemptive work with cultic sacrifice is especially strong in those passages that most scholars agree represent christological hymns used in early Christian worship.[56]

The hymn in Paul's letter to the Philippians (2:6-11),[57] according to many, underscores the dramatic reversal of Adam's sin. Unlike Adam, who was made in the image of God, Christ did not grasp at equality with God, but instead offered his life in humility and obedience to God. Thus in Hebrews, this obedience is compared to the liturgical act of high priestly sacrifice (Heb. 9:11-28). Whereas Israel's high priests would enter the sanctuary once a year to offer animal blood in atonement for the people's sins, Jesus is described typologically as entering the "true" sanctuary—"heaven itself" (Heb. 9:24)—to offer his own blood in sacrifice "to take away the sins of many" (Heb. 9:28).

By this priestly act, this blood-offering, Jesus atones for sin and at the same time reveals the true nature of sacrifice as intended by God from the beginning—man's offering of himself in filial obedience to the divine will. Hebrews explains this through a christological reading of Psalm 40, finding in it a prophecy of Christ's offering of his body on the cross (Heb. 10:5-10).

---

[56] For example, see the redemptive "blood" imagery in Rom. 3:24-25; Eph. 1:3-14; 2:13; Col. 1:15-20; Heb. 1:3; 1 Pet. 1:18-21. On these hymns, generally, see Martin Hengel, "Hymns and Christology," in *Studia Biblica 1978*, ed. E. A. Livingstone, Journal for the Study of the Old Testament Supplement Series 3 (Sheffield: Sheffield Academic, 1980), 173-197; Jack T. Sanders, *The New Testament Christological Hymns: Their Historical Religious Background*, Society for New Testament Studies Monograph Series, 15 (Cambridge: Cambridge University Press, 1971).

[57] Ralph P. Martin, *Carmen Christi: Philippians 2:5-11 in Recent Interpretations and in the Setting of Early Christian Worship*, Society for Biblical Literature Monograph Series 4 (Cambridge: Cambridge University Press, 1967; reprint Grand Rapids: Wm. B. Eerdmans, 1983). See also, N. T. Wright, "*Harpagmos* and the Meaning of Philippians 2:5-11," *Journal of Theological Studies* 37 (1986): 321-52.

Christ's self-offering is shown to be the worship that had been expected originally of Adam and again of Israel as God's firstborn, royal and priestly people. His sacrifice marked the fulfillment of all that Israel's sacrificial system was intended to prepare and instruct Israel for—that through Israel all the nations of the world might learn to make a perfect offering of heart and will to God. Christ makes possible the human vocation of offering priestly service to God.[58]

The New Exodus

As the New Testament presents it, Jesus' sacrificial death brought about a new exodus—liberating God's people from slavery to sin and subjection to death, ending their exile from God, gathering them and all peoples and leading them into the promised land of the heavenly kingdom and the new Jerusalem.

This "new exodus" theme, found in its most developed Old Testament form in the final section of Isaiah, is now widely recognized as a decisive and shaping factor in the New Testament.[59] It is now widely

---

[58] I have in mind here what Yves Congar, O.P., has called the ". . . theology of sacrifice as consisting in *man's offering of himself* (in other words, his loving obedience to God's will) . . ." Referring specifically to Hebrews 10:4-9, he writes: "We are at the heart of the whole work of Jesus, in a word, the work which his Father had given him to do. *It is to this that all God's plan leads*, it is here that all its strands are gathered together, it is from this point that it moves forward to its full implementation. We have seen that after asking for a series of sacrifices consisting in the offering of animals, God had made it known through the prophets that he expected a better, truer sacrifice, man's offering of himself, that is, the loving obedience of his heart." *The Mystery of the Temple: The Manner of God's Presence to His Creatures from Genesis to the Apocalypse* (Westminster, Md.: Newman Press, 1962), 126, 141. See also, Lane, *Hebrews 9-13*, Word Biblical Commentary 47b (Nashville: Thomas Nelson Publishers, 1991), 266: "In the sacrifice of his body on the cross, Christ freely and fully made the will of God his own . . . and eradicated the disparity between sacrifice and obedience presupposed by Psalm 40:6-8. Christ's self-sacrifice fulfilled the human vocation enunciated in the psalm. By virtue of the fact that he did so under the conditions of authentic human, bodily existence and in solidarity with the human family, the new people of God have been radically transformed and consecrated to his service."

[59] See for instance, Carroll Stuhlmueller, *Creative Redemption in Deutero-Isaiah*, Analecta Biblica 43 (Rome: Biblical Institute Press, 1970); F. Ninow, *Indicators of Typology within the Old Testament: The Exodus Motif* (New York: Peter Lang, 2001); Dale C. Allison, Jr., *The New Moses: A Matthean Typology* (Minneapolis: Augsburg-Fortress Press, 1993); Rikki E. Watts, *Isaiah's New Exodus in Mark* (Grand Rapids: Baker Academic, 2000); J. Manek, "The New Exodus in the Books of Luke," *Novum Testamentum* 2 (1958): 8-23; T. F. Glasson, Moses in the Fourth Gospel (Naperville, Ill.: A. R. Allenson, 1963); Stan Harstine, *Moses as a Character in the Fourth Gospel: A Study of Ancient Reading Techniques,* Journal for the Study of the New Testament Supplement Series 229 (Sheffield: Sheffield Academic Press, 2002); Andrew C. Brunson, *Psalm 118 in the Gospel of John: An Intertextual Study on the New Exodus Pattern in the Theology of John* (Tübingen: Mohr Siebeck, 2003); David W. Pao, *Acts and the Isaianic New Exodus* (Grand Rapids: Baker Academic, 2000); Sylvia C. Keesmaat, *Paul and His Story: (Re)-interpreting the Exodus Tradition,* Journal for the Study of the New Testament Supplement Series 181 (Sheffield: Sheffield Academic Press 1999); Mary Rose D'Angelo, *Moses in the Letter to the Hebrews*, Society of Biblical Literature Dissertation Series 42 (Missoula, Mont.: Scholars Press, 1979). See also the seminal work of Jean Danielou, S.J., *From Shadows to Reality: Studies in the Biblical Typology of the Fathers* (Westminster: The Newman Press, 1960), 153-228.

accepted that Jesus is presented as a "new Moses" in the gospels. His passion and death are described as an "exodus" (ἔξοδον Luke 9:31) in a transfiguration scene filled with allusions to the theophanies of the wilderness period. And his death on the cross is described as a paschal sacrifice—that is, in terms of the liturgical sacrifice commanded by God to be offered on the night before Israel's exodus. What the letters of Peter (1 Pet. 1:19) and Paul (1 Cor. 5:7) state explicitly—that Christ was the spotless, unblemished passover lamb—the Gospel of John details typologically.

Announced early in John's gospel as the lamb of God (John 1:29,36), Jesus at the end is condemned to death as "King of the Jews" near the hour when the passover lambs were traditionally slaughtered by the priests in the Temple (19:14). He dies as paschal lamb and king as well as high priest in John's typological account; this latter fact is stressed by the odd detail of Jesus' seamless tunic, similar to that worn by Israel's high priest (19:23; Exod. 28:4; 39:27; Lev. 16:4). Before the first exodus, Moses sprinkled the blood of the paschal lamb on the door posts of the Israelites' homes using a hyssop branch. And in the final moments before the new exodus, a hyssop branch is offered to Jesus on the cross (19:29; Exod. 12:22; see also, Heb. 9:18-20). Finally, the soldiers do not break Jesus' legs because, as John states directly, the paschal lamb was to remain unblemished (19:33, 36; Exod. 2:46).

The effect of John's typology, reflected too in the letters of Paul, Peter and Hebrews and in John's Apocalypse (Rev. 5:6,9; 7:17; 12:1; 15:3), is to present the crucifixion as a liturgical sacrifice. As the first exodus is preceded by the institution of a liturgical memorial, by which Israelites would annually celebrate their establishment as a people of God, so too Christ institutes a memorial of his exodus in the Eucharist.

This typological reading of a new exodus and a new passover is hardly contested. It is also generally accepted that the New Testament writers present the sacraments of baptism and the Eucharist as means by which Christian believers are joined to the new exodus. Baptism is prefigured by the Israelites' passage through the Red Sea, the Eucharist prefigured by the manna and the water from the rock in the desert (1 Cor. 10:1-4; John 6). But a critical aspect of the typology is largely unnoticed in the literature—how the New Testament writers appropriate the Old Testament understanding of the *purpose* for the exodus. As we saw, God's liberation of Israel was ordered to a very specific end—namely, the establishment of Israel as God's royal and priestly people destined to glorify him among the nations.

Echoes of that exodus purpose are clearly heard in Zechariah's canticle at the outset of Luke's Gospel (1:67-79): Mindful of his covenant (Luke 1:73; Exod. 2:24), God has raised up a "horn," the royal son promised to David (Luke 1:69; Ps. 132:17), who will be a new Moses to deliver Israel from the "hand of" its enemies (Luke 1:73; Exod. 3:8) so that it may "serve" God (Luke 1:74; Exod. 3:12; 7:16). The canticle resounds with images and language drawn from the exodus account and from the prophets' and psalmists' hopes for a new deliverance.[60] The goal of this new liberation, as Zechariah sings it, is precisely that of the first exodus—to establish Israel as children of the covenant made with their fathers, as a holy and righteous people that worships in God's presence. Luke even employs here the specific term for the covenant "service" (λατρεύω Luke 1:74) that God intended for Israel.[61]

In 1 Peter, we encounter a rich passage (1 Pet. 1:13-20; 2:1-10) in which the exodus themes are applied to the newly baptized.[62] They are told to "gird up the loins," as the Israelites did on the night of their flight (Exod. 12:11). Peter says they have been "ransomed" (λυτρόω 1 Pet. 1:18), using the same word used to describe Israel's deliverance (Exod. 15:13), by the blood of a spotless unblemished lamb (Exod. 12:5). Their lives are described as a sojourning like that of Israel in the wilderness; they too are fed with spiritual food as the Israelites drank living water from the rock in the desert.

Finally, this passage of 1 Peter culminates with the explicit declaration that the Church is the new Israel—"a chosen race, a royal priesthood, a holy nation." This direct quotation from the Septuagint translation of Exodus 19:6 is joined to a quote from an Isaianic new exodus text that foresees the world-missionary dimension of Israel's royal and priestly vocation as "the people whom I formed for myself, *that they might announce my praise*" (1 Pet. 2:9-10; Isa. 43:21).

The New Priestly Kingdom

Christ's new exodus is ordered to the establishment of the priestly kingdom that God intended in the first exodus. This is the clear literary sense of the New Testament read canonically. It can be traced in the gospels, the epistles, Acts and Revelation. This understanding is enriched by another type found

---

[60] See the review of "scriptural metaphors derived from the exodus" in Joel B. Green, *The Gospel of Luke* (Grand Rapids, Mich.: Wm. B. Eerdmans Publishing, 1997), 110-120.

[61] See Deut. 11:13. In the Septuagint, λατρεύω routinely translates עבד, which, as discussed above, means "to serve or worship [God] cultically, especially by sacrifice." David Mathewson, *A New Heaven and a New Earth: The Meaning and Function of the Old Testament in Revelation* 21:1-22:5, Journal for the Study of the New Testament Supplement Series 238 (Sheffield: Sheffield Academic Press, 2003), 205-206. See also Fitzmyer's conclusion: "The infinitive latreuein, 'to worship' expresses the consequence of the deliverance brought about by Yahweh for his people, expected to result in a way of life that is really a cultic service of him. Though it denotes acts of worship, it is used analogously of the entire way in which the chosen people was to conduct itself." *The Gospel According to Luke*, 1:385. Green, too, sees Zechariah prophesying a new exodus for the same reasons as the first exodus: "This is precisely the purpose of the Exodus. . . . 'To serve' or 'to worship' is used to clarify the nature of the redeemed people, a community whose practices were to be formed in their worship of the Lord God. Thus, the freedom to worship without fear refers to much more than spiritual or cultic practices. Worship or service embraces the whole way of communal life of those who have been delivered." *The Gospel of Luke*, 117.

[62] On this passage, see Danielou, *From Shadows to Reality*, 162-164.

in the New Testament writings—that of the Church as the restored kingdom or house of David. Jesus is portrayed throughout the New Testament as the son of David anticipated in the Old Testament, a priest-king according to the order of Melchizedek.[63] The Church, heir of the royal priestly sonship of Israel, is said to participate in the heavenly high priesthood and royal sonship of Christ.

The redemptive work of Christ is described as priestly. It brings about "purification from sins," Hebrews tells us in language drawn from the Old Testament purification rites (καθαρισμός Heb. 1:3).[64] Through his priestly work, Christ "consecrated" believers (ἁγιάζω) Heb. 2:10; 10:10), as previously God consecrated the Israelites (Exod. 31:13; Lev. 20:8; 21:15; Ezek. 20:12; 37:28). The Christian life is depicted as a living out of this priestly consecration. The believer, Hebrews says, has been consecrated and purified "in order to serve (λατρεύειν) the living God" (Heb. 9:14; 12:28).

The Christian life is seen as a priestly self-sacrificial offering, a worship in the Spirit in which each believer, beginning in baptism, participates personally in Christ's paschal sacrifice (Rom. 6:3; Gal. 3:27). As envisioned in the New Testament, the service to be rendered by the "holy priesthood" of all the faithful is one of offering "spiritual sacrifices acceptable to God through Jesus Christ" (1 Pet. 2:5). Believers are to "present [their] bodies as a living sacrifice, holy and acceptable to God" (Rom. 12:1). In other words, they are to dedicate their whole selves to God, to surrender their wills totally to the will of God.[65] Speaking in the sacrificial vocabulary of the Temple, Paul urges the Philippians to live as "children of God without

---

[63] See Scott W. Hahn, "Kingdom and Church: From Davidic Christology to Kingdom Ecclesiology in Luke-Acts," in *Reading Luke*, eds. Craig Bartholomew, et al. (Grand Rapids, Mich.: Zondervan, 2005); also Hahn, *Kinship by Covenant*, 592-593; Brian M. Nolan, *The Royal Son of God: The Christology of Matthew 1-2 in the Setting of the Gospel*, Orbis Biblicus et Orientalis 23 (Fribourg: University of Fribourg, 1979); Mark L. Strauss, *The Davidic Messiah in Luke-Acts: The Promise and Its Fulfillment in Lukan Christology*, Journal for the Study of the New Testament Supplement Series 110 (Sheffield: Sheffield Academic Press, 1995).

[64] Compare Exod. 29:37; 30:10; Lev. 16:19; 2 Pet. 1:9. See the discussion in Lane, *Hebrews* 1-8, 15.

[65] On this theme in the letters of Paul, see the excellent analysis of Raymond Corriveau, C.Ss.R., *The Liturgy of Life: A Study in the Thought of St. Paul in His Letters to the Early Christian Communities*, Studia Travaux de Recherche 25 (Brusells: Desclée De Brouwer, 1970). See also, Ernest Best, "Spiritual Sacrifice: General Priesthood in the New Testament," *Interpretation* 14 (1960): 273-299. Charles C. Eastwood, *The Royal Priesthood of the Faithful: An Investigation of the Doctrine from Biblical Times to the Reformation* (Minneapolis: Augsburg, 1963); John H. Elliott, *The Elect and the Holy: An Exegetical Examination of 1 Peter 2:4-10 and the Phrase 'Basileion ierateuma'* Novum Testamentum Supplement Series 12 (Leiden: E.J. Brill, 1966); D. Hill, "To Offer Spiritual Sacrifices...(1 Pet. 2:5): Liturgical Formulations and Christian Paranesis in 1 Peter," *Journal for the Study of the New Testament* 16 (1982): 45-63; Eduard Schweizer, "The Priesthood of All Believers: 1 Peter 2:1-10," in *Worship, Theology and Ministry in the Early Church: Essays in Honor of Ralph P. Martin*, eds. M. Wilkins and T. Paige, Journal for the Study of the New Testament Supplement Series 87 (Sheffield: Sheffield Academic Press,1992), 285-293; Thomas F. Torrance, *Royal Priesthood* (Edinburgh: T.&T. Clark, 1955).

blemish" (ἄμωμα Phil. 2:15) and exhorts them in the "sacrifice and liturgy of [their] faith" (τῇ θυσίᾳ καί λειτουργίᾳ τῆς πίστεως ὑμῶν Phil. 2:17). Life itself is here seen as liturgy (λειτουργίᾳ), with Paul adopting the Septuagint word for the ritual worship of God—λατρεύειν—to define the Christian way of life.[66]

The highest expression of this liturgy of life is seen in believers' participation in the cosmic liturgy, the worship in heaven mediated by the high priest Christ. The Eucharist was the "heavenly gift" tasted by those who have "once been enlightened" in baptism (Heb. 6:4). Hebrews describes the Eucharist as a "festal gathering" celebrated by the "church of the firstborn" (ἐκκλεσίᾳ πρωτοτόκων) with the angels on "Mount Zion . . . the city of the living God, the heavenly Jerusalem." In this liturgy in the heavenly sanctuary, the true celebrant is "Jesus, the mediator a new covenant" made in his "sprinkled blood" on the cross (Heb. 12:18-24). The language here again is thick with references to the Old Testament, most pointedly to the covenant theophanies of God at Sinai.[67]

The liturgy of the new covenant, the Eucharist, forms the pattern of life for the firstborn of the new family of God. Like the liberated Israelites, they no longer serve as slaves but as sons. By joining themselves sacramentally to the sacrifice of Christ, the sons and daughters were to offer themselves "through him" as a continual "sacrifice of praise" (Heb. 13:15).[68] The offering of spiritual sacrifices is not only something that Christians *do*—it is of the very substance of their being; it is *who* they are. Nowhere is this more evident than in the frequent descriptions of the Church as a spiritual house or temple and of believers as living temples (1 Cor. 3:16-17; 6:19-20; Eph. 2:21-22; 1 Pet. 2:4-6). The symbolism expressed here marks an unexpected fulfillment of the old covenant's liturgical anthropology—where once God dwelt in a tent, an ark, and a temple, now he has made his dwelling place in the hearts of all who serve him in the liturgy of their lives.

---

[66] See, for example, Acts 24:14; 27:23; Rom. 1:9; 2 Tim. 1:3. See Corriveau, *The Liturgy of Life*, 141-142.

[67] Of course, many recent commentators reject the earliest interpreters of Hebrews and deny that there are Eucharistic references either here or elsewhere in the letter. I am persuaded otherwise. See Hahn, *Kinship by Covenant*, 624-629.

[68] The expression "sacrifice of praise" in Hebrews 3:15 quotes the promise of Psalm 49:14. The phrase δι' αὐτοῦ "through him" was apparently used in the ancient Christian liturgy much as it is used in the Roman liturgy today. Lane, *Hebrews 9-13*, 549.

The Liturgical Consummation of the Canon

The New Testament also depicts the Church fulfilling the mission of Israel—to gather all nations to Zion to offer spiritual sacrifices of praise to God.[69] This is the vision we see in the Bible's last book. John's Apocalypse is a liturgical book. The literary evidence clearly indicates that the book was intended to be read in the liturgy, most likely in the celebration of the Eucharist "on the Lord's day," (Rev. 1:10).[70] The Apocalypse is also a book "about" liturgy. What is unveiled is nothing less than the liturgical reality of creation and the liturgical consummation of human history in Christ. The vision John sees is that of a Eucharistic kingdom, in which angels and holy men and women worship ceaselessly around the altar and throne of God. The vision even unfolds in liturgical fashion, in a series of hymns, exhortations, antiphons and other cultic forms.[71]

Jesus, described throughout the book as "the Lamb," with obvious reference to the lamb of the Passover,[72] brings about a new exodus.[73] Many commentators have noted this, even pointing out the correspondences between the "plagues" inflicted on Pharaoh and the chalices or vials poured out in Revelation. I want to focus on the "end" toward which this new exodus is ordered. In this final book of the canon, we see the fulfillment of the canon's first book: in the new heaven and new earth, the new Jerusalem

---

[69] Wells, *God's Holy People*, 243.

[70] On the liturgical structure of the book, see Vanni, "Liturgical Dialogue as a Literary Form in the Book of Revelation," and Ulfgard, *Feast and Future*.

[71] Gloer, "Worship God! Liturgical Elements in the Apocalypse," at 38-40.

[72] Rev. 5:6,12,13; 6:1,16; 7:9,10,14; 7:17; 12:11;13:8,11; 14:1,4,10; 15:3; 17:14; 19:7,9; 21:9,14,22,23,27; 22:1,3.

[73] On the new exodus typology in Revelation, see Mathews, *A New Heaven and a New Earth*, 62-64. See B. Anderson, "Exodus Typology in Second Isaiah," in *Israel's Prophetic Heritage: Essays in Honor of James Muilenburg*, ed. B. Anderson and W. Harrelson (London: SCM Press, 1962), 177-195; J.S. Casey, "Exodus Typology in the Book of Revelation" (Ph.D. thesis, Southern Baptist Theological Seminary, 1981).

of Revelation, the brethren of the new Adam worship as priests and rule as kings, and the entire universe is revealed to have become a vast divine temple.[74]

This cosmic temple, this new Jerusalem, is revealed to be the body of Christ, the Lamb that was slain (Rev. 21:22). This theme is found throughout the New Testament: Christ's body—destroyed by crucifixion and restored three days later in the resurrection—is the new temple (John 2:18-22; 4:21,23). John's Gospel depicts Jesus' body as the new tabernacle, the new locus of divine presence on earth.[75] Jesus has "pitched a tent" or "tabernacled" (σκηνόω John 1:14) among us, John writes, choosing a word associated in the Septuagint with God's presence dwelling in the tabernacle (Exod. 25:8-9; Zech. 2:10; Joel 3:17; Ezek. 43:7). This theme too has been widely studied. But reading the canonical text liturgically we can see the deeper meaning of this imagery—what God desired in the beginning he has finally brought about at the end of the ages. The divine presence now fills the temple of creation, and God dwells with his people in a covenant relationship that is described in Revelation (21:3)—as in Genesis—in both sabbatical (21:25; 22:5) and nuptial (19:9) terms.[76]

Gathered together into this new paradise, those redeemed by the blood of the Lamb make up a priestly kingdom, as John sees it, quoting God's commission to Israel in Exodus 19:6 (Rev. 1:6; 5:10). But in this new kingdom, the children of Abraham reign with people from every tribe, tongue, and nation (Rev. 5:9; 7:9). Jesus is the "firstborn" of this new family of God, the prophesied root and offspring of David (Rev. 22:16; 3:7) in whom all are made divine sons and daughters of God (Rev. 21:7)—royal sons and priests who will rule with him until the end of ages (Rev. 20:6).

---

[74] For the themes of the new Jerusalem, the new Temple, the new covenant, the new Israel and the new creation in Revelation, see William J. Dumbrell, *The End of the Beginning: Revelation 21-22 and the Old Testament* (Grand Rapids, Mich.: Baker Book House, 1985).

[75] See most recently, Alan R. Kerr, *The Temple of Jesus's Body: The Temple Theme in the Gospel of John*, Journal for the Study of the New Testament Supplement Series, 220. (Sheffield: Sheffield Academic Press, 2002); Mary L. Coloe, *God Dwells with Us: Temple Symbolism in the Fourth Gospel* (Collegeville, Minn.: Liturgical Press, 2001); Raymond E. Brown, *The Gospel According to John,* 2 vols. (Garden City: Doubleday, 1966), 2:32-34.

[76] "The Temple, as symbol of access to the divine presence, is replaced by the Presence itself." C. Deutsch, "Transformation of Symbols: The New Jerusalem in Rev. 21:1-22:5," *Zeitschrift fur die neutestamentliche Wissenschaft* 78 (1987): 106-126. "The dwelling of God with humanity is part of a fuller evocation and transformation, in Rev. 21:3, of the covenant relationship between God and Israel in which God affirms that he is their God and they are his people. Stretching back to the promise to Abraham (Gen. 17:6), affirmed in the context of the exodus (Exod. 6:7; 29:45; Lev. 26:12,45), and again as part of the hope of post-exilic restoration (Ezek. 37:27), this relationship has been implicit in the worship of the people of God recorded in Rev. 7:10,12; 19:1; and is here made explicit." Stephen Pattemore, *The People of God in the Apocalypse: Discourse, Structure and Exegesis* Society for New Testament Studies Monograph Series 128 (Cambridge: Cambridge University, 2004), 201.

In the final pages of the Apocalypse, then, the human vocation given in the first pages of Genesis is fulfilled. Before the throne of God and the Lamb, the royal sons of God are shown worshipping him, gazing upon his face with his name written upon their foreheads, and reigning forever (Rev. 22:1-5). John chooses his words carefully here to evoke the Old Testament promises of God's intimate presence to those who serve him. The word rendered "worship" in most translations of Revelation 22:3 is λατρεύσουσιν. This, as we have seen, is the word used in the Septuagint to translate עבד— the Hebrew word that describes Adam's original vocation as well as the purpose of the exodus and conquest.[77]

Likewise, to "see God's face" has priestly and cultic overtones and may even be a technical term for liturgical worship. The expression is often used in cultic settings to describe the experience of worship in Israel's festivals, including the offering of sacrifice.[78] The name of God written on their foreheads appears to be a reference to the diadem worn by Aaron and succeeding high priests as they entered the Lord's presence in the sanctuary (Exod. 28:36-39; 39:30; Lev. 8:9). The diadem was inscribed with the words "Holy to the Lord" (קדש ליהוה).[79] In the final vision of God's face shedding light upon the people (Rev. 22:5), some scholars hear an allusion to the priestly blessing bestowed by the high priest at the end of the Temple liturgies (see Num. 6:24; Sir. 50:19-20; Ps. 118:27).[80]

At the conclusion of our liturgical reading of the canon, we hear the purpose and meaning of the entire Bible summed up in the refrain of the

---

[77] For the "purpose" of the exodus, see Exod. 3:12; 4:23; 7:16; 9:1,13; 10:3,7,8,24,26; 23:25. Mathews notes that λατρεύω is also used in Rev. 7:15-16 to denote the service of those who stand before the throne in the temple of God. "Thus, the cultic service, which was to be rendered by God's people, and which was the goal of the first exodus, is now fulfilled and carried out in the new Jerusalem where God's people approach the throne and render him worship." *A New Heaven and a New Earth,* 205-206.

[78] Mathews cites Exod. 23:15,17; 34:24; Deut. 16:16; 31:11; Isa. 1:12; Ps. 42:3: "The references from Exodus and Deuteronomy occur in the context of the celebration of Israel's festivals. In Isa. 1:12 the context is specifically the offering of sacrifices (v. 11) and 'beholding the face of God' in Psalm 42:2 is realized in connection with the temple (v. 4). According to Psalm 24:6, those who enter the sanctuary do so to 'seek the face of the God of Jacob.' Moreover, a similar phrase occurred in rabbinic literature (ראות פני שכינה) with reference to the presence of God in the Temple or synagogue. . . . Thus, the goal of cultic worship in the Old Testament is ultimately reached here with the saints serving God before his face." *A New Heaven and a New Earth,* 206-207.

[79] See the discussion in Mathews, *A New Heaven and a New Earth,* 208, n. 98. See also Rev. 7:3; 9:4.

[80] Mathews, *A New Heaven and a New Earth,* 211, notes that God's face shining on his people is "a common metaphor in the Old Testament for divine blessing and salvation (Pss. 4:6; 31:16; 44:3; 67:1; 80:3,7,19; 89:15; 119:135)."

Apocalypse: "Worship God!" (Rev. 14:7; 19:10; 22:9). The human person has been shown from the first pages of Genesis to the last of Revelation to be liturgical by nature, created and destined to live in the spiritual house of creation, as children of a royal and priestly family that offers sacrifices of praise to their Father-Creator with whom they dwell in a covenant of peace and love.[81]

The Bible's Liturgical Trajectory and Teleology

Our liturgical reading of the canonical text reveals a clear liturgical *trajectory* and *teleology*. The story of the Bible is the story of humankind's journey to true worship in spirit and truth in the presence of God. That is the trajectory, the direction toward which narrative leads. This true worship is revealed to be the very purpose of God's creation in the beginning. That is the *teleology* revealed in the canonical text.

The trajectory of Scripture does not terminate with the closing of the final canonical book. The teleology of Scripture includes the proclamation of Scripture in the liturgy. For the believing community that composed, preserved, and continues to meditate upon the Scripture, its "story" continues in the liturgy. The liturgical worship of the new covenant, the Eucharist established by Christ, is at once a remembrance of the story told in Scripture and a gateway into that story.

The formal unity of Scripture and liturgy and the recovery of the canonical text's liturgical teleology and trajectory has important methodological implications for biblical scholarship. Indeed, I would argue that three interpretive imperatives arise from our liturgical reading. These imperatives, which I will consider under the headings *economy*, *typology*, and *mystagogy*, undergird the assumptions of the biblical authors and present themselves as crucial dimensions that must be understood for any authentic interpretation of the text.

The Unity of Scripture: The Divine Economy

Our liturgical reading highlights the importance of what ancient Church writers called "the divine economy"—that is, the divine order of history as presented in the canonical text. The biblical writers everywhere evince a belief in this economy. They see it unfolding in the sequence of covenants that God makes with his people—in creation, after the flood, with Abraham, at Sinai, with David, and finally with Christ.

---

[81] While Congar did not advance a liturgical reading of Scripture *per se*, this reading is anticipated throughout his *The Mystery of the Temple*, see especially, pp. 192; 245-248.

Throughout, the divine economy is presented as the motive for God's words and deeds in sacred Scripture.[82] The biblical writers understood the economy as part of "the mystery of his will, according to his purpose . . . a plan (οἰκονομίαν) for the fulness of time" (Eph. 1:9-10). In this the apostolic witness is faithful to the teaching of Christ, who is shown teaching them to see biblical history fulfilled in his life, death and resurrection (Luke 24:26-27, 44:47).

As we have seen, the liturgy of both the old and new covenants is founded on remembrance and celebration of God's saving words and deeds. Liturgy, then, as presented in the Scripture, is an expression of faith in the divine economy and a means by which believers gain participation in that economy.[83] The Scriptures themselves are regarded by the biblical authors as the divinely inspired testament to the divine economy as it has unfolded throughout history, culminating in the saving event of the cross.

It follows that if our interpretations are to be true to the integrity of the texts, we must pay close attention to this notion of God's economy. The economy gives the Bible its content and unity. The very term "economy" is richly suggestive for the exegete. It translates the Greek οἰκονομία which etymologically derives from οἶκος and νόμος—*household* and *law*. The divine economy is a kind of family law, the law of God's cosmic "household."

The image of God fathering his people runs throughout the Old Testament,[84] a tradition beautifully recapitulated in the teachings of Christ and the early Church.[85] Indeed, the New Testament describes the fatherhood of God and the adoption of all peoples through baptism as the "end" of God's salvific economy.[86] Again we see Scripture ordered to a liturgical consummation—the divine economy culminates "in the fulness of time" with the sending of God's Son and his Spirit, that all may be made adopted children in the sacramental liturgy of baptism.[87]

---

[82] For explanations of God's words and deeds in light of a divine covenant plan, see Exod. 2:24; 6:5; 33:1; Num. 32:11; Deut. 1:8; 9:5; 30:20; 2 Sam. 7:8,10,11, 22-25; 1 Chron. 16:14-18; Jer. 31:31-37; 33:14-26; Luke 1:46-55, 68-79; Acts 2:14-36; 3:12-26; 7:1-51; 11:34-43; 13:16-41.

[83] The purpose of Christian liturgy, says I. H. Dalmais, O.P. is "to express man's *faith* in the divine economy and perpetuate the living effects of the incarnation." *Introduction to the Liturgy*, trans. Roger Capel (Baltimore: Helicon, 1961), 27. See also Jean Danielou, S.J., "The Sacraments and the History of Salvation," in *Liturgy and the Word of God*, Papers given at the Third National Congress of the *Centre de Pastorale Liturgique* (Collegeville, Minn.: Liturgical Press, 1959), 21-32, at 29: "The object of faith is the existence of a divine plan."

[84] See, for example, Exod. 4:22; Deut. 1:31; 32:6; Pss. 89:26; 103:13; Isa. 63:14; 64:8; Hos. 11:1, etc.

[85] For example, Matt. 5:44-45, 48; 7:11.

[86] Rom. 4:11-18; 8:14-23; 2 Cor. 6:2, 161-8; Gal. 3:7-9; 26-29.

[87] Gal. 4:4-6.

This further suggests that the exegete be sensitive to the economy's unfolding according to a divine "fatherly" plan. In this, the interpreter will do well to pay particular attention to what rabbinic and early Church authors described as patterns of divine "condescension" and "accommodation"—God "stooping down" to communicate with his children through words and actions they can readily understand.[88]

The Typological Pattern

The divine economy is comprehended and explained in Scripture through a distinct way of reading and writing that originates in the canonical text and is carried over into the living tradition of the faith community that gives us these texts. We characterize this way of reading and writing broadly as *typology*.

The literature on biblical typology (from the Greek τύπος; see Rom. 5:14; 1 Pet. 3:21) is extensive.[89] What is important for our purposes is to acknowledge the pervasiveness of typological patterns of exegesis in both the Old and New Testaments.[90] We saw this in our overview of the canonical text. To recall but a few examples: The world's creation was portrayed in light of the later building of the tabernacle. The tabernacle in turn was described as a "new creation." Jesus' death and resurrection are seen as a new passover and a new exodus. The Christian sacramental life is illuminated by the exodus event.

These are not mere literary tropes for the biblical authors. The extensive use of typology reflects a profound biblical "worldview." If the economy gives narrative unity to the canonical Scriptures, fashioning them into a single story, typology helps us to understand the full meaning of that

---

[88] See, generally, Stephen D. Benin, *The Footprints of God: Divine Accommodation in Jewish and Christian Thought* (Albany: State University of New York Press, 1993); Second Vatican Council, Dogmatic Constitution on Divine Revelation, *Dei Verbum* (1965), no. 13; Among the Church fathers, see Origen, *Homilies on Jeremiah*, 18.4; St. John Chrysostom, *Homilies on Genesis*, 17:1.

[89] See J. D. Dawson, *Christian Figural Reading and the Fashioning of Identity* (Berkeley: University of California Press, 2002); Christopher R. Seitz, *Figured Out: Typology and Providence in Christian Scripture* (Louisville: Westminster/John Knox, 2001); G. W. Buchanan, *Typology and the Gospel* (New York: University Press of America, 1984); Leonhard Goppelt, *Typos: The Typological Interpretation of the Old Testament in the New*, trans. Donald H. Madvig (Grand Rapids, Mich.: Wm. B. Eerdmans, 1982).

[90] See, for example, Benjamin D. Sommer, *A Prophet Reads Scripture: Allusion in Isaiah 40-66* (Stanford, Calif.: Stanford University Press, 1998); J. Enz, "The Book of Exodus as Literary Type for the Gospel of John," *Journal of Biblical Literature* 76 (1957), 208-215; Michael Fishbane, *Biblical Interpretation In Ancient Israel* (Oxford: Oxford University Press, 1985). "The New Testament . . . did not invent typology, but simply showed that it was fulfilled in the person of Jesus of Nazareth." Jean Danielou, S.J., *The Bible and the Liturgy* (Notre Dame, Ind.: Notre Dame University Press, 1956), 5; see also Danielou, *The Lord of History*, trans. Nigel Abercrombie (New York: Meridian, 1968), 140.

story. It does this by a pattern of analogy or correspondences. What God will do in the future is expected to resemble or follow the pattern of what he has done in the past. What began in the Old Testament is fulfilled partially even within the Old Testament, but definitively in the New, in a way that is both transformative and restorative.

Recognition of this biblical worldview has important hermeneutical implications. The interpreter of the Bible enters into a dialogue with a book that is itself an exegetical dialogue—a complex and highly cohesive interpretive web in which the meaning of earlier texts is discerned in the later texts and in which later texts can only be understood in relation to ones that came earlier. In order to read the texts as they are written the exegete needs to acknowledge the authors' deep-seated belief in both the divine economy and in the typological expression of that economy. This is the teaching that the Scriptures themselves attribute to Christ. Words and deeds found in the Law, the prophets, and the Psalms, are signs that find fulfillment in him (Luke 24:44).

From our liturgical reading, we see that three moments in the economy of salvation stand out as having decisive typological significance for the entire canonical text—creation, the exodus, and the Davidic kingdom.[91] These in turn should have special significance for the exegete. The first Adam is not only a living being but a type of the new Adam, the life-giving Spirit who is to come (Rom. 5:14; 1 Cor. 15:45). The exodus is more than an event in the life of Israel. It is a sign of the future liberation of all peoples by the cross of Jesus. Solomon is not only a historical leader of Israel, the son of David. He is a sign of a "greater than Solomon"—the Son of David who is to come.

We must remain mindful that the foundation of all authentic biblical typology is the historical and literary sense of the text. Typology is not an arbitrary eisegesis. For the biblical authors, God uses historical events, persons, and places as material and temporal symbols or signs of future events and divine realities. The prophets can speak of a "new exodus" only because they presuppose the historical importance of the original exodus. The exegete must see the literal and historical sense as fundamental to his or her approach to Scripture.

Mystagogy: Living the Scripture's Mysteries

The final hermeneutical imperative that emerges from our liturgical reading is *mystagogy*. From the Greek, mystagogy means "doctrine of the mysteries." Mystagogy recognizes that the same typological patterns by which the divine economy is comprehended in Scripture continue in the Church's sacramental liturgy.

---

[91] For just a few of the citations, see the prophets' announcement of a new creation (Isa. 4:5; 65:17; 66:22; Jer. 31:35-36; Ezek. 36:8-11), a *new exodus* (Isa. 51:9-11; Jer. 16:14-15; Ezek. 29:3-5), and a *new kingdom* (Isa. 9:2-7; Jer. 23:5-6; Ezek. 34:23-24).

As we noted at the start of this paper, the canon was a liturgical enactment—the Scriptures come to us as the authoritative texts to be used in Christian teaching and worship. But as it was written and passed on to us, Scripture has more than an instructional or exhortative function. When proclaimed in the Church's liturgy, Scripture is intended to "actualize" what is proclaimed—to bring the believer into living contact with the *mirabilia Dei*, the mighty saving works of God in the Old and New Testament.

Mystagogy focuses our attention on the deep connection between the written "Word of God"—the Scripture itself—and the creative Word of God described in the pages of the Old and New Testaments. From the first pages to the last, we see expressed the biblical authors' faith that God's Word is living and active and possesses the power to bring into being what it commands. Creation, as seen in Scripture, is the work of the Word.[92] The early Christians identified this Word as Jesus.[93] The apostolic preaching was depicted as a "ministry of the Word" (Acts 6:4). The divine Word, experienced in the apostolic Church, had such efficacy that it could literally raise the dead (Acts 9:36-41).

The Church's traditional understanding of the sacramental liturgy is built on this belief in the performative power of the Word of God as a "divine speech act."[94] Proclaimed sacramentally and accompanied by the ritual washing of water, the Word brings the Spirit upon people, making them sons and daughters of God through a real sharing in his life, death and resurrection (Rom. 6:3; Gal. 4:6; 1 Pet. 1:23). Proclaimed as

---

[92] See, for instance, Pss. 32:9; 148:5; Isa. 55:10-11; 2 Pet. 3:5; Louis Bouyer, "The Word of God in Israel," in *The Meaning of Sacred Scripture* (South Bend, Ind.: University of Notre Dame Press, 1958), 1-14; "The Word of God and the Berakah," in *Eucharist: Theology and Spirituality of the Eucharistic Prayer* (Notre Dame, Ind.: University of Notre Dame, 1968), 29-49. Lucien Deiss, C.S.Sp., *God's Word and God's People* (Collegeville, Minn.: Liturgical Press, 1974), xvii: "The word of God is all-powerful and possesses a sovereign efficacy. God speaks and the universe exists; he commands and all things come into being. Wherever he sends his word, it acts as a messenger empowered by him and everywhere accomplishes its mission in an irresistible way."

[93] John 1:1-3; Rev. 19:13. For the efficacy of "the Word" in the New Testament, see Craig A. Evans, *Word and Glory: On the Exegetical and Theological Background of John's Prologue* Journal for the Study of the Old Testament Supplement Series 305 (Sheffield: Sheffield Academic Press, 1993); "The Agent of the New Exodus: The Word of God," in Pao, *Acts and the Isaianic New Exodus*, 147-180; Yun Lak Chung, " 'The Word of God' in Luke-Acts: A Study in Lukan Theology" (Ph.D. diss., Emory University, 1995); Leo O' Reilly, *Word and Sign in the Acts of the Apostles: A Study in Lucan Theology* Analecta Gregoriana, 243 (Rome: Editrice Pontificia Universita Gregoriana, 1987); Jerome Kodell, " 'The Word of God Grew: The Ecclesial Tendency of Λόγος in Acts 6:7; 12:24; 19:20," *Biblica* 55 (1974): 505-519.

[94] On divine speech acts, see T. Ward, *Word and Supplement: Speech Acts, Biblical Texts and the Sufficiency of Scripture* (New York: Oxford University Press, 2002); R. S. Briggs, *Words in Action: Speech Act Theory and Biblical Interpretation* (Edinburgh: T&T Clark, 2001); Kevin Vanhoozer, "From Speech Acts to Scripture Acts: The Covenant Discourse and the Discourse of the Covenant," in Craig Bartholomew, et. al., *After Pentecost: Language and Biblical Interpretation* (Grand Rapids, Mich.: Zondervan Press, 2001), 1-49.

commanded in the Eucharistic liturgy, the Word brings about true participation in the one body and blood of Christ (1 Cor. 10:16-17). The Word in the sacramental liturgy continues the work of the Word in Scripture. This pattern, too, is shown originating in the pages of Scripture. The interpretation of Scripture is ordered to the celebration of baptism (Acts 8:29-38) and the Eucharist (Luke 24:27-31). The New Testament also gives us numerous passages in which the sacraments are explained "typologically" that is, according to events and figures in the Old Testament (1 Cor. 10; 1 Pet. 3:20-21). This paschal catechesis is at the heart of what early Church writers called *mystagogy*.[95]

At a minimum, then, our interpretations of Scripture must respect the mystagogic content of the New Testament. In this exegetes will do well to recall that the sacramental liturgy afforded the first interpretive framework for the Scriptures. But on a deeper level, the exegete must appreciate the *mystagogic intent* of the Bible. The exegete must always be conscious that the Word he or she interprets is written and preserved for the purpose of leading believers to the sacramental liturgy where they are brought into a covenant relationship with God.[96]

Toward a Liturgical Hermeneutic

I believe that, as a natural outgrowth of the past century's scientific exegesis of the Bible, we are prepared for the development of a new hermeneutic. It is a hermeneutic that will reflect the last century's fundamental rediscovery of Scripture's liturgical sense as expressed in the formal and material unity of Scripture and liturgy. This formal and material unity—Scripture being both *for* and *about* liturgy—necessitates a new biblical-theological reading of the canonical text, a reading that I have tried to sketch in this paper. As we have seen, this reading has the potential to offer extraordinary unitive, explanatory, and interpretive power. Further, it suggests certain

---

[95] See, generally, Enrico Mazza, *Mystagogy: A Theology of Liturgy in the Patristic Age* (New York: Pueblo Publishing Co., 1989).

[96] "The sacraments are simply the continuation in the era of the Church of God's acts in the Old Testament and the New. This is the proper significance of the relationship between the Bible and the liturgy. The Bible is a sacred history; the liturgy is a sacred history. . . . [The sacraments] are the divine acts corresponding to this particular era in the history of salvation, the era of the Church. . . . The sacramental acts are, therefore, only saving actualizations of the passion and resurrection of Christ." Jean Danielou, "The Sacraments and the History of Salvation," 28,31. See also J.A. DiNoia, O.P. and Bernard Mulcahy, O.P., "The Authority of Scripture in Sacramental Theology: Some Methodological Observations," *Pro Ecclesia* 10 (2001), 329-345, at 330: "The sacramental economy is a divine arrangement . . . by which grace is given by God in virtue of the passion, death, and resurrection of Christ. It is a divine provision which . . . employs or deploys the natural signification of things, actions and words to the divine end of bringing us progressively closer to the triune God and closer to one another in the triune God."

exegetical imperatives—concern for the principles of economy, typology, and mystagogy—that arise integrally from a liturgical reading of Scripture.

These principles, along with a biblical-theological reading of the canonical text that illuminates Scripture's liturgical trajectory and teleology, are the foundations for a hermeneutic that is at once literary and historical, liturgical and sacramental. As I hope this paper has suggested, this hermeneutic is capable of integrating the contributions of historical and literary research while at the same time respecting the traditional meanings given to the Bible by the believing community in which the Bible continues to serve as the source and wellspring of faith and worship.

What is emerging is a *liturgical hermeneutic.* It is an interpretive method that recognizes the liturgical content and "mission" of the Bible—its mystagogic purpose in bringing about, through the sacramental liturgy, the communion of believers with the God who has chosen to reveal himself in Scripture. It is, then, a hermeneutic that grasps the profound union of the divine Word incarnate in Christ, inspired in Scripture, and proclaimed in the Church's sacramental liturgy.

Much work remains to be done. But, I believe this understanding of Scripture has great potential to renew the study of the Bible from the heart of the Church. Reading Scripture liturgically, we will find no tension between letter and spirit, between the literary and historical analysis of Scripture and the faithful contemplation of its religious and spiritual meaning.

Rediscovering St. Thomas Aquinas as Biblical Theologian

• Christopher T. Baglow •

Our Lady of Holy Cross College, New Orleans

It is necessary to begin by asserting a well-established fact: St. Thomas Aquinas sees a unity between sacred Scripture and sacred doctrine.[1]

My purpose in this short note is to suggest that Thomas's basic insight—as articulated in his theological writings and modeled in his own exegetical work—has promising implications for modern biblical scholarship and exegesis.

For Thomas, Scripture and doctrine are phases in the broader dynamism of God's revelation of himself to humanity. In the *Summa Theologiae* (I,I,3), he declares that sacred doctrine is a single science because sacred Scripture has a single formal object—namely, divine revelation. That he moves from articles dealing with issues of sacred doctrine to articles regarding sacred Scripture without beginning a new *quaestio* may be the most compelling proof of their unity in his mind. Even God's knowledge and God's will get distinct *quaestiones* in the *Summa*—yet not so sacred Scripture and sacred doctrine.

Perhaps this is because the distinction between the two is much less important for Thomas than the fact that the two derive from the true center and source of all revelation—the divine Son of God.

In his commentary on John 14:6 ("I am the way, and the truth and the life"), Thomas notes that the divine person of the Son, being both man and God, is both the way for humanity and its end, or goal (*terminus*). This insight he finds signified by John's use of the words *via* and *veritas*.[2] Thus, the incarnational pattern described by John provides a wonderful analogy for understanding scriptural revelation for Thomas. As human words, the words of Scripture are a way by which the human mind can traverse to

---

[1] This has been observed by innumerable scholars. For a classic explanation of this point, see J. Van der Ploeg, "The Place of Holy Scripture in the Theology of St. Thomas," *The Thomist* 10 (1947): 410-413. For Thomas on the relation of Scripture and sacred doctrine, see for example, *I Scriptum super libros Sententiarum*, Prol., 1, 1-5; *Quaestiones de quodlibet*, 7, 14-16; *Super Epistolam ad Galatas*, 4:24 [252-54], *Quaestiones disputata de potentia*, 4.1; *Exposito super librum Boethii de trinitate*, Praef., 2.1-4.

[2] *Super Evangelium S. Ioannis Lectura*, 14:5-6 [1865-1872]. For an analysis of revelation as it is treated in this passage and elsewhere, see A. Blanco, "Word and Truth in Divine Revelation: A Study of the Commentary of St. Thomas Aquinas on John 14:6," in L. Elders, ed., *La Doctrine de la Thomas d'Aquin tenu a Rolduc, les 4 et 5 Novembre 1989* (Vatican City: Libreria Editrice Vaticana, 1990), 27-48.

understanding. But because they are at the same time divine speech, these human words become also the medium by which divine truth and salvation are communicated to us.

Scripture participates in this pattern of the incarnation, by which God reveals the truth about himself and makes a way to himself. Yet so also does doctrine. Hence, scriptural revelation cannot be broken away or separated from the later articulations of revelation in doctrine. To do so would be tantamount to separating Christ's presence in human history in his life and death from his ongoing presence to the Church in his resurrection.

We come to know and experience Christ's presence in the Church gradually, by progressive stages that always begin with reflection on Christ's saving presence in history. In the same way, we come to know the proper articulation of the truths of faith through a reflection on Scripture—a reflection in which those truths are identified, crystallized, and made foundational.

As Thomas says in the introduction to his *Compendium Theologiae* (in reference to the creed), "that which he handed down clearly and expansively in the various volumes of sacred Scripture for those eager to learn, for those with little leisure he included the teaching concerning the salvation of humanity in a summary form." [3] In other words, the content of that "summary form"—sacred doctrine—is identical to the content of the more "expansive" teaching found in Scripture.

The 'Science' of Sacred Scripture

Therefore Scripture is fundamental to the science that is sacred doctrine. In fact, as we noted above, he gives both the name "science" (*scientia*).[4] But how can Scripture, which is so overwhelmingly narrative and event-oriented, be scientific in the way that theology is scientific—with its generally conceptual and expository nature? Thomas never poses the question. For him, Scripture is given "through the mode of teaching" (*per modum cuiusdam doctrinae*). That is, Scripture itself is *doctrinal*, a matter of teaching and instruction. Scripture is a science because it causes knowledge in those who read it, thereby fulfilling the formal definition of *scientia*.[5]

---

[3] *Compendium Theologiae*, I, 1. See also *Summa Theologiae*, II-II, 1,9, ad 1.

[4] *Summa Theologiae*, I, 1, 8.

[5] See *Scriptum super libros Sententiarum*, Prol. 1.1.; *Summa Theologiae*, II-II, 171, 6.

Yet this is not to say that Thomas neglects the immediacy of scriptural revelation as an encounter with God. Drawing conclusions from God's activity does not mean that the divine activity itself is neglected or ignored. To the contrary, in doctrine, the divine activity narrated in Scripture is appropriated in all its relevance for the Church. Thomas's own epistemology offers us, at least in part, the rationale for this position. Thomas says that when a person understands something, the thing understood itself is present in the one who understands, not simply a conceptual representation of that thing.

Therefore, the scriptural narratives of encounters and events demand a response from the believer since they are now part of the believer's understanding. To formulate doctrines is an extension of the believer's response to the encounter with God in reading Scripture. These doctrinal responses, when correct, bear the authority of Scripture itself, Thomas adds, "since the whole science [of Scripture/sacred doctrine] is contained virtually in its principles" (*cum tota scientia virtute contineatur in principiis*).[6]

But what is the process by which Scripture reaches its fruition in doctrine, by which doctrine reveals and realizes its fundamental identity with Scripture? Thomas never systematically answers this question. But it can be easily deduced from his writings that for him, doctrinal formulation and theological argumentation are first and foremost matters of hermeneutics. In accessing Scripture, as in any task of interpretation, there is a definite goal which is involved, namely that of understanding (*intelligere*).

Thomas turns often to the etymology of *intelligere* in his theory of interpretation. It is *intus legere*—"to read within," that is, to discover the essence of a thing (what Thomas often refers to as *quod quid est*) or to apprehend what a speaker or writer has intended.[7] In the case of Scripture, the interpreter seeks to understand the intention of the divine author. This, Thomas presumes, will require assistance on the part of God and his grace if the interpreter is to pierce through to the divine truth contained in the sacred page.

In addition, the interpreter, in trying to grasp not only individual truths but to make connections and draw insights between the multiple truths and insights found in Scripture, must respect the "aggregate" nature of the Scripture.

---

[6] *Summa Theologiae*, I. 1, 7. See L. Elders, "Aquinas on Holy Scripture as the Medium of Divine Revelation," in *La doctrine de la revelation divine de saint Thomas d'Aquin*, p. 135.

[7] T. F. Torrance, "Scientific Hermeneutics According to St. Thomas Aquinas," *Journal of Theological Studies* 13 (1962): 261.

'Canonicity' and 'Soteriological Purpose'

The principle of the "canonicity" of Scripture is fundamental to Thomas's approach to Scripture. For Thomas, Scripture has one "author," God, who works through the instrumentality of the many human authors of the individual books of Scripture. Because God is the "author" of all Scripture, any reflection on any single text must be read within "the canon"—the totality of the different sacred writings considered by the Church to be canonical.

After interpretation, the second part of the movement from sacred Scripture to sacred doctrine is *theological argumentation*, or what Thomas sometimes calls "the science of divine realities" (*scientia divina*).[8] This involves the use of one's intellectual powers, again with the assistance of grace, to comprehend the truths revealed in Scripture, for the purpose of drawing conclusions from those truths.

This process begins with faith—again, a gift of God. Faith enables us to grasp the primary truth of God revealed in the canon. In grasping this primary truth, we come to accept by faith other truths revealed in Scripture. These truths in turn become the first principles in what Thomas considers to be the science of sacred Scripture/sacred doctrine.

Despite its fundamental dependence on the supernatural origin of its principles, theological argumentation is truly a human science for Thomas. It relies on reason for its elucidation and development, makes use of logical argumentation, and even has recourse to philosophical authorities who do not begin with faith as the theologian does.[9] This science is essentially concerned with instruction, with the transmission of the truths revealed in Scripture. It is intended to culminate in the reception of these truths, first by the theological interpreter, but ultimately by the believer.

Through this science, which begins in Scripture, a body of sources of theological instruction develops which becomes authoritative, especially magisterial sources.[10] These sources, however, remain always subordinate to Scripture itself and in the service of an ever continuing quest for deeper understanding. Scripture always remains central. As Thomas claims:

---

[8] *Exposito super librum Boethii de trinitate*, Praef., 2,2.

[9] *Exposito super librum Boethii de trinitate*, Praef., 2,3.

[10] *Summa Theologiae*, II-II, 5,3, ad 2. See also E. Persson, *Sacra Doctrina: Reason and Revelation in Aquinas*, trans. R. Mackenzie (Philadelphia: Fortress Press, 1970), 70, who notes that for Thomas "the teaching of the Church is to be understood essentially as the interpretation of Scripture."

"Only the canonical scriptures are the standard of faith" (*sola canonica scriptura est regula fidei*).[11]

It is apparent, then, that Thomas's understanding of the process by which sacred doctrine is drawn from Scripture is based on certain fundamental presuppositions about Scripture itself. We saw above that he presumes Scripture to be of both divine and human authorship and that he presumes the canonical form of Scripture to be fundamental in interpretation.

Thomas also insists that the principles found in Scripture are not subject to proof because they are matters of faith and beyond the ability of the human mind to establish them. "This science," he says, "treats *chiefly* [italics mine] of those things which, by their sublimity, transcend human reason" (*ista scientia est principaliter de is quae sua altitudine rationem transcendunt*).[12]

Thomas acknowledges that there are other things and facts treated in Scripture—such as narrative, historical or geographical details—that do not transcend reason. These are not unimportant to Thomas. But he repeatedly affirms a *soteriological purpose* for Scripture. His writings clearly suggest that the doctrinal enterprise must give priority to identifying those saving truths, including the speculative and practical truths of morality, to which Scripture itself gives a central place. Details in Scripture that do not refer to God's action, message or designs, do not merit the theologian's attention *except* in reference to the central content of revelation—to those truths which have import for salvation.[13]

Thomas also presumes that there is an inexhaustible depth to the meaning of sacred Scripture—that Scripture has both a literal sense (*sensus literalis*) and a spiritual sense (*sensus spiritualis*). Thomas actually has more to say on this subject than he does on any other aspect of theological method, although in the *Summa* it occupies only a single article. The basic division of the senses of Scripture which he asserts there deserves to be quoted in full:

---

[11] *Super Evangelium S. Ionnis Lectura,* 21:24 [2656]; see also *Summa Theologiae,* 1,1,8, ad 2.

[12] *Summa Theologiae,* I, 1, 5.

[13] *Quaestiones de quodlibet,* 7, 15; I *Scriptum super libros Sententiarum,* Prol. 1,3.; *Summa Theologiae,* I, 1, 4. See also J. Boyle, "St. Thomas and Sacred Scripture," *Pro Ecclesia* 4 (1996): 93, who says that this soteriological principle "governs all of Thomas's thought" on sacred Scripture.

> The author of sacred Scripture is God, in whose power
> it is to signify his meaning not by words only (as man
> can also do), but also by things themselves. So whereas
> in every other science things are signified by words, this
> science has the property, that the things signified by
> words have themselves also a signification. Therefore,
> that first signification whereby words signify things
> belongs to the first sense, the historical or literal. That
> signification whereby things signified by words have
> themselves also a signification is called the spiritual
> sense, *which is based on the literal, and presupposes it*
> [italics mine].[14]

The end of the quote is of the greatest importance for the theological
process. Thomas holds that only the literal sense of Scripture is available
to theological argumentation. That is because he maintains that all the
truths necessary for salvation—the only proper "content" of doctrine and
theology—are to be found in the literal sense of Scripture.[15]

It is not that he denies the possibility or utility of the spiritual
senses. Rather, he insists on an essential, foundational status for the literal
sense. To be legitimate, all spiritual interpretation must be based on the
literal sense. The spiritual sense of a specific text or passage must in no
way conflict with its literal sense. This rules out any allegorizing that does
not first deal with the literal meaning of the text.

Finally, Thomas urges a certain humility and restraint on the part
of the theologian. Because of the dignity and depth of Scripture, but also
because of the limitations of the human interpreter, Thomas would advise
exegetes not to settle too quickly or firmly on a single interpretation: "The
authority of Scripture is in no way derogated if it is explained in various
ways, yet without violating the faith. This is because the Holy Spirit has
made it fertile with more truth than any man may find in it."[16]

In his own reading of Scripture, Thomas listens to the voices of
many extra-biblical *auctoritates* in his attempt to determine the meaning
of the text. At times he offers two interpretations and then chooses one of

---

[14] *Summa Theologiae,* I, 1,10. Thomas derives this principle from Hugh of St. Victor—see *De scripturis,* 3; *Didascalicon, 5-6.*

[15] *Summa Theologiae,* I, 1, 10, ad 1.

[16] II *Scriptum super libros Sententiarum,* 12,1,2, ad 7. This translation is taken from R. G. Kennedy, "Thomas Aquinas and the Literal Sense of Sacred Scripture" (Ph.D. diss., University of Notre Dame, 1985), 231. See also *Quaestiones disputata de potentia,* 4,1; *Quaestiones de quodlibet,* 3,4, ad 10; *Summa Theologiae,* I, 68, 1.

the two as the better explanation.[17] At other times, he dismisses earlier interpretations in favor of his own.[18] Most often, Thomas simply sets out two explanations of the text (sometimes including his own) and refuses to decide between them.[19]

Yet his caution should not be misinterpreted as a lack of vigor. Never does Thomas abandon his quest for the best possible interpretation. This always means giving priority to the rule of faith offered by the rest of Scripture—either in itself or as it has been elaborated formally in established Christian doctrine.[20]

Reading the 'Bread of Life' Discourse

In his theological writings and biblical commentaries Thomas achieves the fundamental identification of Scripture and doctrine that he asserts in his teaching. By looking at an example drawn from perhaps his most significant exegetical writing, the *Lectura super Ioannem*, I would like to suggest that Thomas's method and example have much to offer modern biblical scholars. The *Lectura* is a work far different from the *Summa* and the other systematic theological works of Thomas. But as we will see in this short consideration of Thomas's six lectures on Jesus' "Bread of Life" discourse (John 6:26-72), it is no less theological or doctrinal.

Thomas begins his lectures on John 6 in the usual manner: he divides the text according to its content. For him, the chapter has two parts: "First he [John] describes a visible miracle, in which Christ exhibited bodily food. Secondly, he considers spiritual food (6:26-72)." Thomas's reserve is perhaps the most remarkable aspect of this division. His generic characterization of the discourse shows a profound attention to the text and a conscious decision to eschew an immediate "spiritual" interpretation in terms of Catholic sacramental theology.

As the chapter moves into the discourse (John 6:26), Thomas continues to show such reserve, avoiding the many opportunities the chapter presents for reading Catholic doctrine into the text. As he refrains from the easy, sacramental interpretation, he analyzes the meaning of the terms such as "food," "bread," and "life"—drawing on other scriptural passages, mainly from Johannine and Wisdom sources.

---

[17] See *Super Epistolam ad Ephesios*, 3:10 [161].

[18] See *Super Epistolam ad Ephesios*, 2:15 [116].

[19] See *Quaestio disputata de potentia*, 4,1; *Super Evangelium S. Ioannis Lectura*, 6:27 [898].

[20] For an argument which proves that Thomas held there to be only one literal sense of any given verse of Scripture, see Kennedy, "Thomas Aquinas and the Literal Sense of Sacred Scripture," 212-232.

He comes up with a three-fold distinction: spiritual food as "God himself" *(ipse Deus)*, as "obedience to the divine commands" *(obedientia divinorum mandatorum)* and as "Christ himself" *(ipse Christus)*, that is, as the flesh of Christ "joined to the Word of God" *(coniuncta verbo dei)*.[21] This distinction allows him to follow the transitions of the text and to unify them, ultimately making a rich identification between the first kind of spiritual food (God himself) and the third kind (Christ himself) based on a sapiential understanding of Christ as the Word. The flesh of Christ, he says, is given its power as spiritual food because of its ineffable closeness to the person of the Word, who is Wisdom itself. His flesh is bread because Wisdom is bread, an identification made possible through the inter-textual citation of the Book of Sirach (15:3).[22] This three-fold distinction allows him to discuss spiritual bread from the perspective presented in the Johannine text itself: how it gives life (in v. 33)[23] and how it is imperishable (v. 35).[24]

Until he reaches verse 50, Thomas refuses to give a solely Eucharistic interpretation to the spiritual bread that Jesus speaks of. If he has preferred any one of its three meanings, it has been the first (that is, God himself), especially as the Son, the life-giving Word of God. He has only given brief, cursory references to the Eucharist, never actually using the term, and has only used the word *sacramentum* twice. This is understandable—Christ's references to food "which endures to eternal life" (v. 27), "true bread from heaven" (v. 32), and finally to himself as the bread of life have not been significantly different in meaning from the "living water" discourse at the well (John 4:10-15). Indeed, Thomas uses similar language to describe this new discourse as he does that earlier one,[25] in which he makes no mention of an obviously tempting interpretation, namely, that the "living waters" refer to baptism. What makes John 6 different, however, is that the text itself takes a decidedly sacramental turn in the final verses, introducing new terms such as "eat," "flesh," and "blood." Only when these appear does Thomas's exposition turn to the Eucharist.

Prompted by the scriptural text itself, then, in verse 52, Thomas begins identifying a theology of the Eucharist in the text. He makes the distinction directly: "So what he said above, 'I am the living bread,' pertained to the power of the Word; but what he is saying here pertains to the sharing of his body, that is, to the sacrament of the Eucharist."[26] Here

---

[21] *Super Evangelium S. Ioannis Lectura*, 6:27 [898].

[22] *Super Evangelium S. Ioannis Lectura*, 6:35 [914].

[23] *Super Evangelium S. Ioannis Lectura*, 6:35 [914].

[24] *Super Evangelium S. Ioannis Lectura*, 6:37 [921].

[25] *Super Evangelium S. Ioannis Lectura*, 4:10, 13-14 [577, 586-587].

[26] *Super Evangelium S. Ioannis Lectura*, 6:52 [959].

Thomas pauses to offer a short account of basic eucharistic doctrine in the mode of a *quaestio*.[27] This allows him to maintain his strict adherence to the text while also availing himself of a pedagogical opportunity.

Yet his actual interpretation of the final verses of John 6 are by no means tangential; in fact, they are strikingly acute. In the grumbling response of "the Jews" to Jesus, Thomas develops his interpretation on an entirely new level. He discerns the drama in the text—the crisis of belief versus unbelief — and approaches it as a commentary on the way in which spiritual food is received. As he explains how we take the bread of life he does so in a way that is broader than a purely sacramental interpretation. As he explains it, we take the bread of life by believing in Christ with a faith made living by love. Thus, Christ is in us in two ways: "In our intellect through faith, so far as it is faith, and in our affections through love, which informs or gives life to our faith."[28] The grumblers represent for Thomas one way of eating material bread that symbolizes spiritual bread, be it manna or Eucharist. The grumblers eat the bread "as a sign only" (*ad signum tantum*). They are distinguished by Thomas from those who taste the "spiritual food" contained in the material bread.[29]

Building on this new distinction, Thomas develops an ecclesial element of his interpretation, introducing further distinctions between spiritual, spiritual/sacramental, and insincere sacramental receptions of the Eucharist, particularly in his exegesis of verse 57: "He who eats my flesh and drinks my blood abides in me and I in him."[30]

In this ecclesial interpretation, Thomas asserts that Christ is the cause of the unity of the Church because the spiritual eating makes us a part of him in the mystical body of the Church. To receive Christ in faith, therefore, means to share in the unity of the Church.[31] Thomas draws together the three themes he discerned in the early discourse—Christ as spiritual bread, the inaccessibility of spiritual bread to those who do not believe, the Eucharist as spiritual bread—to draw a still deeper insight into the text: that the spiritual food received in faith is source of unity among those who believe in Christ.

Respecting the principle of an identity between sacred Scripture and sacred doctrine, Thomas is able to discern a meaning in the Johannine text that is missed by modern exegetes—namely, that the grumblers lack a certain unity that is constituted by spiritual eating, a unity that is a precursor to the unity to be constituted by the Eucharist, which Thomas

---

[27] *Super Evangelium S. Ioannis Lectura*, 6:52 [960-964].

[28] *Super Evangelium S. Ioannis Lectura*, 6:48 [951].

[29] *Super Evangelium S. Ioannis Lectura*, 6:49 [954].

[30] *Super Evangelium S. Ioannis Lectura*, 6:57 [976].

[31] *Super Evangelium S. Ioannis Lectura*, 6:54 [969].

refers to as the unity of the Mystical Body, or the Church. The unbelieving Jews are divided, grumbling, arguing, disputing, both with Christ and one another. The cause of their grumbling and dissension, as Thomas interprets it, is their inability to perceive the spiritual food in the material. They understand the words of Jesus in a carnal way, as if he is speaking of material food.

Thomas contrasts the divisions among the Jews with the unity of the apostles, which allows Peter to speak for the whole group.[32] Thomas discovers then in the textual narrative, a drama that captures a primitive ecclesiology—the unity of the Church caused first by the person of Christ and then by his person in the Eucharist. In so doing, Thomas has also drawn together Christology, sacramentology, spirituality, and a theology of grace. Or perhaps, it is better to say that Thomas draws a theological model from the text in which he respects the organic unity of these elements.

Thomas handling of this important text from John is emblematic of his approach to Scripture throughout his exegetical corpus. As a practical consequence of his guiding insight—the fluidity and even identity of Scripture and doctrine—he is able to join the exegetical and the theological, to bring the scriptural text into "conversation" not only with other scriptural texts, but with the whole of the Church's doctrinal and liturgical tradition.

At all times the literal text of Scripture remains central and determinative of the interpretation. Thomas is never seen "reading into" the text. Rather, with his understanding of the continuity of Scripture and doctrine, we see Thomas bringing to his exegetical work a fresh perspective, one informed and illuminated by the Church's rich interpretive tradition, as it is reflected in its liturgy and doctrinal teaching. As a result, he is able to draw out from the text extraordinary depths of meaning unavailable to a strictly historical and literary reading.

We see in Thomas's exegetical practice that important Catholic doctrines are connected to their vital biblical source, and in the process revitalized and deepened. All this he does within a conservative, carefully moderate, exegetical context that has important lessons to teach modern interpreters.

What Thomas's principally has to teach exegetes today is the importance of recovering the Scriptures as primary theological documents. As M. Barth observed in his commentary on Ephesians: "Since Ephesians is a theological document, it must be explained in theological terms—or else the exposition would not be literal."[33] What Barth says of Ephesians is true for the other works of the New Testament, which only further underscores the significance for modern exegesis and theology of Thomas's insights on the unity of Scripture and doctrine.

---

[32] *Super Evangelium S. Ioannis Lectura*, 6:69 [1001].

[33] M. Barth, *Ephesians*, 2 vols., Anchor Bible Series (Garden City: Doubleday, 1974), 1:60.

THE SPIRITUAL SENSE IN DE LUBAC'S HERMENEUTICS OF TRADITION

• Marcellino D'Ambrosio •

Crossroads Initiative

In the introduction to the first volume of *Exégèse Médiévale*,[1] Henri de Lubac, S.J., observes that the surge of interest in the scientific study of Scripture during the mid-twentieth century had the unfortunate consequence of casting long shadows upon the ancient hermeneutic of the Church, making it appear quaint, outmoded, and even obsolete.

Some critical exegetes even expressed the opinion that ancient spiritual exegesis was a kind of pedagogue or temporary substitute for scientific exegesis. Its historical role was to "preserve the Bible within a very pure and very exalted sphere of ideas and sentiments, until minds reached sufficient maturity to be able to understand the past and to be given the direct explanation of the texts."[2]

Others seemed to assume that the ancient distinction between literal and spiritual senses can be entirely attributed to ignorance in the field of science; hence the conviction expressed by a few scientific exegetes that the progress made in their particular discipline has shattered the traditional distinction in its very principle.

De Lubac frankly thinks that such ideas smack of "a modern self-sufficiency" and "a-priori thinking."[3] While he is ready to grant that ancient commentaries obviously contained outmoded elements—"to tell the truth, a lot of trash"[4]—he staunchly maintains that not everything about the ancient expositors can be explained simply by the fact that they lived in a "pre-critical" age.

---

[1] *Exégèse Médiévale*, 4 vols. (Paris: Aubier, 1959-1964). English translation (partial): Henri de Lubac, *Medieval Exegesis*, trans. M. Sebanc (Grand Rapids: W.B. Eerdmans, 1998, 2000).

[2] Dom Wilmart, "Un repertoire d'exegese compose en Angleterre vers le debut du XII siercle," in *Memoriale Lagrange* (Paris: J. Gabalda, 1940), 312, cited in de Lubac, *The Sources of Revelation* (New York: Herder & Herder, 1968), 65. *Sources,* an accessible English translation which I will use throughout this paper, is an anthology of which draws from the four volumes of *Exégèse Médiévale and Histoire et Espirit* (Paris: Cerf, 1950).

[3] *The Sources of Revelation*, 65, 150.

[4] *Exégèse Médiévale*, 1/2:661.

Beneath exegetical procedures which seem so strange to us today, de Lubac argued, we find a "deeply pondered theology" which retains a "permanent value" and lies not only at "the heart of all Christian exegesis, but at the heart of Christian faith itself."[5] Speaking elsewhere of the traditional commentators, de Lubac likewise affirms that "a sacred element lies at the heart of their exegesis, an element which is one of the treasures of the faith."[6] Considered in its doctrinal foundations rather than in its implementation, ancient exegesis for de Lubac touches upon the substance and rhythm of the Christian mystery and thus must be perpetually retained by the Christian community.

Thus, de Lubac sees the ancient doctrine of the dual meaning of Scripture—spiritual as well as literal—as a non-negotiable part of the Christian patrimony. Indeed, he says, it is an "inalienable datum of tradition."[7] In support of this contention, de Lubac recalls that allegorical or spiritual interpretation of the Old Testament is precisely the usual exegetical practice of the New Testament authors themselves.[8] For him, it is axiomatic that "the exegesis of all Christian generations will have to conserve as an absolute norm the exegesis of the first generation." [9]

He also points to the fact that such has been the unanimous teaching of the fathers and doctors from the first centuries of the Church down to the present day and has been recently confirmed by the very papal documents which legitimized and mandated the development of scientific exegesis within the Catholic Church. He quotes Pope Leo XIII who, speaking of the allegorical or figurative sense of Scripture, affirms that "this

---

[6] *The Sources of Revelation*, 66-67.

[7] *The Sources of Revelation*, 158.

[8] De Lubac rejected efforts to attribute "allegorical interpretation" to the influence of Greek philosophy on the early Church. He traces the origin of Christian allegorism back to Paul, to the author of the Letter to the Hebrews, and to other writers of the canonical New Testament texts. De Lubac points out that the belief of the Christian allegorists that everything in the Old Testament is a figure or "type" of Christ and the Church comes from Paul's figurative interpretation of the symbols of the Exodus and desert trek in 1 Cor. 10:1-11. Moreover, both the word and the concept of allegory were inserted into the Christian exegetical tradition by Paul when he interpreted Hagar and Sarah as an allegory of synagogue and Church in Gal. 4:21-24: "Both the word and idea of Christian allegory come from St. Paul." See "Hellenistic Allegory and Christian Allegory," in *Theological Fragments* (San Francisco: Ignatius, 1989), 165-6; See *Exégèse Médiévale,* 2/2:62.

[9] *Exégèse Médiévale*, 2/2:109.

method of interpretation has been received by the Church from the apostles and has been approved by her own practice, as the liturgy attests."[10]

Pope Pius XII, observes de Lubac, says much the same thing in *Divino Afflante Spiritu*.[11] And in *Dei Verbum*, the Second Vatican Council's Dogmatic Constitution on Divine Revelation, de Lubac sees many aspects of the traditional hermeneutic endorsed as *necessary* for biblical interpretation today:

> In two consecutive paragraphs devoted to scriptural inter-
> pretation, what, really, does the third chapter of *Dei
> Verbum*, on divine revelation, say if not that we must first,
> by purely scientific study, determine as best we can the
> "intention" of each of the human authors and that only
> then, in order to better grasp the meaning, should we read
> it and interpret it as a whole "in the light of the same
> Spirit who caused it to be written"? When the sixth chap-
> ter advised us to "study the holy fathers, those of the East
> as well as those of the West," so as to obtain this increased
> understanding, does this not indicate that there must still
> be profit to be derived from a study of the exegetical tradi-
> tion which stemmed from the fathers? And when we are
> told, in the constitution's introduction and frequently
> throughout the text, that the Word of God contained in
> Scripture is none other than the Word made flesh, and
> that "the entire revelation of the Most High God is ful-
> filled" in Jesus Christ, do we not hear the traditional
> theme of the *Verbum abbreviatum*?

---

[10] Pope Leo XIII, Encyclical *Providentissimus Deus* (1893), no. 322, cited in *The Sources of Revelation*, 150, n. 8. De Lubac also adduces this encyclical in support of the enduring relevance of patristic exegesis in *Exégèse Médiévale*, 1/1:357, n. 2.

[11] *The Sources of Revelation*, 150, n. 8. Though de Lubac does not quote any specific texts, he could have cited no. 26: "For what was said and done in the Old Testament was ordained and disposed by God with such consummate wisdom, that things past prefigured in a spiritual way those that were to come under the new dispensation of grace. Wherefore the exegete, just as he must search out and expound the literal meaning of the words, intended and expressed by the sacred writer, so also must he do likewise for the spiritual sense, provided it is clearly intended by God. For God alone could have known this spiritual meaning and have revealed it to us. Now our Divine Savior himself points out to us and teaches us this same sense in the holy gospel; the apostles also, following the example of the Master, profess it in their spoken and written words; the unchanging tradition of the Church approves it; and finally the most ancient usage of the liturgy proclaims it, wherever may be rightly applied the well-known principle: the rule of prayer is the rule of faith."

... the Council, in its chapter on the Old Testament, using an expression whose most famous exponent was St. Augustine, no less forcefully declares the mutual implications of the two testaments: *Novum in Vetere latet, Vetus in Novo patet.* Thus it canonizes the key idea which, since apostolic times, has dominated the doctrine of spiritual understanding of the Scriptures as elaborated through the ages. The Council thus affirms—or rather confirms—the foundation of what was in the beginning and will always remain the Christian newness.[12]

Typology and the Dialectic of the Covenants

While de Lubac was encouraged by the various attempts during the forties and fifties to reappropriate the valid, fruitful insights of the traditional spiritual exegesis of the Church, he did not regard every approach as equally felicitous. He agreed with most commentators that "allegorical exegesis" ought to be ruled out as a name for this renewed figurative exposition given the connotations of artificiality and subjectivism that the term allegory had borne for the last century or two. Yet he had serious reservations about the widespread enthusiasm for the distinction whereby "typology" is promoted as an objective, biblical form of historical figurism and "allegory" is rejected as a Hellenistic form of *eisegesis* that evacuates history.

De Lubac perceived an inherent narrowness in the terminology of "typology." First of all, this rather recent[13] term refers solely to a result, namely a correspondence between different historical events, without in any way alluding to the spiritual process responsible for accomplishing that result. "Typology" does not explain the unique passage from prophecy to gospel. Therefore, it is not sufficient to show with proper forcefulness the work accomplished by Jesus Christ.

---

[12] *The Sources of Revelation,* viii-ix.

[13] De Lubac is well aware of Paul's use of the words *typoi* and *typikos* in 1 Cor. 10:6 and 11 respectively. He also recognizes the subsequent use which the exegetical tradition has made of these terms and their Latin equivalents. What he perceives to be of recent origin is the practice of referring to the study of the correspondence between biblical events as "typology" and distinguishing this sharply from "allegory."

It does not provide a fundamental explanation either of the New Testament's roots in the Old or, more importantly, of its emergence and sovereign freedom. Having assumed the task of establishing "corelations among historical realities at different moments in sacred history," it lacks the ability to show that the New Testament is something other than a second Old Testament which, at its term, would still leave us completely within the thread of history.[14]

Typology, as customarily defined, had already occurred within the Old Testament. To see the New Testament as a typological fulfillment of the Old, then, says nothing about the eschatological quality of the Christ-event and the definitive, final, and unsurpassable character of the new covenant which it initiated. In its exclusive emphasis upon continuity and correspondence, typology neglects the other side of the traditional dialectic of the covenants.

De Lubac here stresses the critical necessity of preserving the perspective of the New Testament writers and the fathers of the Church—the Christian theology of history which, in large measure, consists in the theology of the two covenants and their interrelationship. In de Lubac's mind, it would be hard to exaggerate the importance of the relationship between the covenants for the thought of the early Church, or for that matter, the entire history of Christian thought. Fundamentally, he reminds us, both Testaments are only successive parts of one, unified divine plan of salvation. This profound unity of the divine plan compels recognition of both the organic continuity of New Testament and Old and "the unique and incomparable summit" of the salvation history in the coming of the Lord Jesus.[15]

Just as it fails adequately to account for the relation between the covenants, so does typology fail to express "the connection between spiritual understanding and the personal conversion of the Christian,

---

[14] *The Sources of Revelation*, 144.

[15] For a fuller treatment of de Lubac's understanding of the "dialectic of the two Testaments," see Marcellino D'Ambrosio, "Henri de Lubac and the Recovery of the Traditional Hermeneutic" (Ph.D. diss., Catholic University of America, 1991), 152-160.

or the relationship between 'New Testament' and 'new man,' between newness of understanding and newness of spirit." In fact typology really only corresponds to the first phase of the threefold spiritual sense which the medieval distich calls *allegoria*.[16]

To narrow down the figurative interpretation of the ancient tradition to typology would be completely to eliminate the existential, interior element from the interpretation process. This is completely unacceptable to de Lubac since, for the ancient tradition, personal assimilation, whether it take the form of moral application (tropology) or mystical "volatus"[17] ("practical" anagogy), *is a sine qua non* of true understanding. Thus, in de Lubac's view, typology stops the spiritual impulse of traditional spiritual understanding at the half-way mark. "Even in its best features, it still remains apart from the great Pauline inspiration which gives life to the entire doctrine."[18]

De Lubac is equally cool to the attempt to account for traditional figurative exegesis by recourse to a *sensus plenior*. It seems to him that this well-meaning effort of certain scientific exegetes to preserve the spiritual sense by absorbing it into the literal meaning is doomed to failure. Though the spiritual meaning really is, in one sense, a *sensus plenior* and is contained within or under the letter of the scriptural text, it can only be perceived in the light of Christ, within the Church, by the Church. Faith, not exegetical science, is the key to its discovery, he argues.[19]

The Spiritual 'Understanding' of Scripture

If we want to obtain a complete view of the more-than-literal meaning of Scripture as passed on to us by the Church's traditional hermeneutic, there is, in de Lubac's opinion, only one truly adequate term by which this meaning can be designated—*the spiritual sense*. There are many reasons for this choice, not the least of which is that it is the term formally countenanced by Scripture itself, exploiting the Pauline distinction between the letter (or flesh) and the spirit while at the same time reminding us that we are dealing with the meaning that proceeds from the Holy Spirit.

---

[16] See the *Catechism of the Catholic Church*, no. 118.

[17] *Volatus* is the term of Gregory the Great which de Lubac customarily employs to designate the more contemplative, existential dimension of anagogy. Aware, of course, that this terminology was far from universal, he insists nonetheless that this form of interpretation—which tends towards mystical union with the heavenly Christ is, in the main, an integral aspect of the traditional hermeneutic. See *Exégèse Médiévale*, 1/2: 639-640, citing Gregory, *Homilies on Ezekiel*, 1.1, h. 3, nos. 1, 15.

[18] *The Sources of Revelation*, 144-145.

[19] *The Sources of Revelation*, 150-152.

Given that there is an evangelical relationship between the notions of "spirit" and "truth," this terminology also alludes to the most essential characteristic of the figurative sense — that it proceeds from the "truth" of the New Testament, in contrast to the "shadows" of the Old. Moreover, in light of Paul's statement in 2 Corinthians 3:17 that the "Lord is the Spirit," it is only appropriate that the meaning related to Christ be known as the "spiritual" sense.

Finally, "spiritual" also connotes "interior" and thereby recalls to our awareness the fact that "the Christian mystery is not something to be curiously contemplated like a pure object of science, but is something which must be interiorized and lived." The meaning which leads us to the realities of the spiritual life and which can only be the fruit of a spiritual life is aptly named the "spiritual sense."[20]

Likewise, de Lubac thinks it appropriate to retain the traditional usage whereby the term "spiritual understanding" refers to the activity which leads both to the spiritual sense in its threefold extension and to the figurative literal meanings. This is because, "whether our purpose be to discover an advance indication of Christ, to abandon the seemingly carnal meaning of certain prophecies, to understand a parable, or to obtain greater penetration into the teachings of Jesus in the Sermon on the Mount," the same intellectual process is at work under the influence of the same Spirit, despite the objective diversity of spiritual and figurative literal sense.[21]

This, for de Lubac, leads to what is perhaps the key point of all: if we hope to recapture anything of the ancient Church's spiritual exposition of Scripture, we must pass beyond an objective cataloging of symbolic correspondences to a reappropriation of this dynamic spiritual movement which animated traditional exegesis and is called "spiritual understanding."

All Christian experience, in all its phases, is comprised within this all-encompassing movement of the Spirit.

> This amounts to saying that this understanding cannot lead to results which are completely controllable by a particular method or which are apt to be gathered together into a definitive canon. It amounts to saying that it can never be made completely objective. It always envelops and transcends what has been grasped, and is, at the same time, enveloped and transcended by what it has as yet been unable to grasp.[22]

---

[20] *The Sources of Revelation*, 16-19.

[21] *The Sources of Revelation*, 20.

[22] *The Sources of Revelation*, 23.

While de Lubac does not deny that there are some spiritual interpretations of Scripture which have more objective validity than others, he frankly admits that spiritual understanding has an inherently subjective aspect which cannot be excised without neutralizing the entire process and rendering it spiritually profitless. Thus, it can never be judged from a purely objective viewpoint or reduced to a scientific discipline.

Here again, de Lubac insists on the distinction between the literal and spiritual senses—what he terms "the religious meaning of the Bible" (*sens religieux de la Bible*) and "the spiritual meaning of Scripture" (*sens spirituel de l'Ecriture*).

The "religious meaning" is the meaning which Scripture had for its human author and its original audience. It essentially takes the form of a careful and scrupulously objective reconstruction of the religious consciousness and institutions of the Old Testament in their original context and for their own sake. The scientific exegete who carries out this important investigation "will always be attentive to differences in historical situations. . . . All his attention is directed towards reconstituting the past."

Ancient Meaning 'Received in Sign'

What de Lubac calls "the spiritual meaning" also has to do with the history of Israel's religion, but is altogether different in its motivation and perspective. The investigator who seeks to uncover this meaning is driven by no backward-orientated curiosity, no desire to reconstitute the past for the past's sake. Rather, by means of a deeply meditated Christian faith, he or she "interprets the Jewish past solely from the viewpoint of the Christian present."

Instead of seeking to elucidate the feelings or thoughts of the Old Testament writers, the exegete will search the Scriptures for the deeper, symbolic meaning of the extrinsic facts and objective institutions of ancient Israel usually without making any attempt "to fill the gap between the primary meaning of those institutions or facts, as understood and lived by the majority of ancient Jews, and the Christian meaning received, in sign, by them."[23]

Moreover, the careful objectivity and reserve so necessary for the historian are basically inappropriate for us when we approach the text as spiritual interpreters. We must not hold ourselves at an objective distance from the text, but must rather allow God, through the text, to speak to us here and now.

---

[23] *The Sources of Revelation*, 26-27, 20-31.

Thus, it would be inaccurate to say that in spiritual interpretation we question the text as we would any other document from the past. Rather, de Lubac says, making his own the words of the poet, Paul Claudel, "it would be more exact to acknowledge that it is Scripture which is questioning us, and which finds for each of us, through all time and all generations, the appropriate question."[24]

The Christian is not simply to choose whatever of these two exegetical approaches is more congenial to him. For de Lubac, the spiritual sense ought normally to be the ultimate goal when Christians approach the Bible as Christians. We must, as believers, come to the Bible expecting to receive more than "understanding of the past" or even, for that matter, moral or doctrinal instruction. We must become aware that, in pursuing the spiritual sense, we "are accomplishing a religious activity according to the total logic of our faith."[25]

For de Lubac as for his friend, Hans Urs von Balthasar, spiritual exegesis thus leads to an encounter with the living God, a meeting which changes us: "Just as the Eucharist is not a simple remembrance of something which happened in the past, but the perpetual reactualization of the body of the Lord and of his sacrifice, in the same fashion is Scripture less a question of history than of the form and vehicle of God's Word uttered unceasingly, and uttered even now." [26]

De Lubac affirms, with the traditional hermeneutic, that before any such understanding of the Old Testament can be undertaken in the light of the New, the New must be understood historically in light of the Old. Here too we see the importance of the religious meaning — what the tradition calls the "literal sense"—of the Bible as the indispensable basis or foundation of the spiritual sense.

Both the religious and the spiritual senses of Scripture are, then, irreducible in de Lubac's scheme of things. Though they are interrelated in a number of ways, they nonetheless have different ends and are attained by different methods. Their relative autonomy must be preserved. Spiritual exegesis must not interfere with or try to substitute for historical science.

On the other hand, the scientific exegete must bear in mind that his science does "not exhaust what the Christian is to expect from the Word of God. Whatever may be the superiority which we have acquired or which

---

[24] Claudel cited in *The Sources of Revelation*, 73.

[25] *The Sources of Revelation,* 65, 73.

[26] Von Balthasar, "Die Schrift als Gottes Wort," *Schweizer Rundschau (1949),* cited and translated in *The Sources of Revelation*, 74. Von Balthasar's piece is translated as "Scripture as the Word of God," *Downside Review* 68 (1950).

we still have yet to acquire from the scientific point of view, it is this that the ancients, including the medievals, never cease and never will cease to remind us." [27]

Henri de Lubac's voluminous study of ancient Christian exegesis is clearly more than a work of historical reconstruction. He has successfully demonstrated that the Catholic exegetical and dogmatic tradition is unanimous in affirming both literal and spiritual senses of Scripture and that this has been consistently reaffirmed over the past hundred years by the very same magisterial documents which have so zealously promoted a more rigorously historical and critical methodology for Catholic literal exegesis.

Moreover, his insistence that this hermeneutic is fundamental to the New Testament authors' understanding of Christ and the salvation history which led up to him seems unassailable. It is hard to see, in light of the evidence he adduces for this, how one could entirely reject spiritual exegesis of the Old Testament without completely rejecting the New Testament's interpretation of the Old and thereby endangering the foundation of the Church's faith.

All in all, de Lubac's proposal for the recovery of spiritual exegesis proves to be a modest and reasonable one which is historically well-informed and philosophically well-meditated. It is neither reactionary nor pre-critical, but rather proceeds from an enthusiastic acceptance of and broad acquaintance with modern critical exegesis. In fact, the recovery de Lubac envisions takes the form of a "fusion of horizons" between ancient and modern exegesis whereby each is critiqued, purified, and widened in light of the other.

Though many features of ancient exegesis inevitably succumb to the critique of modern historical science, the fundamental principles and structure of the traditional hermeneutic emerge from the crucible virtually intact. The primary impact of modem scientific exegesis upon this ancient hermeneutic is to increase the sophistication and religious value of this first phase of exegesis. As significant as this is, however, de Lubac contends that a focus on sound literal interpretation is not *per se* modern and constitutes no contradiction with ancient exegesis. Indeed, it marks no essential modification in the Church's traditional process of reading and applying the Scriptures:

> If the impossible could have happened and the methods and results of the criticism such as we possess them today would have suddenly appeared to these ancients, they would have no doubt manifested the same ability to assim-ilate them as we. Yet, these ancients, who would have

---

[27] *Exégèse Médiévale*, 2/2: 93.

become the most shrewd in criticism and the most versed in biblical science of all those of our school, would have had to add the following in order to remain faithful to themselves: "This new world of human knowledge is precious to us. If it obliges us to revise many things regarding our opinion and exegetical procedures, our subtle principles will not be any obstacle to this at all, and we will labor with you to make this new science greater still. But, for our part, know that it does not substantially change an essential problem. And although these new lights which you bring to us can be a great help in the examination of this problem, it is essentially of another order." [28]

In de Lubac's view, sound literal exegesis of the Old Testament, though more valuable today than ever, nonetheless remains preliminary and preparatory in the Christian's total approach to the sacred text. Despite its religious value, it remains primarily an exercise in historical reconstruction.

De Lubac is correct in insisting that the ultimate objective of the Christian must be the religious activity whereby the mystery of Christ—which is the ultimate object of the biblical text, is spiritually appropriated in faith: "The essential thing for the Christian who receives the Word of God will never cease to be the assimilation of the Spirit of which history is the bearer and to be nourished by the fruit which history has matured." [29]

---

[28] *Exégèse Médiévale,* 2/1:128.

[29] *Histoire et Espirit* (Paris: Aubier, 1950), 282.

To the New Student
of Sacred Scripture

• Hugh of St. Victor •

To the eager student, first of all it ought to be known that sacred Scripture has three ways of conveying meaning—namely, *history*, *allegory*, and *tropology*.

Often, in one and the same literal context, all may be found together, as when a truth of history both hints at some mystical meaning by way of allegory and equally shows by way of tropology how we ought to behave.

To be sure, all things in the divine utterance must not be wrenched to an interpretation such that each of them is held to contain history, allegory, and tropology all at once. Even if a triple meaning can appropriately be assigned in many passages, nevertheless it is either difficult or impossible to see it everywhere. It is necessary, therefore, so to handle the sacred Scripture that we assign individual things fittingly in their own places, as reason demands.

It ought also to be known that in the divine utterance not only words but even things have a meaning—a way of communicating not usually found to such an extent in other writings. The philosopher knows only the significance of words. But the significance of things is far more excellent than that of words because, while the latter was established by usage, nature dictated the former. The latter is the voice of men, the former the voice of God speaking to men. The latter, once uttered, perishes; the former, once created, subsists. The unsubstantial word is the sign of man's perceptions; the thing is a resemblance of the divine idea.

Therefore, what the sound of the mouth—which all in the same moment begins to subsist and fades away—is to the idea in the mind, the whole extent of time is to eternity. The idea in the mind is the internal word, which is shown forth by the sound of the voice, that is, by the external word. And the divine wisdom, which the Father has uttered out of his heart, invisible in itself, is recognized through creatures and in them.

From this it is most surely gathered how profound is the understanding to be sought in the sacred writings, in which we come through the word to a concept, through the concept to a thing, through the thing to its idea, and through its idea arrive at truth. Because certain less well instructed persons do not take account of this, they suppose that there is nothing subtle in these matters on which to exercise their mental abilities; they turn their attention to the writings of philosophers instead, precisely because, not knowing the power of truth, they do not understand that in Scripture there is anything beyond the bare surface of the letter.

That the sacred utterances employ the meaning of things, moreover, we shall demonstrate by a particular short and clear example. The Scripture says: "Watch, because your adversary the Devil goeth about as a roaring lion" (1 Pet. 5:8). Here, if we should say that the lion stands for the Devil, we should mean by "lion" not the word but the thing. For if the two words "Devil" and "lion" mean one and the same thing, the likeness of that same thing to itself is not adequate. It remains, therefore, that the word "lion" signifies the animal, but that the animal in turn designates the Devil. And all other things are to be taken after this fashion, as when we say that worm, calf, stone, serpent, and other things of this sort signify Christ. . . .

The Foundation Is History

In the order of study of sacred Scripture, history precedes allegory and tropology. In this question it is not without value to call to mind what we see happen in the construction of buildings—where first the foundation is laid, then the structure is raised upon it, and finally, when the work is all finished, the house is decorated by the laying on of color.

So too, in fact, must it be in your instruction. First you learn history and diligently commit to memory the truth of the deeds that have been performed, reviewing from beginning to end what has been done, when it has been done, where it has been done, and by whom it has been done. For these are the four things which are especially to be sought for in history—the person, the business done, the time, and the place.

Nor do I think that you will be able to become perfectly sensitive to allegory unless you have first been grounded in history. Do not look down upon these least things. The man who looks down on such smallest things slips little by little. If, in the beginning, you had looked down on learning the alphabet, now you would not even find your names listed with those of the grammar students. I know that there are certain fellows who want to play the philosopher right away. They say that stories should be left to pseudo-apostles. The knowledge of these fellows is like that of an ass. Don't imitate persons of this kind. "Once grounded in things small, you may safely strive for all."[1]

But, you say, "I find many things in the histories which seem to be of no utility: why should I keep busy with this sort of thing?" Well said. There are indeed many things in the Scriptures which, considered in themselves, seem to have nothing worth looking for. But if you look at them in the light of the other things to which they are joined, and if you begin to weigh them in their whole context, you will see that they are as necessary as they are fitting. Some things are to be known for their own sakes. But others, although for their own sakes they do not seem worthy of our labor,

---

[1] Marbodus, *De ornamentis verborum*, Prologus (*P.L.* CLXXI, 1687).

must by no means be carelessly skipped—because without them the former class of things cannot be known with complete clarity. Learn everything. You will see afterwards that nothing is superfluous.

You ask if I have any opinion about the books which are useful for this study. I think the ones to be studied most are: Genesis, Exodus, Joshua, the Book of Judges, and that of Kings, and Chronicles. Of the New Testament, first the four Gospels, then the Acts of the Apostles. These eleven seem to me to have more to do with history than do the others.

This, then, my student, is what I propose to you. All things were brought forth in order: move along in order yourself. Following the shadow, one comes to the body: learn the figure, and you will come to the truth.

I am not now saying that you should first struggle to unfold the figures of the Old Testament and penetrate its mystical sayings before you come to the gospel streams you must drink from. But just as you see that every building lacking a foundation cannot stand firm, so also is it in learning.

The foundation and principle of sacred learning is history, from which, like honey from the honeycomb, the truth of allegory is extracted. As you are about to build, therefore, "lay first the foundation of history; next, by pursuing the 'typical' meaning, build up a structure in your mind to be a fortress of faith. Last of all, however, through the loveliness of morality, paint the structure over as with the most beautiful of colors."[2]

Until the End of the Ages, God's Mercies Do Not Slacken

You have in *history* the means through which to admire God's deeds, in allegory the means through which to believe his mysteries, in morality (*tropology*) the means through which to imitate his perfection.

Read, therefore, and learn that "in the beginning God created heaven and earth" (Gen. 1:1). Read that in the beginning he planted "a paradise of pleasure wherein he placed man whom he had formed" (Gen. 2:8). Him sinning God expelled and thrust out into the trials of this life. Read how the entire offspring of the human race descended from one man; how, subsequently flood destroyed sinners; how, in the midst of the waters, the divine mercy preserved the just man Noah with his sons; next, how Abraham received the mark of the faith, but afterwards Israel went down into Egypt; how God thereafter led the sons of Israel out of Egypt by the hand of Moses and Aaron, brought them through the Red Sea and through the desert, gave them the Law and settled them in the land of promise; how often he delivered them as sinners into the hands of their enemies and

---

[2] Gregory the Great, *Moralium libri*, Episula missoria iii (*P.L.* LXXV, 513C).

afterwards freed them again when they were penitent; how first through judges, then through kings, he rules his people.

"He took his servant David from following the ewes great with young" (Ps. 78:70-71). Solomon he enlightened with wisdom. For the weeping Ezekiel he added on fifteen years. Thereafter he sent the straying people captive into Babylon by the hand of Nebuchadnezzar. After seventy years he brought them back. At last, however, when that time was already declining, he sent his Son into our flesh, and he, having sent his apostles into all the world, promised eternal life to those repentant. He foretold that he would come at the end of the ages to judge us, to make a return to each man according to his deeds—namely, eternal fire for sinners, but for the just, life and the kingdom of which there shall be no end. See how, from the time when the world began until the end of the ages, the mercies of God do not slacken.

The Mysteries of Allegory

After the reading of history, it remains for you to investigate the mysteries of allegories, in which I do not think there is any need of exhortation from me, since this matter itself appears worthy enough in its own right. Yet I wish you to know, good student, that this pursuit demands not slow and dull perceptions but matured mental abilities which, in the course of their searching, may so restrain their subtlety as not to lose good judgment in what they discern. Such food is solid stuff, and, unless it be well chewed, it cannot be swallowed. You must therefore employ such restraint that, while you are subtle in your seeking, you may not be found rash in what you presume; remembering what the Psalmist says: "He hath bent his bow and made it ready. And in it he hath prepared the instruments of death" (Ps. 7:13-14).

You remember, I suppose, that I said above that Divine Scripture is like a building, in which, after the foundation has first been laid, the structure itself is raised up; it is altogether like a building, for it too has its structure. For this reason, let it not irk us if we follow out this similitude a little more carefully.

Take a look at what the mason does. When the foundation has been laid, he stretches out his string in a straight line, he drops his perpendicular, and then, one by one, he lays the diligently polished stones in a row. Then he asks for other stones and still others; and if by chance he finds some that do not fit with the fixed course he has laid, he takes his file, smoothes off the protruding parts, files down the rough spots and the places that do not fit, reduces to form, and so at last joins them to the rest of the stones set into the row. But if he finds some to be such that they cannot either be made smaller or be fitly shaped, he does not use these lest perhaps while he labors to grind down the stone he should break his file.

Pay attention now! I have proposed to you something contemptible to gapers but worthy of imitation to those who understand. The foundation is in the earth, and it does not always have smoothly fitted stones. The superstructure rises above the earth, and it demands a smoothly proportioned construction. Even so the divine page, in its literal sense, contains many things which seem both to be opposed to each other and, sometimes, to impart something which smacks of the absurd or the impossible. But the spiritual meaning admits no opposition; in it, many things can be different from one another but none can be opposed.

The fact, also, that the first course of stones to be laid upon the foundation is placed flush with a taut cord—and these are the stones upon which the entire weight of the others rests and to which they are fitted—is not without its meaning. For this is like a sort of second foundation and is the basis of the entire superstructure. This foundation both carries what is placed upon it and is itself carried by the first foundation. All things rest upon the first foundation but are not fitted to it in every way. As to the latter foundation everything else both rests upon it and is fitted to it. The first one carries the superstructure and underlies the superstructure. The second one carries the superstructure and is not only under the superstructure but part of it.

The foundation which is under the earth we have said stands for history, and the superstructure which is built upon it we have said suggests allegory. Therefore, that basis of this superstructure ought also to relate to allegory. The superstructure rises in many courses of stones, and each course has its basis. Even so, many mysteries are contained in the divine page and they each have their bases from which they spring.

Constructing the Spiritual Building

Do you wish to know what these courses are? The first course is the mystery of the Trinity, because this, too, Scripture contains, since God, three and one, existed before every creature. He, from nothing, made every creature—visible, namely, and invisible. Behold in these the second course. To the rational creature he gave free judgment, and he prepared grace for it that it might be able to merit eternal beatitude. Then, when men fell of their own will, he punished them; and when they continued to fall, he strengthened them that they might not fall further.

What the origin of sin, what sin, and what the punishment for sin may be: these constitute the third course. What mysteries he first instituted for man's restoration under the natural law: these are the fourth course. What things were written under the Law: these, the fifth course. The mystery of the incarnation of the Lord: this, the sixth course. The mysteries of the New Testament: these, the seventh course. Finally, the mysteries of man's own resurrection: these, the eighth course. Here is the whole of divinity, this is that spiritual structure which is raised on high—built, as it were, with as many courses of stones as it contains mysteries.

See now, you have come to your study. You are about to construct the spiritual building, the spiritual structure. Already the foundations of history have been laid in you. It remains now that you found the bases of the superstructure. The very bases of your spiritual structure are certain principles of the faith—principles which form your starting point. Truly, the judicious student ought to be sure that, before he makes his way through extensive volumes, he is so instructed in the particulars which bear upon his task and upon his profession of the true faith, that he may safely be able to build onto his structure whatever he afterwards finds.

Do you wish that I should teach you how such bases ought to be laid? Look back at those things which I listed for you a moment ago. There is the mystery of the Trinity. First learn briefly and clearly what is to be believed about the Trinity, what you ought unquestionably to profess and truthfully to believe. Afterwards, when you have begun to read books and have found many things obscurely, many things clearly, and many things doubtfully written, take those things which you find clear and, if it should be that they conform, add them to their proper base. The doubtful things interpret in such a way that they may not be out of harmony. Of those things that are obscure, if you cannot penetrate to an understanding of them, pass over them so that you may not run into the danger of error by presuming to attempt what you are not equal to doing. Do not be contemptuous of such things, but rather be reverent toward them, for you have heard that it is written: "He made darkness his hiding-place" (Ps. 18:12). But even if you find that something contrary to what you have already learned should be held with the firmest faith, still it is not well for you to change your opinion daily—unless first you have learned what the universal faith, which can never be false, orders to be believed about it.

Thus should you do concerning the mystery of the altar, thus concerning the mystery of baptism, that of confirmation, that of marriage, and all which were enumerated for you above. You see that many who read the Scriptures, because they do not have a foundation of truth, fall into various errors and change their views almost as often as they sit down to read. But you see others who, in accordance with that knowledge of the truth upon which, interiorly, they are solidly based, know how to bend all scriptural passages whatever into fitting interpretations and to judge both what is out of keeping with sound faith and what is consonant with it.

Ezekiel and the Spirit of Interpretation

In Ezekiel you read that the wheels follow the living creatures, not the living creatures the wheels. It says: "When the living creatures went, the wheels also went together by them: and when the living creatures were lifted up from the earth, the wheels also were lifted up with them" (Ezek. 1:19). So it is with the minds of holy men. The more they advance in virtues or in knowledge, the more they see that the hidden places of the Scriptures are profound. Those places which, to simple minds and minds still tied to earth, seem worthless—to minds which have been raised aloft seem sublime. For the text continues: "Whithersoever the Spirit went, thither as the Spirit went the wheels also were lifted up withal, and followed it: for the Spirit of life was in the wheels" (Ezek. 1:20). You see that these wheels follow the living creatures and follow the Spirit.

Still elsewhere it is said: "The letter killeth, but the spirit quickeneth" (2 Cor. 3:6), because it is certainly necessary that the student of the Scripture adhere staunchly to the truth of the spiritual meaning— the high points of the literal meaning, which itself can sometimes be wrongly understood too, should not lead him away from this central concern in any way whatever. Why was that former people—who received the Law of life — reproved, except that they followed the death-dealing letter in such a way that they did not have the life-giving Spirit?

I do not say these things in order to offer anyone the chance to interpret the Scriptures according to his own will, but in order to show the man who follows the letter alone that he cannot long continue without error. For this reason it is necessary both that we follow the letter in such a way as not to prefer our own sense to the divine authors, and that we do not follow it in such a way as to deny that the entire pronouncement of truth is rendered in it. Not the man devoted to the letter "but the spiritual man judgeth all things" (1 Cor. 2:15).

In order, therefore, that you may be able to interpret the letter safely, it is necessary that you not presume upon your own opinion, but that first you be educated and informed, and that you lay, so to speak, a certain foundation of unshaken truth upon which the entire superstructure may rest. You should not presume to teach yourself, lest perhaps when you think you are introducing you are rather seducing yourself. This introduction must be sought from learned teachers and men who have wisdom — who are able to produce and unfold the matter to you both through the authorities of the holy fathers and the evidences of the Scriptures and, once you have already had this introduction, to confirm the particulars they have taught you by reading from the evidences of the Scriptures.

So the matter appears to me. Whoever is pleased to follow me in this, I accept with pleasure. Whoever thinks things ought not to be done in this way, let him do what he pleases: I shall not argue with him. For I know that a number of people do not follow this pattern in learning. But how certain of these advance, this too I am not unaware of.

If you ask what books are best for this study, I think: the beginning of Genesis on the works of the six days; the three last books of Moses on the mysteries of the Law; Isaiah; the beginning and end of Ezekiel; Job; the

Psalter; the Canticle of Canticles; two gospels in particular, namely those of Matthew and John; the Epistles of Paul; the canonical Epistles, and the Apocalypse. But especially the Epistles of Paul, which even by their very number show that they contain the perfection of the two Testaments.[3]

---

[3] *Original editor's note:* There are 14 Pauline epistles—the number 14 being twice seven, the perfect number, in biblical numerology.

THE SACRAMENT OF SACRED SCRIPTURE

• F. X. Durrwell, C.Ss.R. •

The sacraments exist to make contact between men and the Word of God at the point when that Word is pronounced for our salvation: in the man Jesus and in his action redeeming us. Their name, "sacraments," means "mysteries," because by them the mystery of the redemption that is in Christ Jesus is accessible to mankind.

Holy Scripture, too, is a kind of sacrament—not one of the seven, of course, yet comparable to them because intended like them to link us with the Word of salvation in the redeeming Christ. That once-spoken Word came from the Father, and with it have come many words to us—like circles spreading out from the Word falling into the sea of mankind, spreading to the beginnings of centuries and the ends. These words are at work for God's designs, intended to lead men to the center from which they grow, the mystery of salvation which is in Christ. One may say that Scripture is also, in its own way, a sacrament to incorporate us into the redeeming Christ.

From patristic times, theology has seen a real analogy between the two mysteries of Scripture and the incarnation. As Bossuet said: "He [the Word] took a kind of second body, I mean, the Word of his gospel." Through the action of the Holy Spirit in the Virgin Mary, God's own thought—his Word—was clothed in human nature, with its imperfections, and dwelt among us. Through another action of the Holy Spirit, in the sacred writers, in the womb of their intellect, God's thought was introduced into humanity, taking the form of human thought, and again dwelt among us. The Word has put off its glory, taken the form of a servant, and come to dwell among us.

In the office for the Blessed Sacrament, the Church sings her happiness at possessing the incarnate Word in her midst in the Eucharist: "Neither is there, nor has there been, any other nation so great, that hath gods so nigh them, as our God is present to all our petitions." The words are taken from Deuteronomy, and were used by the Jews to express the pride they felt in having a God who spoke to them, and whose thought and will for them they possessed in the sacred scrolls they carried with them (Deut. 4:7-8). This praise, which we now sing of the incarnation and the Eucharist, was first uttered to glorify Scripture, which was a sort of first incarnation of God's thought.

The Book of Life

Having sung at length the divine origins of Wisdom and its eternal prerogatives, Sirach concludes: "All these things are the book of life and the [book of the] covenant of the Most High . . . who filleth up Wisdom as the waters of Phison, and as the Tigris in the days of the new fruits" (Sir. 24:3, 9, 22-23). In Scripture God's Wisdom is already incarnate, flowing in the sacred book like a river between its banks. Israel made that divine presence an object of worship. The tables of the Law were placed in the Ark; in the synagogues, the Bible, contained in a cupboard facing the people, was the only object of worship. No one touched it till he had washed his hands, and then with much reverence.

Similarly, there is an intense presence of God in the books of the New Testament, but closer and more evident. Before becoming human in the thoughts and words of men, God's Wisdom, which wrote the New Testament, took human flesh, and it is that incarnate Wisdom—Christ in his glory—who dwells among us in the books of the New Testament. For it is he who is the author of the New Testament. Augustine said: "The members [the apostles] wrote what the Head inspired them to. Christ dictated to them, as to his hands, which of his words and actions he wanted us to know about."

One text in St. John shows us that the opened side of Christ in glory is the source whence the books of the New Testament flow:

> If any man thirst, let him come to me, and let him that believeth in me drink. As the Scripture saith: *Out of his belly shall flow rivers of living water.*

From Christ's belly the rivers will flow—we should translate this Hebrew phrase by saying they will flow from Christ's heart. And "this he said of the Spirit which they should receive who believed in him" (John 7:37-39). He said it of the Holy Spirit whose tremendous outpouring in the last days had been spoken of by the prophets. From Christ's sacred Body where the soldier's lance struck him, as from the rock of Sinai, would flow the rivers of the New Testament, all the graces of the kingdom, and also those of Scripture—the graces by which Scripture would be inspired, by which it would be read and understood, by which it would give life to the world. All these rivers will flow from that open side on the day of his redeeming glory. The evangelists came, and each drank from that spring. "He drank the rivers of the gospel from the sacred fount of the Lord's heart," we say of the apostle John in the office for his feast.

Refuge and Communion

The New Testament is not Christ's book because it tells his story. It is his book because it is born out of the wound in his heart, born like a child. Every word of Scripture is a grace of the Spirit of Jesus, a thought of everlasting life which flowed from his heart along with his blood.

With their sure instincts, the saints felt this redeeming presence in the New Testament. St. Ignatius of Antioch wrote: "I take refuge in the gospel as in the flesh of Jesus Christ." St. Ignatius sought his refuge in the gospel, in the revelation of the Christian mystery, for that gospel was like a sacrament of the redeeming Christ—like a field in which, as St. Jerome said, the treasure was hidden, the treasure of Christ himself.

In Christian worship Holy Scripture is forever linked with that supreme sacrament of Christ's body and the redemption, the Eucharist. The same name is used for both: "This chalice," our Lord said, "is the New Testament." This book also we call the New Testament. Chalice and book, each in its own way, contain the new covenant, the mystery of our redemption in Christ. The analogy is tremendous: "I think myself that Christ's Body is [also] his gospel," says St. Jerome, "the bread of Christ and his flesh is the divine Word and heavenly doctrine." The early Church, struck by the resemblance between these two sacraments of Christ's presence, placed together, as on "two tables" side by side, the bread of Christ and the Book, inviting the faithful to sit equally at both, to feed upon their Savior and upon the salvation that was in him.

For, in every form, Christ's presence among men has that same purpose—to create a communion of salvation with men. Scripture too establishes a communion, different from the Eucharist but real nonetheless, a communion of thought between two people who love each other and talk together, one of whom is Christ.

Whenever we read his Scriptures with faith, Christ speaks. It was long ago that he inspired his apostles, and centuries have passed since. But though the human writing of the Book was something that happened in the past, the inspired words still live in the moment when they are spoken by Christ. Augustine says: "This was written for us, and preserved for us; it is recited for us and will also be recited for our descendants, right up to the end of time."

The redeeming action of Christ in glory knows no succession of time. He speaks to the heart of the Church in eternity. The thoughts formulated by the apostles and put into writing at a given moment of history are addressed to the Church of all the ages in an eternal present. Men are coming into existence now, are now reading Christ's word with faith, are hearing Christ speaking to them now.

Because Scripture is an everlasting word, always being said, the epistle to the Hebrews introduces all its quotations from Scripture by saying, "The Holy Spirit saith" or "The Holy Spirit doth testify" (Heb. 3:7; 10:15)—all in the present tense.

Christ speaks to us at this moment, but not like a friend far away communicating by letter (see Acts 17:27; Eph. 3:17). We sit at his feet and listen to him: "The gospel is the very mouth of Christ," Augustine says, a sacrament of his words to us. There is no human intermediary between his word and our mind; the sound we hear is actually his voice. According to St. Thomas, God has two far from equal ways of teaching us: he speaks through an intermediary in human books of religious instruction, but "he speaks directly to our minds in sacred Scripture."

This communion with Christ in thought is even closer than that between two people speaking together. When we look for the truth hidden in the text of Scripture, Christ can communicate the meaning of his words directly to our minds. When we hear the words of Scripture, "the Master is in our hearts" and communicates the same understanding of the truths they express that he himself has. He arouses in us his own sentiments: "Let the word of Christ dwell in our hearts in all its riches" (Col. 3:16). It is a wonderful communion of mind and heart—the communion of Mary of Bethany, of the disciples on the road to Emmaus.

'A Substantial Bread'

This communion, too, is effective, giving eternal life. Of Scripture as of the Eucharist it can be said, *Pinguis est panis*—it is a substantial bread. For Christ lives now only in his redemptive act, given to God for mankind, immortal in his death for them, and forever an instrument of God's action in raising up to eternal life. Every presence and every action of Christ works redemption. When he appeared in the evening of Easter day, he sent the apostles out to forgive sins. In the same way he made them write the pages of the New Testament—for the remission of sins and the salvation of men.

Scripture bestows a Spirit of life on those who read it with faith: "Was our heart not burning within us, whilst he spoke?" (Luke 24:32); "The Word of God is living and effectual" (Heb. 4:12), the "sword of the Spirit" (Eph. 6:17). If ordinary human words, noble or degraded, can transform a man by their psychological dynamism, how much more must the Word of God penetrate and pierce to the very depths of the soul (see Heb. 4:12).

It is not merely that God's Word contains the thoughts of Christ, lofty and profound, which can stir up man's heart. But it is spoken *for me* and *for my salvation*. It is spoken by my Savior, in the grace of the Holy Spirit who flows from his pierced side. The gospel is a sacrament of salvation, in which "the Holy Spirit works in efficacious words."

The Fathers seem to have been unable to find images strong enough to describe the banquet of redemption offered on the table of Scripture. The gospel, according to St. Jerome, is true food and true drink. Scripture is an ocean of fullness, says St. Ambrose, a cup from which we drink Christ, a cup that is a river whose waves delight the city of God. It is the cure for all our ills: "Take and drink; all sickness of soul finds its remedy in Scripture." The Eucharist, says St. John Chrysostom, makes us as fierce lions in face of the devil. Scripture also, says St. Athanasius, puts our adversary to flight, for "in Scripture the Lord is present, and the demons, who cannot bear his presence, cry: 'I beg you, do not torment us before our time.' They burn simply from seeing the Lord present."

Thus the banquet of Scripture feeds and strengthens just as does the eucharistic banquet of Christ's immolated flesh; and like it, it has its joys, that great comfort which made the Maccabees say, "We needed none of these things, nor any one, having for our comfort the holy books that are in our hands" (1 Macc. 12:9). Scripture and the Eucharist are the life-force and the joy of the Church, because they are for her a communion in the Body given and Blood shed for us. Other than that banquet there exists only what this life can offer us: "We have in this world only this one good thing: to feed upon his flesh and drink his blood, not only in the [eucharistic] sacrament, but in the reading of Scripture."

Despite its own efficaciousness, Scripture does not enter into any kind of competition in our souls with that other sacrament of presence and communion, the Eucharist; it does not supplant it, or make it unnecessary. The central point of Christian worship is the incarnate Word in his eternal sacrifice. It is by the Eucharist that Christ is present to us in the reality of his body, in the reality of his immolation and his glory. So Scripture must collaborate with the sacrament to unite believers with the redeeming Christ.

In the Mass, the Splendor of Scripture

In the Mass, the splendor of Scripture comes to surround the sacred Body of Christ on all sides, as the royal purple of the incarnate Word in his immolation, as the veil of the Holy of Holies in which the eternal sacrifice is offered—a veil which is not there to hide but to reveal the way into the sanctuary. It was in this way, through the veil of the Scriptures, that the world of the Old Testament was brought to Christ.

Many non-Catholic Christians read Scripture more assiduously than many Catholics, but do not feed on the Eucharist. Among a lot of them there is a profound tendency not to accept the incarnation of the Word in its ultimate reality, but to prefer what seems to be a worship of God's transcendence—to prefer at least in practice, the spoken Word to the personal Word, to remain in the Old Testament, on the threshold of the fullness of the incarnation. Many Catholics have a tremendous devotion to the Eucharist, but neglect Scripture. Many of them, perhaps, do not therefore know the personal Word as well as they might, and are not in the best possible dispositions to receive him in the Eucharist. For the secret of opening one's heart to that one Word is contained most fully in Scripture.

VATICAN II AND THE TRUTH OF SACRED SCRIPTURE

• Augustin Cardinal Bea, S.J. •

Biblical inspiration is intimately connected with the question of the firmness and faithfulness with which it hands down to man the great treasure of revelation.

Dei Verbum, the Second Vatican Council's Constitution on Divine Revelation, says of the divine books: "Inspired by God and committed once and for all to writing, they impart the Word of God himself without change" (no. 21). The intimate connection between this faithfulness and certainty of Holy Scripture—called by theologians "inerrancy"—and its divine inspiration is also noted in the Constitution. Indeed, the inerrancy of Scripture is presented as the logical conclusion of the doctrine on inspiration: "Therefore, since everything asserted by the inspired authors or sacred writers must be held to be asserted by the Holy Spirit, it follows that the books of Scripture must be acknowledged as teaching firmly, faithfully, and without error that truth which God wanted put into the sacred writings for the sake of our salvation" (no. 11).

Let us consider briefly the composition of this passage. It clearly consists of two parts: the premise and the conclusion to be deduced from it. The premise is this: "Everything asserted by the inspired authors or sacred writers must be held to be asserted by the Holy Spirit." This statement is in its turn presented as a conclusion derived from what has gone before, for it is introduced with "therefore." The previous argument is that if God has so moved the inspired authors that, although writing as true authors, they nevertheless wrote "all and only those things which he wished to be written" (no. 11), then there can be no doubt that all that these authors assert is to be considered as asserted by the Holy Spirit which has inspired them.

The second part of our text, the conclusion deduced from the premise, is this: "The books of Scripture . . . teach firmly, faithfully, and without error that truth which God wanted put into the sacred writings for the sake of our salvation." This conclusion presupposes a self-evident truth—that God surely obtains what he desires, and that he cannot make a mistake or cause a mistake to be made. This obvious presupposition is explicitly formulated further on in this same chapter of the Constitution (no. 13).

Concerning the proof of the doctrine of the inerrancy of Scripture, the document itself quotes as its foundation passages from St. Augustine, St. Thomas Aquinas, and the Council of Trent and some recent documents of the supreme magisterium of the Church.

The doctrine of inerrancy was put forward and expounded chiefly by Leo XIII in his encyclical, *Providentissimus Deus*, which is largely dedicated to establishing and defining this doctrinal point. The encyclical first expounds the doctrine of inspiration in order to affirm that of inerrancy, asserting: "Therefore it is so impossible for divine inspiration to contain any error that, by its very nature, it not only excludes even the slightest error but must of necessity exclude it, just as God, the Supreme Truth, must also necessarily be absolutely incapable of promoting error."

The encyclical therefore concludes: "Consequently, any who were to admit that there might be error in the authentic pages of the sacred books must certainly either betray the Catholic concept of divine inspiration or make God himself the author of error." The encyclical bases this teaching on the doctrine of the popes, from among whom it quotes largely St. Gregory and St. Augustine. The same theme of inerrancy is fully dealt with also in the encyclical *Spiritus Paraclitus*, which illustrates with particular care St. Jerome's doctrine about this. The teaching of Leo XIII on this question is recalled by Pius XII's encyclical *Divino Afflante Spiritu*.

The Inerrancy of Scripture in Scripture

The source and foundation of this conviction held by the first fathers of the Church and the magisterium concerning the inerrancy of Scripture is Scripture itself—or more precisely the way in which Christ and the apostles used and quoted it.

According to the New Testament, there exists a collection of writings which are called "Scripture" (see John 2:22; 10:35; Gal. 3:8; 1 Pet. 2:6; 2 Pet. 1:20) or "the Scriptures" (Matt. 21:42; 22:29; John 5:39; Acts 17:2, 11; 18:24; Rom. 15:4), or the "Holy Scriptures" (Rom. 1:2). This collection is considered by both Christ and the apostles to be of divine origin and to it is attributed divine authority. With the words "it is written," Christ repeatedly appealed to the Scriptures as to an irrefutable authority (Matt. 4:4-10; 22:31, 43; John 10:34-35). So did the apostles (Acts 15:15-18; Rom. 1:17).

The divine origin of these Old Testament books is also implied by their being called simply "oracles of God" (Rom. 3:2) or described as "prophetic"and their words as "prophecies"(see Matt. 13:14; 15:7; Rom. 16:26; 1 Pet. 1:10; 2 Pet. 1:19-20)—prophetic being the term used to describe a man who brings to other men the message, the Word of God.

Moreover, in a series of texts, Christ and the apostles, referring to the Old Testament, affirm that God himself is present in these writings because he himself speaks in them, or because the human authors speak "in the Holy Spirit" or are "inspired by the Holy Spirit" (Acts 1:16-18; 2:30-31; Matt. 22:31-32, 43; 2 Pet. 1:19-21; 2 Tim. 3:16-17). Hebrews introduces a quotation from Psalm 95 with the words: "the Holy Spirit says" (Heb. 3:7; 4:4-5; 9:8; 10:15). Moreover, in Matthew, quotations from the Old Testament are introduced with the words: "All this took place to fulfil what the Lord had spoken by the prophet. . ." (Matt. 1:22; see also 2:15). Because God was considered the Author of Scripture, it was considered necessary and inevitable that the Scripture should "be fulfilled" (Matt. 5:18-19; Luke 24:44; Acts 1:16 etc.). This argument from Scripture is summed up in the encyclical *Spiritus Paraclitus*:

> Who is there who does not know and remember that when speaking to the people, either on the mountain by the lake of Genazareth, in the synagogue of Nazareth or in the city of Capernaum, Jesus our Lord drew the principal points and proofs of his doctrine from the sacred books? Was it not from these that he took invincible weapons for his discussions with the Pharisees and the Sadducees? Whether he was teaching or discussing he always derived his assertions and examples from every part of Holy Scripture; he refers, for example, to Jonah, to the inhabitants of Nineveh, to the Queen of Sheba and Solomon, to Elijah and Elisha, to David, Noah, Lot, the inhabitants of Sodom, and Lot's own wife.

'Truth . . . For the Sake of Our Salvation"

Let us now proceed to determine the meaning of the Constitution's doctrine on inerrancy. We have already said that it does not use here the theological term itself, but instead, for greater precision, says that the Scriptures "teach firmly, faithfully and without error." The basic idea of the absolute truth of the Scriptures is always the same, although it may be differently expressed. The Constitution expresses most forcefully the notion that Scripture absolutely guarantees the faithful transmission of God's revelation.

On the other hand, it is more difficult to define another point of our text—that is, the object of the infallible teaching of Scripture, "the truth which God wanted put into the sacred writings for the sake of our salvation."

At first sight, the meaning of these words seems clear and obvious. In fact, the whole Constitution illustrates the truth—the revelation of God is intended to bring about man's supernatural salvation. It is therefore to be expected that the truth taught by Scripture should be with reference to this salvation. Nevertheless, there is a certain difficulty here which needs to be explained.

In order to understand this point let us re-consider the preparatory work for this Constitution. An earlier *schema* or draft (the third in succession), said that the sacred books teach "truth without error." The following *schema*, the fourth, inspired by words of St. Augustine, added the adjective "saving," so that the text asserted that the Scriptures taught "firmly, faithfully, wholly and without error the saving truth." In the voting which followed, one hundred and eighty-four council fathers asked for the adjective "saving" to be removed, because they feared it might lead to misunderstandings, as if the inerrancy of Scripture referred only to matters of faith and morality, whereas there might be error in the treatment of other matters. The Holy Father, to a certain extent sharing this anxiety, decided to ask the drafting commission to consider whether it would not be better to omit the adjective, as it might lead to some misunderstanding. After a long and wearisome debate, with much discussion and several ballots, the present text was accepted, the adjective "saving" being omitted: "the truth which God wanted put into the sacred writings for the sake of our salvation."

This incident concerns us only in so far as it helps us to understand more precisely the meaning of the present definitive text of the Constitution. The actual question is as follows: It is evident that the purpose which God wished to be expressed in Scripture was the revelation of God to man, in the fullest sense, a revelation by means of "deeds and words," which aims at man's eternal salvation. Now we must consider whether the "truth" (that is, the truth "which God wanted put into the sacred writings for the sake of our salvation") implies some limit set to the inerrancy of Scripture—meaning that it taught "without error," not everything that it asserts, but only all that concern our salvation (or those things also which closely and directly affect our salvation).

Let us explain at once what we mean. In order to describe those manifestations of God occurring in "deeds and words," which form the "history of salvation" (see no. 2), Scripture must necessarily set them in an authentic historical framework. Our question, therefore, about the possible existence of a limit set to inerrancy refers, not to the events in which God truly reveals himself, but to those events which form their historical setting and which Scripture frequently describes in great detail. Does the inerrancy asserted in this document cover also the account of these historical events? In other words, is the historical background also described "without error"?

In the 'Background' of Salvation History

For my own part I think that this question must be answered affirmatively, that is, that these "background" events also are described without error. In fact, we declare in general that there is no limit set to this inerrancy, and that it applies to all that the inspired writer, and therefore all that the Holy Spirit by his means, affirms.

Our reasons are these. First of all, the Constitution itself says that in Holy Scripture the truth and holiness of God must always remain inviolable (see no. 13). This thought, which re-occurs in various forms in the documents of the magisterium of the Church, is here clearly understood in a sense which excludes the possibility of the Scriptures containing any statement contrary to the reality of the facts.

In particular, these documents of the magisterium require us to recognize that Scripture gives a true account of events, naturally not in the sense that it always offers a complete and scientifically studied account, but in the sense that what is asserted in Scripture—even if it does not offer a complete picture—never contradicts the reality of the fact.

If therefore the Council had wished to introduce here a new conception, different from that presented in these documents of the supreme teaching authority, which reflects the beliefs of the early fathers, it would have had to state this clearly and explicitly.

Let us now ask whether there may be any indications to suggest such a restricted interpretation of inerrancy. The answer is decidedly negative. There is not the slightest sign of any such indication. On the contrary everything points against a restrictive interpretation.

First of all: even at that stage of the discussion when the Conciliar Theological Commission put forward the term "the saving truth," it explained that by this expression it did not mean to restrict the inerrancy of the Bible to matters of faith and morals. In order to show that this had not been its intention, it explained that the text spoke of "truth" in the singular, not of "truths," as if it had wished to discriminate between those which are necessary for salvation and others which are not. Moreover, in spite of this prudent explanation, the word "saving" was finally eliminated from the text and replaced with another expression—in order to prevent any possibility of implying that the inerrancy was restricted.

Does the text of *Dei Verbum* we have before us now imply a restrictive interpretation of inerrancy? Here also the answer is firmly negative. The first proof of this is seen in the fact that all those (and in the first place the pope himself) who had been anxious to prevent the possible misunderstandings that might have arisen from the expression "the saving truth" have instead accepted the present form. This means they consider that this does not present the same danger of misunderstanding. In fact, the phrasing we now have does not admit of any such interpretation because the idea of salvation is no longer directly linked with the noun "truth," but with the verbal expression "wanted put into the sacred writings." In other words, the phrase in which the text speaks of salvation explains God's purpose in causing the Scriptures to be written, and not the nature of the truth enshrined therein.

Let us then conclude: all that the inspired writers assert is asserted through them by the Holy Spirit. Consequently, in all their assertions the sacred books teach "firmly, faithfully and without error, what God wanted put into them for the sake of our salvation." The paragraph we are commenting upon (no. 11) ends with St. Paul's words: "All Scripture is inspired by God and useful for teaching, for reproving, for correcting and, for training in righteousness; that the man of God may be perfect, equipped for every good work" (2 Tim. 3:16-17, *Greek text*).

John A. Davies, *A Royal Priesthood: Literary and Intertextual Perspectives on an Image of Israel in Exodus 19:6.* Journal for the Study of the Old Testament Supplement Series 395 (London: T & T Clark International, 2004).

God's designation of Israel as "a kingdom of priests and a holy nation" (Exod. 19:6), made in the preamble to the covenant at Sinai, has engendered centuries of interpretive and theological debate, beginning with its use by the New Testament writers (1 Pet. 2:5, 9; Rev. 1:6; 5:10; 20:6). In this important study, John Davies seeks to fix the exegetical meaning of Israel's collective priesthood in the context of the exodus narrative and the larger Old Testament canon.

Davies argues that the Sinai covenant is a "treaty of grant" by which God grants to Israel the unprecedented privilege of standing before him as a "royal company of priests." This is a novel interpretive approach to Sinai, which is usually regarded as a type of "kinship" covenant (M. D. Guinan), or a "treaty" type (K. A. Kitchen). In finding a grant treaty at Sinai, Davies is also at odds with Moshe Weinfeld, who first formulated the notion of "the covenant of grant." And while Davies marshalls a number of interesting insights, his argument remains unconvincing.

He is on surer footing in his careful literary and intertextual analysis, which also makes judicious use of comparative ancient Near Eastern materials. Israel's priestly character, he argues, should be understood in terms of the holiness required to serve in God's presence. This is the purpose of the redemptive act of the exodus—to establish this priestly people in "the heavenly court of the divine king."

Offering a fresh interpretation of the liturgical ratification of the Sinai covenant (Exod. 24), focusing on the blood rite and the covenant meal eaten in the presence of God, he helps us see close parallels between the Sinai liturgy and the later Levitical ordinations (Lev. 8-9). In a useful and insightful review of the Old Testament priesthood, he sees the Levites not as competing with or supplanting Israel's royal priestly vocation but instead serving it—by providing a model of that vocation while at the same time "facilitating" the people's growth in holiness.

Davies' patient exegesis opens up fruitful areas for further biblical theological reflection. For instance, he connects the Levitical priesthood with the portrayal of the tabernacle as "an ideal or restored cosmos where God and man meet." The priests are "a visible reminder of the glory and honor to which God has called the whole people (Deut. 26:19; Isa. 17:3; 62:2; Jer. 13:11). . . . The priest is the living symbol of blessing and well-being, of life to the full, of all that humanity should be and could become in relation to God."

Reading anew a difficult passage of Hosea (6:4-7), he makes a plausible case that the prophet is comparing Israel's unfaithfulness to Adam's failure as "the archetypal priest-king in the primal paradise-garden." Davies writes: "If Hosea has as part of his shared presupposition pool with his readers the story of Genesis 2, with Adam as the idyllic priest-king (see Ezek. 28:12-15; *Jub.* 4:23-26), together with the notion that Israel at Sinai was constituted as the new humanity, the true successors to Adam (see 4 *Ezra* 3:3-36; 6:53-59; 2 *Bar.* 14:17-19), then it makes sense to compare the breach of the Sinai covenant (see Hos. 4:1,2) with the rebellion in the garden (Gen. 3; compare Ezek. 28:16-17)."

David W. Pao, *Acts and the Isaianic New Exodus* (Grand Rapids, Mich.: Baker Academic Press, 2002)

Although a couple of years old now, David Pao's study—together with Rikki E. Watts's *Isaiah's New Exodus and Mark* (1997) and Mark L. Strauss' *The Davidic Messiah in Luke–Acts* (1995)—has significantly advanced our appreciation of the narrative and theological self-understanding of the early Church as reflected in the New Testament.

The importance of Old Testament citation and allusion in Luke-Acts has long been recognized. Pao's contribution is to underscore how these scriptural statements, especially in Acts, return again and again to Israel's founding story—the exodus—as that story was interpreted and transformed in the prophecies of Isaiah. As Isaiah used the exodus to explain the identity and destiny of the Israelites in their exile and rebuilding, Pao finds that this story is used in Acts to bolster the "claim by the early Christian community to be the true people of God in the face of other competing voices."

As in Isaiah, the new exodus in Acts is different than the first exodus. First, it involves not Israel's captivity in Egypt, but its exile among the nations; second, it entails a restoration of Israel to Zion, not to Sinai. Finally, it envisions a restoration that includes not only Israel, but all nations accompanying Israel in an eschatological pilgrimage toward a messianic banquet (Isa. 25).

Pao observes the critical role that Isaianic motifs play in the literary structure of the narrative. The missionary task given by Christ to the apostles (Acts 1:8) provides an outline for the entire book that follows the stages of Isaiah's new exodus (Isa. 40:1-11)—beginning with the restoration of Jerusalem and the reconstitution of the people of God, and continuing with the people of God's vocation to be a "light" to the Gentiles.

Pao's study has important implications for a biblical theology of the Church, an ecclesiology that is rooted in the pattern of promise and fulfillment with special reference to the Davidic covenant and kingdom. It also should encourage a new examination of the narrative unity of Luke and Acts. Strauss has shown us how Luke's Christology draws on the expectations of a Davidic Messiah. And although Pao leaves this theme underdeveloped, his research suggests that the Isaianic new exodus in Acts is ordered to a Davidic kingdom ecclesiology.

Stephen Pattemore, *The People of God in the Apocalypse: Discourse, Structure, and Exegesis.* Society for New Testament Studies Monograph Series 128 (Cambridge: Cambridge University Press, 2004)

The Book of Revelation is seldom approached in terms of its ecclesiology, despite the fact that it depicts the unveiling of the bride of the Lamb, the Church. The book's use of Old Testament citation and allusion has received much attention. However, Stephen Pattemore has made a real contribution in showing how these citations and allusions shape the book's implicit ecclesiology. In particular, Pattemore stresses the importance of the Zion traditions and anticipates a rereading of the Apocalypse in light of the ecclesiology implicit in the cluster of Davidic themes and images that converge in John's visions.

Pattemore looks at Revelation through the lens of Relevance Theory, a tool in the linguistic field of pragmatics that studies how authors and their audiences communicate and recognize inferences and intentions. John and his audience, he argues, share a "mutual cognitive environment" that includes not only the Old Testament, but also the liturgy, in which John's words were originally meant to be heard.

From this common intellectual and imaginative tradition, John develops a "messianic ecclesiology," especially in his vision of the "souls under the altar" (Rev. 6:9-11). Pattemore argues that John wanted his hearers to discover their identity as members of the messianic people of God and their task as a "martyr Church." John's intent, as Pattemore sees it, is to encourage the persecuted Church in bearing witness to "the Lamb who was slain" by mirroring Christ's self-sacrifice in their own willingness to offer up their lives. Pattemore shows how the "new exodus" motif and the vision of the "new Jerusalem" as holy city and bride of God function to encourage believers in their suffering for the faith. Through these familiar images, John assured them that they, like the Old Testament people of God, would find victory and deliverance into God's presence.

G. K. Beale, *The Temple and the Church's Mission: A Biblical Theology of the Dwelling Place of God.* New Studies in Biblical Theology 17 (Downers Grove, Ill.: InterVarsity Press, 2004).

G. K. Beale's comprehensive study begins at the end of the Bible—with John's much-studied vision of a "new heaven and a new earth" (Rev. 21:1). Why, he inquires, does John describe this new creation as a temple-city, drawing explicitly on a wealth of Old Testament accounts of Solomon's temple and expectations of an eschatologically restored temple?

Ranging widely over the biblical text, with keen sensitivity to inner-biblical exegesis and the ways in which the Scriptures are interpreted in rabbinic, Qumranic and other intertestamental sources, Beale traces the temple theme in Scripture. The temple was already implicit in creation and the sabbath liturgy shows us this cosmic temple, he recognizes. And as Christ brings about a new creation, then not surprisingly the temple emerges with great theological prominence and significance in his ministry. The new creation is a temple in John's apocalypse, he concludes, because the cosmos was intended from the beginning to be God's great temple, the site of his "rest" together with his people, who were created to serve and rule in this temple.

Beale considers the theological and practical implications of his findings for Christian faith and practice. He reminds us that in the Davidic kingdom it was not the palace but the temple that was the principal architectural sign of God's indwelling presence and God's own kingship. The messianic role of the Davidic figure, in turn, is that of both king and temple-builder. This of course has implications for our understanding of Jesus' messianic project and the kingdom ecclesiology of the New Testament. Beale also shows us the importance of the liturgy and the priestly role of God's people in liturgical sacrifice as the principal expression of their worship.

Concluding where he began, Beale suggests that redemption as presented in Scripture proceeds "from God's unique presence in the structural temple in the Old Testament to the God-man, Christ, the true temple. As a result of Christ's resurrection, the Spirit continues building the end-time temple, the building materials of which are God's people, thus extending the temple into the new creation in the new age. This building process will culminate in the eternal new heavens and earth as a paradisiacal city-temple."

Charles Kannengiesser et. al., *Handbook of Patristic Exegesis: The Bible in Ancient Christianity,* 2 vols. (Leiden: Brill, 2004).

Charles Kannengiesser and a team of renowned scholars set themselves an ambitious task—to retrieve the hermeneutical system of the early Church for biblical scholars and the common believer. As he notes, this tradition has long been "relegated to the realm of erudite curiosities, irrelevant . . . and dispensable for serious theology."

But in more than 2,000 pages of essays and comprehensive annotated bibliographies, Kannengiesser makes the case that this hermeneutical legacy is anything but a dead letter. The *Handbook* demonstrates the centrality of the Scriptures to the patristic worldview and in turn how that biblical worldview was foundational to the development of Western culture.

Notable are the *Handbook's* authoritative discussion of the literal and spiritual senses in the patristic interpreters; the detailed look at how each book of the canon was used and interpreted in the early Church; the insightful essays on early exegetes such as Augustine and Origen; and the treatment of Scripture's use in apologetics *vis-a-vis* the synagogue and the early heretical movements.

The loss of the patristic patrimony has had enormous implications for believers, and Kannengiesser hopes that its retrieval will be equally momentous: "The recent situation, seen through the eyes of the common believer, is that of a sophisticated field of scientific research called biblical exegesis, which has very little connection with actual church communities. The exegesis of the biblical text was detached from its founding religious culture by the very fact of its secular study . . . and therefore was often deeply alienated from the believing church assemblies. In a word, the need for the academic study of Scripture in its traditional status (as exemplified in ancient Christianity) cannot be detached from the need to give the Bible back to the churches. The fundamental issue is to conceive the task of exegesis as a spiritual exercise *within* a necessary submission to academic constraint and sophistication."

Jeremy Driscoll, O.S.B., *Theology at the Eucharistic Table: Master Themes in the Theological Tradition.* Studia Anselmiana 138 (London: Gracewing Publishing, 2003).

This collection of journal articles and conference papers should establish Jeremy Driscoll as one of our finest contemporary writers on the Bible and the liturgy. His key insight is that the Church's theological understandings grow through its daily encounter with the Word of God in the liturgy. In this sense, Driscoll gives us an extended meditation on what Irenaeus of Lyons said in the second century: "Our way of thinking is attuned to the Eucharist and the Eucharist in turn confirms our way of thinking."

In this wise and slender volume, Driscoll studies an impressive array of topics—the ancient Eucharistic prayer attributed to Hippolytus; the trinitarian theology that undergirds Origen's exegetical corpus; the contemporary contributions of Marsili, Fisichella, Lafont, and von Balthasar; the role of liturgy in catechesis; and the theological significance of adoration of the Blessed Sacrament. In an introductory essay, written especially for this volume, he identifies his "master themes" of theology: ecclesiology; the dynamic interrelation of Word and sacrament; the paschal mystery; anamnesis, epiclesis, and eschatology; the revelation of the trinitarian mystery; moral theology; spiritual theology; and missiology.

In each of these themes, Driscoll says: "Theology truly shows itself . . . as an *intellectus fidei*, a rational effort to understand the faith that is professed and celebrated in the liturgy, an effort undertaken so that, returning to the liturgy according to its rhythms, faith may be professed and celebrated ever more deeply and with ever greater understanding."

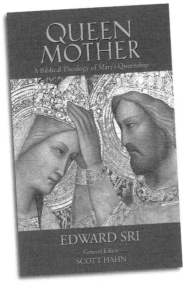

THE ST. PAUL CENTER
FOR BIBLICAL THEOLOGY
Reading the Bible from the Heart of the Church

Promoting Biblical Literacy for Ordinary Catholics . . .

- Free Online Bible Studies—*for beginners, intermediate, and advanced students*
- Online Library of Scripture, Prayer, and Apologetics—*more than 1,000 resources*
- Online Bookstore—*hundreds of titles*
- Popular Books & Textbooks—*on the Bible, the sacraments, and more*
- Workshops—*including parish-based training for Bible-study leaders*
- Pilgrimages—*to Rome and other biblical sites*

. . . and Biblical 'Fluency' for Clergy, Seminarians, and Teachers

- Homily Helps—*lectionary resources for pastors, and RCIA leaders*
- Reference Works—*including comprehensive Bible dictionary*
- *Letter & Spirit*—*journal of biblical theology*
- Scholarly Books and Dissertations—*on topics of Scripture, liturgy, and tradition*
- Studies in Biblical Theology and Spirituality—*reissues of classic works in the field*
- Seminars and Conferences—*including ecumenical dialogues and themes*

ST. PAUL CENTER
FOR BIBLICAL THEOLOGY

2228 Sunset Boulevard, Suite 2A
Steubenville, Ohio 43952-2204
(740)264-7908
www.SalvationHistory.com